The East India Company and the Politics of Knowledge

The East India Company is remembered as the world's most powerful, not to say notorious, corporation. But for many of its advocates from the 1770s to the 1850s, it was also the world's most enlightened one. Joshua Ehrlich reveals that a commitment to knowledge was integral to the Company's ideology. He shows how the Company cited this commitment in defense of its increasingly fraught union of commercial and political power. He moves beyond studies of orientalism, colonial knowledge, and information with a new approach: the history of ideas of knowledge. He recovers a world of debate among the Company's officials and interlocutors, Indian and European, on the political uses of knowledge. Not only were these historical actors highly articulate on the subject but their ideas continue to resonate in the present. Knowledge was a fixture in the politics of the Company – just as it seems to be becoming a fixture in today's politics.

JOSHUA EHRLICH is Assistant Professor at the University of Macau.

The East India Company and the Politics of Knowledge

JOSHUA EHRLICH

University of Macau

CAMBRIDGE
UNIVERSITY PRESS

Shaftesbury Road, Cambridge CB2 8EA, United Kingdom

One Liberty Plaza, 20th Floor, New York, NY 10006, USA

477 Williamstown Road, Port Melbourne, VIC 3207, Australia

314–321, 3rd Floor, Plot 3, Splendor Forum, Jasola District Centre,
New Delhi – 110025, India

103 Penang Road, #05–06/07, Visioncrest Commercial, Singapore 238467

Cambridge University Press is part of Cambridge University Press &
Assessment, a department of the University of Cambridge.

We share the University's mission to contribute to society through the
pursuit of education, learning and research at the highest international
levels of excellence.

www.cambridge.org
Information on this title: www.cambridge.org/9781009367950

DOI: 10.1017/9781009367967

First published 2023

A catalogue record for this publication is available from the British Library.

Library of Congress Cataloging-in-Publication Data.
Names: Ehrlich, Joshua, 1987– author.
Title: The East India Company and the politics of knowledge /
Joshua Ehrlich, University of Macau.
Description: Cambridge, United Kingdom ; New York, NY : Cambridge
University Press, 2023. | Includes bibliographical references and index.
Identifiers: LCCN 2022060967 (print) | LCCN 2022060968 (ebook) |
ISBN 9781009367950 (hardback) | ISBN 9781009367967 (epub)
Subjects: LCSH: East India Company – History. | Elite (Social sciences) –
India | Learning and scholarship – Political aspects – History. |
Education – India – History – 19th century. | India – Colonization. |
India – History – British occupation, 1765–1947.
Classification: LCC DS465 .E176 2023 (print) | LCC DS465 (ebook) |
DDC 954.03/1–dc23/eng/20230131
LC record available at https://lccn.loc.gov/2022060967
LC ebook record available at https://lccn.loc.gov/2022060968

ISBN 978-1-009-36795-0 Hardback

For my family

Contents

Acknowledgments

In the summer of 2013, I encountered the following statement in a prospectus for the London Literary Lyceum penned in 1783 by Jacques-Pierre Brissot:

> Commerce may be rendered subservient to the promotion of Science, and the same ship that carries the East-India Company's orders to Calcutta, may likewise carry the new instruments or the new work, and may bring back the Indian book for the Student of Gottingen, or the professor of oriental Languages at Paris.[1]

These words intrigued me. Why, at a time when the East India Company was conquering and ruling vast swathes of India, did the expatriate *philosophe* Brissot describe it in stubbornly mercantile terms? Why, at a time when its actions were drawing criticism from numerous quarters, did he envision the Company as an enlightened benefactor? I soon discovered that Brissot's rhetoric was scarcely original: Advocates of the Company had employed it for some years and would do so for many more. To explain this rhetoric, I would need to revisit the Company's ideology, its political–commercial constitution, and its engagements with knowledge.

This project first took shape as a doctoral dissertation at Harvard University. All those who guided and supported me in that undertaking have, and will ever have, my sincerest gratitude. I must mention specifically my committee members Sugata Bose and Emma Rothschild, and my writing group mates Kit Heintzman and Joe La Hausse de Lalouvière. But I am indebted to a hundred others and I hope they will forgive me for not listing their names here.

[1] Jacques-Pierre Brissot, *London Literary Lyceum; or, an Assembly and Correspondence Established at London* [London, 1783], p. 9.

In 2018, after defending my dissertation, I began the process of developing it into a book. I received more help than I had any right to expect from more individuals than I can now hope to remember. Sujit Sivasundaram and Robert Travers were abiding sources of inspiration and models of generosity. Peter Marshall, as ever, was an attentive reader of my work and an indispensable cicerone to the world of the Company. Nick Abbott, Ben Gilding, Nick Groom, Jessica Patterson, and Callie Wilkinson offered astute comments on the manuscript. Nick Abbott, Daniel Morgan, and Chander Shekhar lent expert advice on, and assistance with, Persian texts. (Any errors in translation are my own.) Many friends and colleagues kindly invited me to present my research virtually or in person; I would like to thank in particular Thomas Ahnert, Divya Cherian, Barry Crosbie, Beth Harper, Parimala Rao, Paris Spies-Gans, and Hiroki Ueno. Special thanks go to Rosane Rocher, who provided wisdom and reassurance at a pivotal juncture. I am profoundly grateful for the aid I also received, in abundance, from the following individuals: Mario Cams, Rishad Choudhury, Scott Connors, Richard Delacy, Rajeev Kinra, Nathan Kwan, Peter Mandler, Mohit Manohar, Dinyar Patel, Bhavani Raman, Holly Shaffer, Asheesh Siddique, and Ian Stewart.

I am deeply grateful too for the help rendered to me by archivists, librarians, and research assistants, especially during the COVID-19 pandemic. While confined to Macau, I came to rely upon an international network stretching from Cambridge, Massachusetts, to Delhi to the Isle of Bute. I would like to thank above all Lynsey Nairn, Syed Shahid, Sadie Sunderland, Robbie Wilson, the Resource Sharing staff at Harvard Library, and the Asia, Pacific, and Africa Collections staff at the British Library. It is no exaggeration to say that without their contributions *The East India Company and the Politics of Knowledge* could not have been written.

My greatest debt is to David Armitage, who, more than anyone, has taught me what it means to be a historian. David's input over the past decade has sharpened and enriched this book immeasurably.

Finally, I would like to thank my family, especially my parents, Paul and Vicky, and my partner, Susan. I dedicate this book to them in small but heartfelt recompense for their steadfast love and encouragement.

Note on the Text

Outside of direct quotations, Persian and other non-English names and terms have generally been rendered according to modern scholarly convention. But certain contemporary renderings have been preserved: The decision has been made to sacrifice some consistency for the sake of ease of reference. In lieu of a glossary, definitions of non-English words are provided throughout the text.

Abbreviations

AJ	*Asiatic Journal*
BL	British Library
DMW	Marquess Wellesley, *The Despatches, Minutes, and Correspondence, of the Marquess Wellesley, K. G., During His Administration in India*, ed. [Robert] Montgomery Martin, 5 vols. (London, 1836–7)
GCPI	General Committee of Public Instruction
GIED	Lynn Zastoupil and Martin Moir, eds., *The Great Indian Education Debate: Documents Relating to the Orientalist-Anglicist Controversy, 1781–1843* (Richmond, UK, 1999)
HC Deb	House of Commons Debate, in *Parliamentary Debates from the Year 1803* (London, 1803–) unless otherwise stated
HL Deb	House of Lords Debate, in *Parliamentary Debates from the Year 1803* (London, 1803–) unless otherwise stated
JRAS	*Journal of the Royal Asiatic Society of Great Britain and Ireland*
LWJ	Sir William Jones, *The Letters of Sir William Jones*, ed. Garland Cannon, 2 vols. (Oxford, 1970)
MAS	*Modern Asian Studies*
MWH	G. R. Gleig, *Memoirs of the Life of The Right Hon. Warren Hastings*, 3 vols. (London, 1841)
NAI	National Archives of India
NLS	National Library of Scotland
PCFW	Proceedings of the College of Fort William, National Archives of India, Home Miscellaneous
PP	Parliamentary Papers
TNA	The National Archives (UK)

Introduction

The weight of the occasion was palpable. Representatives of the state and, surrounding them, members of the press and public filled the august chamber. At the front of this great assembly sat the diminutive company executive, flanked by his lawyers and facing a committee of legislators. In the hearings that followed, one speaker after another accused the executive and the company of grave offenses. Under his leadership, had the company not exceeded its bounds at home and abroad, amassing power to rival that of an independent state? Had it not subverted governments, trampled individual rights, caused violence, all in the name of profit? In and out of doors, the executive and his advocates put forward various defenses. One stood out for its boldness. They claimed that the company had been concerned not merely with profit but, moreover, with gathering and disseminating the world's knowledge. Under the executive's leadership, had it not fostered research, sponsored scholars, and endowed colleges? The committee would have none of this. Its members denounced the company's involvement in science and the humanities as window dressing or, worse, another outlet for its greed. Neither side, however, could hope to settle conclusively what had become a sprawling debate over the proper relations among companies, states, and knowledge. Indeed, this debate remains unsettled – over two centuries later.

If this scene seems familiar, this may be because ones like it have transpired around the world in recent years. Charged by critics in government and the media with malfeasance or overreach, technology giants, in particular, have committed themselves to the cause of knowledge.[1] Nor have they been alone. These encounters have

---

[1] Hence Google's stated mission "to organize the world's information." For a skeptical view, see Jean-Noël Jeanneney, *Google and the Myth of Universal Knowledge*, trans. Teresa Lavender Fagan (Chicago, 2007).

played out against the backdrop of a growing "knowledge sector," into which corporate idealism and investment have increasingly flowed. By encroaching on science, education, and other spheres long deemed the preserves of states, companies seem to have mixed commerce, politics, and knowledge as never before.[2] And yet the scene described above took place not recently but rather in the eighteenth century. The occasion was the impeachment of Warren Hastings in the British House of Commons. The company in question was the East India Company.

While the East India Company has been known to posterity as, among other things, "the world's most powerful corporation," several generations of its advocates echoed Hastings' claim that it was also the world's most enlightened one.[3] It is easy to dismiss this claim. From its setting up in 1600 until its winding down in 1858, the Company was distinguished for profit seeking on a global scale. Beginning in the middle of the eighteenth century, moreover, it subjugated vast swathes of the Indian subcontinent and beyond. The Company was no benevolent organization. And yet, to assume that its interest in knowledge was merely incidental, or instrumental, is to overlook the significance of knowledge in its ideology.[4] The greatest challenge for the Company's advocates was to justify to audiences in Britain and India its dual character as a company and a state. When this union came under intense strain, beginning in the 1770s, they made the support of knowledge a cornerstone of its legitimacy.

[2] See, for example, Richard S. Ruch, *Higher Ed, Inc.: The Rise of the For-Profit University* (Baltimore, 2001); Derek Bok, *Universities in the Marketplace: The Commercialization of Higher Education* (Princeton, 2003); Sheldon Krimsky, *Science in the Private Interest: Has the Lure of Profits Corrupted Biomedical Research?* (Oxford, 2003); Jennifer Washburn, *University Inc.: The Corporate Corruption of Higher Education* (New York, 2006); Philip Mirowski, *Science-Mart: Privatizing American Science* (Cambridge, MA, 2011); Tressie McMillan Cottom, *Lower Ed: The Troubling Rise of For-Profit Colleges in the New Economy* (New York, 2018).

[3] Tirthankar Roy, *The East India Company: The World's Most Powerful Corporation* (New Delhi, 2012).

[4] This book understands ideology simply as "a language of politics deployed to legitimate political action." For this definition, which summarizes comments by James Tully on the work of Quentin Skinner, see Aletta J. Norval, "The Things We Do with Words – Contemporary Approaches to the Analysis of Ideology," *British Journal of Political Science* 30 (2000), p. 320.

The East India Company and the Politics of Knowledge is about a moment, like the present one, in which the roles of companies and states overlapped in the realm of knowledge. It reveals how the Company, like many companies today, drew upon ideas about knowledge to legitimize its evolving mix of concerns. The Company may not have been a lineal ancestor of today's "knowledge enterprises," but it generated a rich body of thought and debate on many of the questions they raise.[5] Is knowledge a public good or a private commodity? Are the values of scholarship and business compatible? Should companies be entrusted to provide education and promote intellectual discovery? For that matter, should states? Can states effectively tend transnational fields of knowledge? Are they less, or are they more, likely than companies to corrupt knowledge? These are questions for our time, but they did not originate in it. To address them requires a historical perspective.

Accordingly, the book aims not only to show how "the politics of knowledge" and "ideologies about knowledge" shaped the politics and ideology of the Company but also to develop a general approach to the study of these phenomena in history.[6] The history *of ideas* of knowledge promises to do for knowledge what other approaches have begun to do for the company and the state: It promises to recover that concept's past meanings and uses and make them available in the present. As pursued in this book, it offers a reminder that the company, the state, and knowledge have been fluid concepts relatable to each other in myriad ways. To restore a sense of the historical amplitude and interrelation of these concepts is to empower stakeholders, citizens, and scholars to mold them anew.

*　　　＊ ＊ ＊ ＊ ＊*

[5] For cautions about drawing structural analogies between the Company and the modern corporation, see Philip J. Stern, "English East India Company-State and the Modern Corporation: The Google of Its Time?," in Thomas Clarke, Justin O'Brien, and Charles R. T. O'Kelley, eds., *The Oxford Handbook of the Corporation* (Oxford, 2019).

[6] The business theorist Peter Drucker coined these terms to describe what he saw as future phenomena unprecedented in history. Peter F. Drucker, *The Age of Discontinuity: Guidelines to Our Changing Society* (New York, 1969), pp. 340–7.

The histories of the company, the state, and knowledge have been studied often, yet seldom have they been studied together. Indeed, the history of the East India Company has never been studied in the context of the relations among these three entities. Even much-discussed episodes in its annals, like the Hastings trial, have not been seen to involve the kinds of questions raised above. Why this should be so, why the Company's political ideas about knowledge remain to be investigated, requires explanation.

Most often linked have been the histories of the company and the state, and the link has been best established for the early modern period. Historians of the Company, prominently, have challenged modern distinctions between companies and states by demonstrating the extent to which trade and politics once blurred into each other. And yet only rarely and tentatively have they carried this line of inquiry beyond the middle of the eighteenth century. While these historians have illuminated the origins of the Company's hybrid constitution, they have scarcely inquired into its later persistence.

In the South Asian context, these origins can be traced at least as far back as the sixteenth century. At that time, even powerful rulers of the subcontinent like the Mughals governed according to a "shared and layered" understanding of sovereignty.[7] The Mughal administrative center functioned as more of a "coordinating agency" than a commanding authority.[8] It expanded its reach by incorporating local powerholders, who, more often than not, had one foot in the world of trade. Sometimes they came from that world, as evidenced by the Hindustani proverb, "the father a merchant, the son a nawab."[9] In any case, they increasingly relied for capital and credit

[7] Sugata Bose, *A Hundred Horizons: The Indian Ocean in the Age of Global Empire* (Cambridge, MA, 2006), p. 25.

[8] Muzaffar Alam, *The Crisis of Empire in Mughal North India: Awadh and the Punjab, 1707–48*, 2nd edn (New Delhi, 2013), p. 5.

[9] Thomas Roebuck, *A Collection of Proverbs and Proverbial Phrases in the Persian and Hindoostanee Languages*, ed. H. H. Wilson (Calcutta, 1824), part 2, p. 27 [translation amended]. For examples, see Muzaffar Alam and Sanjay Subrahmanyam, introduction to Alam and Subrahmanyam, eds., *The Mughal State, 1526–1750* (Delhi, 1998), pp. 53–5.

on merchant bodies, which they wooed and rewarded with "'shares' in sovereignty."[10] This pattern of exchange fueled not only the "commercialization" of Indian politics, but also, in turn, the political rise of the Company.[11] For by the seventeenth and eighteenth centuries, powerholders were granting extensive rights not only to local merchant bodies but also to European ones.[12]

Nowhere was this phenomenon more pronounced than in Bengal, where the Company first acquired extensive territory. From the turn of the eighteenth century, as the ruling nawabs claimed more and more independence from Delhi, commercial interests captured more and more of the newly accessible political sphere.[13] One sign of the growing interpenetration of politics and trade was the appearance among political elites of a solicitude, even a sense of responsibility, toward merchants.[14] Another was the rise of a group of Asian "merchant princes," who acted as middlemen among bazaar, court, and factory.[15] Both developments facilitated the Company's gradual insinuation into the politics of the province. At least as significant in this respect was the local reformulation of Mughal ideas of government and sovereignty. By mid-century, nobles and bureaucrats were espousing the happiness and welfare of the people as the ultimate

[10] Farhat Hasan, *State and Locality in Mughal India: Power Relations in Western India, c. 1572–1730* (Cambridge, 2004), p. 126.

[11] The classic account is C. A. Bayly, *Indian Society and the Making of the British Empire* (Cambridge, 1987).

[12] P. J. Marshall, introduction to Marshall, ed., *The Eighteenth Century in Indian History: Revolution or Evolution?* (Delhi, 2003), pp. 21–3. For a detailed study, see David Veevers, *The Origins of the British Empire in Asia, 1600–1750* (Cambridge, 2020).

[13] Philip B. Calkins, "The Formation of a Regionally Oriented Ruling Group in Bengal, 1700–1740," *Journal of Asian Studies* 29 (1970). On the extent of commercialization in Bengal, see John R. McLane, *Land and Local Kingship in Eighteenth-Century Bengal* (Cambridge, 1993), p. 6; and, for a later period, Rajat Datta, *Society, Economy, and the Market: Commercialization in Rural Bengal, c. 1760–1800* (Delhi, 2000).

[14] Kumkum Chatterjee, *Merchants, Politics and Society in Early Modern India: Bihar, 1733–1820* (Leiden, 1996); Tilottama Mukherjee, *Political Culture and Economy in Eighteenth-Century Bengal* (New Delhi, 2013), ch. 5.

[15] Sushil Chaudhury, "Merchants, Companies and Rulers: Bengal in the Eighteenth Century," *Journal of the Economic and Social History of the Orient* 31 (1988); Chatterjee, *Merchants*, chs. 3–4.

test of a good ruler, displacing, or at least downgrading, once paramount considerations of pedigree and faith.[16] Might even the rule of a foreign trading company be rendered legitimate? This was the question that loomed on the eve of the Company's ascendancy.

Meanwhile, the same question was being asked in Britain. For here as well, commerce and politics mixed, and concepts that would later be reserved for one or the other sphere straddled the two. In the early modern archipelago, the state was a diffuse complex of individuals and institutions that included ones devoted to trade.[17] Companies were knots within the tangled and indistinct webs of market, state, and society.[18] Corporations ranged from business associations to municipal and national governments, and even to the Crown.[19] And sovereignty – composite rather than unitary – extended to these and many other kinds of entities.[20] All of this explains why, as works focused on the seventeenth century have shown, the Company formed part of the English state and even a state in its own right.[21] All of this also explains how the Company managed to gain a foothold in both Britain and India, half a world apart. To quote one study,

[16] Kumkum Chatterjee, *The Cultures of History in Early Modern India: Persianization and Mughal Culture in Bengal* (New Delhi, 2009), pp. 165–80.

[17] Michael J. Braddick, *State Formation in Early Modern England, c. 1550–1700* (Cambridge, 2000).

[18] Phil Withington, *The Politics of Commonwealth: Citizens and Freemen in Early Modern England* (Cambridge, 2005), chs. 5–6; Phil Withington, *Society in Early Modern England: The Vernacular Origins of Some Powerful Ideas* (London, 2010), ch. 4.

[19] Henry S. Turner, *The Corporate Commonwealth: Pluralism and Political Fictions in England, 1516–1651* (Chicago, 2016).

[20] For "composite," "fragmented," "layered," or "divisible" sovereignty as an enduring feature of European states and empires, see J. H. Elliott, "A Europe of Composite Monarchies," *Past and Present* 137 (1992); Charles Tilly, *Coercion, Capital, and European States, AD 990–1990* (Malden, MA, 1992); Lauren Benton, *A Search for Sovereignty: Law and Geography in European Empires, 1400–1900* (Cambridge, 2010); Alison L. LaCroix, *The Ideological Origins of American Federalism* (Cambridge, MA, 2010).

[21] Philip J. Stern, "'A Politie of Civill and Military Power': Political Thought and the Late Seventeenth-Century Foundations of the East India Company-State," *Journal of British Studies* 47 (2008); Philip J. Stern, *The Company-State: Corporate Sovereignty and the Early Modern Foundations of the British Empire in India* (Oxford, 2011); Rupali Mishra, *A Business of State: Commerce, Politics, and the Birth of the East India Company* (Cambridge, MA, 2018).

imarat (government) and *tijarat* (trade) were "adjunct and at times overlapping spheres" for Europeans as well as South Asians.[22] As another has it, "blurring the boundaries between politics and trade" was a game Europeans already knew how to play.[23] The public–private, politico-economic constitution of the Company was unexceptional, whether judged by Indian or by British standards.[24] It may even have been typical across an early modern world that abounded with "company-states" and other hybrid entities.[25] By the late eighteenth century, however, company-states were under pressure; by the early nineteenth century, they were anomalous.[26] What demands further consideration is how the Company was able to adapt to these changing circumstances.

For all of the attention to the ideas and arrangements that shaped the Company's hybrid constitution in the seventeenth century, there has been little to those that sustained it from the middle of the eighteenth century. Generations of commentators have narrated the history of the Company following the Battle of Plassey in 1757 as one of utter transformation: from trade to empire, and from independence to integration with the British government. Revisionist claims that the Company was a state, and was part of other states, long before that watershed have not sparked a parallel interest in the ways in which it remained a company long thereafter. To be sure, there have been hints in this direction. Recent works have pointed out that the Company's organizational structure was essentially constant;

---

[22] Sanjay Subrahmanyam, "Of *Imârat* and *Tijârat*: Asian Merchants and State Power in the Western Indian Ocean, 1400 to 1750," *Comparative Studies in Society and History* 37 (1995), p. 750.

[23] Jon E. Wilson, "Early Colonial India beyond Empire," *Historical Journal* 50 (2007), p. 958.

[24] On the Company as a constitutional entity, see William A. Pettigrew, "Corporate Constitutionalism and the Dialogue between the Global and Local in Seventeenth-Century English History," *Itinerario* 39 (2015).

[25] Stern, *Company-State*, p. 3; Andrew Phillips and J. C. Sharman, *Outsourcing Empire: How Company-States Made the Modern World* (Princeton, 2020), chs. 1–2.

[26] Timothy Alborn, *Conceiving Companies: Joint-Stock Politics in Victorian England* (London, 1998), p. 7; Phillips and Sharman, *Outsourcing Empire*, ch. 3.

that its "commercial sovereignty" found defenders well into the nineteenth century; that regulation by the British government was sporadic and often resembled collusion; and that, until the very end, the Company paid a dividend and maintained a role in commercial affairs.[27] Still, these facts have barely registered in broader assessments of how the later Company was conceptualized, justified, and criticized. Histories of the ideological foundations and false starts of the Raj have largely neglected the Company qua company.[28] Their common, if variously woven, thread has been a concern with efforts to legitimize British rule over subjects and territories. What remains to be studied is how these efforts related to those to legitimize the Company state. How did the Company's supporters defend its "commercial sovereignty" when others increasingly saw it as a territorial ruler? This book reveals one important answer: They turned to ideas about knowledge.

* * * * *

[27] Respectively, H. V. Bowen, *The Business of Empire: The East India Company and Imperial Britain, 1756–1833* (Cambridge, 2006), pp. 182–9; Anna Gambles, *Protection and Politics: Conservative Economic Discourse, 1815–1852* (Woodbridge, UK, 1998), pp. 158–65; Douglas M. Peers, *Between Mars and Mammon: Colonial Armies and the Garrison State in India, 1819–1835* (London, 1995), pp. 21–4; Anthony Webster, *The Twilight of the East India Company: The Evolution of Anglo-Asian Commerce and Politics 1790–1860* (Woodbridge, UK, 2009), pp. 13, 106, 160–1. The phrase "commercial sovereignty" had been used in reference to the Company as early as the 1770s, for example, in John Morrison, *The Advantages of an Alliance with the Great Mogul* (London, 1774), p. 99.

[28] For example, Thomas R. Metcalf, *Ideologies of the Raj* (Cambridge, 1995); Sudipta Sen, *Distant Sovereignty: National Imperialism and the Origins of British India* (New York, 2002); P. J. Marshall, *The Making and Unmaking of Empires: Britain, India, and America c. 1750–1783* (Oxford, 2005); Robert Travers, *Ideology and Empire in Eighteenth-Century India: The British in Bengal* (Cambridge, 2007); James M. Vaughn, *The Politics of Empire at the Accession of George III: The East India Company and the Crisis and Transformation of Britain's Imperial State* (New Haven, 2019); Robert Travers, *Empires of Complaints: Mughal Law and the Making of British India, 1765–1793* (Cambridge, 2022). Popular histories have more often treated the later Company as a company but have generally ignored its ideology. They have also risked overstating similarities between the Company and the modern corporation. For example, Nick Robins, *The Corporation That Changed the World: How the East India Company Shaped the Modern Multinational*, 2nd edn (London, 2012); William Dalrymple, *The Anarchy: The East India Company, Corporate Violence, and the Pillage of an Empire* (London, 2019).

If knowledge is power, as the aphorism goes, then it would seem to follow that knowledge is political. The venerable history of political thought has not dealt much with knowledge, however, nor has the upstart history of knowledge dealt much with political thought. This book attempts to remedy this mutual oversight by adapting the methods of the old field to the concerns of the new one. In doing so, it also addresses some of the limitations of previous studies of the Company's engagements with knowledge. The history *of ideas* of knowledge does not obviate existing approaches but does challenge and supplement them. Knowledge debates in the present would benefit from an understanding of knowledge debates in the past, including prominently those of the Company.

The East India Company and the Politics of Knowledge is intended at one level as a contribution to the history of knowledge. As an outgrowth of social history, cultural history, and the history of science, however, that field has inherited a cultural-structural emphasis.[29] Leading studies have chronicled the rise and fall of institutions, forms, or systems – "from Alexandria to the Internet," for instance, or "from Gutenberg to Google."[30] They have eschewed the characteristic focus of contextualist intellectual history on the utterances and aims of historical actors.[31] The first classic in the field has examined "intellectual environments rather than intellectual problems," including the culture but not the contents of political discourse.[32] Other studies have analyzed discourse from a Foucauldian perspective equally dismissive of authorship and agency.[33] A history

---

[29] On these various origins, see Johan Östling et al., introduction to Östling et al., eds., *Circulation of Knowledge: Explorations in the History of Knowledge* (Lund, 2018).

[30] Ian F. McNeely with Lisa Wolverton, *Reinventing Knowledge: From Alexandria to the Internet* (New York, 2008); Peter Burke, *A Social History of Knowledge*, 2 vols. (Cambridge, 2000–2012), vol. II, p. 1.

[31] The classic statement of this method is Quentin Skinner, "Meaning and Understanding in the History of Ideas," *History and Theory* 8 (1969).

[32] Burke, *Social History of Knowledge*, vol. I, p. 4.

[33] On this tendency, see Suzanne Marchand, "How Much Knowledge Is Worth Knowing? An American Intellectual Historian's Thoughts on the *Geschichte des Wissens*," *Berichte zur Wissenschafts-Geschichte* 42 (2019), pp. 142–4.

of cultures or structures of knowledge may offer something "more than intellectual history."[34] It also surely offers something less. To examine past "knowledge economies," "knowledge revolutions," and the like by analogy with those of today may be valid, but such phenomena are difficult to delimit without a genealogy, not to say a definition, of the concept of knowledge. For that matter, if another aim of the history of knowledge is to inform present knowledge debates, then the field must be devoted in part to the recovery of past such debates in the terms in which they were waged.

What is needed, in other words, is a history *of ideas* of knowledge that might elucidate the concept of knowledge and its discursive uses past and present. This approach promises to enrich not only the history of knowledge but also the history of ideas, including the history of political thought. Intellectual historians in the contextualist tradition have yet to respond adequately to the claim at the heart of Michel Foucault's famous power/knowledge coupling: that power and knowledge are so closely and innately related as to be inseparable from each other.[35] While these historians have focused often on power, in a political connection, and sometimes on its relations with certain branches of knowledge, seldom if ever have they treated the concept of knowledge at large or its political implications.[36] A recognition that this concept is analytically meaningful forms the basis – perhaps the only common one – of the new history of knowledge. A recognition that it has been so too for historical actors ought to form the basis of a distinct yet complementary history of ideas of knowledge. Studies under this heading might track changing meanings of the word "knowledge" and of its cognates and alternatives – a

[34] Daniel Speich Chassé, "The History of Knowledge: Limits and Potentials of a New Approach," *History of Knowledge* (3 Apr. 2017), https://historyofknowledge .net/2017/04/03/the-history-of-knowledge-limits-and-potentials-of-a-new-approach/.
[35] See especially Michel Foucault, *Discipline and Punish: The Birth of the Prison*, trans. Alan Sheridan, 2nd edn (New York, 1995), pp. 27–8.
[36] J. G. A. Pocock, for instance, has treated "the politics of historiography" but not the larger politics of knowledge. J. G. A. Pocock, "The Politics of Historiography," *Historical Research* 78 (2005).

method that has been extended to countless other concepts.[37] Or they might examine how ideas of or about knowledge "arose in the competitive context of political argument" – the method adopted in this book.[38] Both methods can yield an answer to Foucault in the form of proof that the power–knowledge relationship has been contingent, subject to endless rethinking and remaking. In addition, the latter method, by recovering past knowledge debates, can be expected to furnish present ones with new resources.

The East India Company's engagements with knowledge comprise a fitting subject for the kind of history proposed above, not least because other kinds have been tried extensively and have exemplified the tendencies it seeks to overcome. The first sustained interest in the subject can be traced to the postwar rise of area and imperial studies in the Euro-American academy, which spurred not only research on other parts of the world but also research on the history of such research. Among the fruits of this agenda were works on the orientalist scholarship of officials in the Company's employ. Early efforts suggested that the changing patterns of this scholarship were linked to changing political ideas and ideologies.[39] Before this line of intellectual history had progressed very far, however, the cultural turn came early in the form of David Kopf's *British Orientalism and the Bengal Renaissance* (1969).[40] Kopf characterized the decades

---

[37] Examples of this method include Quentin Skinner, "A Genealogy of the Modern State," *Proceedings of the British Academy* 162 (2009); Keith Tribe, *The Economy of the Word: Language, History, and Economics* (Oxford, 2015); Michael Sonenscher, *Capitalism: The Story Behind the Word* (Princeton, 2022). Worries lest historians of knowledge "make a fetish of words" are premature, considering that they have yet to try this method in earnest. For these worries, see Martin Mulsow and Lorraine Daston, "History of Knowledge," in Marek Tamm and Peter Burke, eds., *Debating New Approaches to History* (London, 2019), p. 177.

[38] David Armitage, *The Ideological Origins of the British Empire* (Cambridge, 2000), p. 5. For that matter, this method need not be limited to strictly political argument.

[39] Raymond Schwab, *La Renaissance Orientale* (Paris, 1950); George D. Bearce, *British Attitudes towards India, 1784–1858* (Oxford, 1961); S. N. Mukherjee, *Sir William Jones: A Study in Eighteenth-Century British Attitudes to India* (Cambridge, 1968).

[40] David Kopf, *British Orientalism and the Bengal Renaissance: The Dynamics of Indian Modernization 1773–1835* (Berkeley, 1969).

around 1800 as a high moment in the British study of India, and ascribed its passing to the shift from an "Orientalist" (east-facing) official culture to an "Anglicist" (west-facing) one. It is difficult to overstate the influence of what might be called the Orientalist-Anglicist thesis. Until Kopf, the two terms used together denoted rival parties in a debate on Indian education in the 1830s. But since Kopf, they have also denoted rival cultural formations, the conflict between which supposedly raged "for at least six decades."[41] One sign of the staying power of the Orientalist-Anglicist thesis has been the appearance over the years of a host of minor variations. The shift from "Orientalism" to "Anglicism" has been reprised as one from "Indomania" to "Indophobia," or from "pluralism" to "philistinism."[42] Meanwhile, although Kopf's wholesale admiration for British orientalism has gone out of fashion, his cultural-structural approach to the subject has only become more entrenched.

Edward Said's *Orientalism* (1978) embraced such an approach even as it recast Western scholarship on the East as a tool of political domination. Rather than treat knowledge as a concern of political thought and thinkers, Said followed Foucault in subsuming it and politics alike into an agentless "discourse."[43] Hence, the many studies of "colonial knowledge" in India that have come in the wake of Said – and in that of the likeminded anthropologist Bernard Cohn – have emphasized the generalities of power and culture over particular political utterances and aims.[44] Hence, too, these studies have

---

[41] William A. Green and John P. Deasy, Jr., "Unifying Themes in the History of British India, 1757–1857: An Historiographical Analysis," *Albion* 17 (1985), p. 27; Lynn Zastoupil and Martin Moir, introduction to *GIED*.

[42] Respectively, Thomas R. Trautmann, *Aryans and British India* (Berkeley, 1997); Michael J. Franklin, *Orientalist Jones: Sir William Jones, Poet, Lawyer, and Linguist, 1746–1794* (Oxford, 2011).

[43] Said paid more attention than Foucault to individuals, but likewise saw them as largely passive vessels of culture. See Edward Said, *Orientalism* (New York, 1978), pp. 11, 202.

[44] See Shruti Kapila, preface to Kapila, ed., An Intellectual History for India, special issue of *Modern Intellectual History* 4 (2007), pp. 3–4. For an overview of studies of "colonial knowledge," see Tony Ballantyne, "Colonial Knowledge," in Sarah Stockwell, ed., *The British Empire: Themes and Perspectives* (Malden, MA, 2008).

tended to dismiss debates surrounding the Company's engagements with knowledge as mere epiphenomena of an essentially continuous "cultural project of control."[45] Such studies have been productive in two respects. They have focused attention on power, a theme largely absent from earlier works on orientalism. And they have shown that the Company's scholarly interests went beyond orientalism to include, in fact, nearly every conceivable domain. There has long been a tension between these two tendencies: between the increasing ramification of "colonial knowledge" and the continued ascription of it, in all of its forms, to an "impulse to dominate and control."[46] If it is simplistic to treat knowledge as neutral or innocent, then it is equally simplistic to reduce the spectrum of human motivation to a primal will to power. Accepting a key role for the workings of power ought to mark the beginning, not the end, of essays in the politics of knowledge. Further questions must be asked. What ideas did historical actors form of the relations between knowledge and power? To what political uses did they put them? By failing to address these questions, studies of "colonial knowledge" have elided the complex agency not only of the "colonizer" but also of the "colonized."

This last point has been urged in support of alternative approaches, notably that of C. A. Bayly's *Empire and Information* (1996). By fixating on "colonial knowledge," Bayly argued, Said's followers risked ignoring "Indians and *their* knowledge as thoroughly as the most hidebound colonial administrative history."[47] This argument was typical of the "Cambridge school" of Indian history, which held that the Raj was built upon and sustained by "Indian agency."[48] Yet the Cambridge

---

[45] For the quote, see Nicholas B. Dirks, foreword to Bernard S. Cohn, *Colonialism and Its Forms of Knowledge: The British in India* (Princeton, 1996), p. ix.

[46] For the quote, see Gauri Viswanathan, *Masks of Conquest: Literary Study and British Rule in India* (New York, 1989), p. 3.

[47] C. A. Bayly, *Empire and Information: Intelligence Gathering and Social Communication in India, 1780–1870* (Cambridge, 1996), p. 314 [emphasis added]. For a thorough analysis of the disagreement, see William R. Pinch, "Same Difference in India and Europe," *History and Theory* 38 (1999).

[48] This is not to be confused with the Cambridge school of intellectual history.

school itself gave little scope to agency, Indian or other, at the level of ideas.[49] In *Empire and Information*, Bayly was concerned far less with the minds of Company officials or "native informants" than with the structures into which they fit.[50] None of the structures he identified – "the information order," "knowledge communities," "the Indian ecumene" – would have meant anything to these individuals. Nor, for that matter, would his definition of "knowledge." Whereas contemporaries were apt to distinguish the "knowledge" of a scholar from the "information" of a news writer or the "intelligence" of a spy, Bayly used such terms interchangeably. "Knowledge," in the words of one distinguished follower, was simply "what it took to govern."[51] This functionalist stance has proved useful in identifying certain forms and practices, like writing and print, that served as "technologies of rule."[52] Again, however, it has tended to obscure the ideas about knowledge that historical actors themselves developed and deployed. Among Bayly's keenest insights in *Empire and Information* was one that belied his methodological commitments. For the Company, he submitted, scholarship "was not a homogenous mode of gaining power" but "rather an arena of debate."[53] Taking this proposition seriously requires adopting an altogether different approach: It requires attending to the ideational terms in which such debate was undertaken.

---

[49] Only in a later phase and in a somewhat different context did Bayly address this omission. See C. A. Bayly, *Recovering Liberties: Indian Thought in the Age of Liberalism and Empire* (Cambridge, 2011).

[50] This approach was inspired by the sociologist Manuel Castells, for whom, as Bayly put it, "Knowledge itself is a social formation." Bayly, *Empire and Information*, p. 4.

[51] Sujit Sivasundaram, *Islanded: Britain, Sri Lanka, and the Bounds of an Indian Ocean Colony* (Chicago, 2013), p. 20.

[52] See, for example, Miles Ogborn, *Indian Ink: Script and Print in the Making of the English East India Company* (Chicago, 2007); Bhavani Raman, *Document Raj: Writing and Scribes in Early Colonial South India* (Chicago, 2012).

[53] Bayly, *Empire and Information*, p. 360. "Debate" seems preferable to related notions of "dialogue," "conversation," and "co-production," as it invites particular attention to the political sphere. Cf., respectively, Eugene F. Irschick, *Dialogue and History: Constructing South India, 1795–1895* (Berkeley, 1994); Thomas R. Trautmann, *Languages and Nations: The Dravidian Proof in Colonial Madras* (Berkeley, 2006); Kapil Raj, *Relocating Modern Science: Circulation and the Construction of Knowledge in South Asia and Europe, 1650–1900* (Basingstoke, 2007).

The potential for such an approach has occasionally come into view. Cultural-structural biases have been, if not corrected, then at least identified. One historian has countered Kopf's Orientalist-Anglicist thesis by pointing up the flexibility of contemporary British and Indian political rhetoric.[54] Another has rebutted the "sweeping ... discourse" of Said and his followers by stressing the "intricate dialectics" between intellectual and political pursuits.[55] A number of studies have heeded the call for nuance and specificity. Most have done so by focusing on particular scholarly fields or individuals. Thus, disciplinary histories have suggested that the Company's interest in certain kinds of knowledge reflected not a simple drive to dominate but rather complex and shifting concerns.[56] And biographical treatments have revealed that scholar-officials in the Company's employ, though instruments of power, could be subtle and idiosyncratic thinkers.[57] Increasingly, historians have explored the intellectual worlds not only of the Company's British personnel but also of its non-British interlocutors and intermediaries. Studies of Asian, Eurasian, and continental European knowledge patrons, go-betweens, and entrepreneurs have done much to overturn facile conflations of knowledge and power.[58] At the same time, the view

[54] Travers, *Ideology and Empire*, pp. 15–16.
[55] Rosane Rocher, "British Orientalism in the Eighteenth Century: The Dialectics of Knowledge and Government," in Carol A. Breckenridge and Peter van der Veer, eds., *Orientalism and the Postcolonial Predicament: Perspectives on South Asia* (Philadelphia, 1993), p. 215.
[56] For example, Richard H. Grove, *Green Imperialism: Colonial Expansion, Tropical Island Edens and the Origins of Environmentalism, 1600–1860* (Cambridge, 1995), chs. 7–8; Jessica Patterson, *Religion, Enlightenment and Empire: British Interpretations of Hinduism in the Eighteenth Century* (Cambridge, 2021).
[57] For example, Rosane Rocher and Ludo Rocher, *The Making of Western Indology: Henry Thomas Colebrooke and the East India Company* (Abingdon, UK, 2012); Tobias Wolffhardt, *Unearthing the Past to Forge the Future: Colin Mackenzie, the Early Colonial State and the Comprehensive Survey of India*, trans. Jane Rafferty (New York, 2018).
[58] For example, Rosie Llewellyn-Jones, *A Very Ingenious Man, Claude Martin in Early Colonial India* (Delhi, 1992); Muzaffar Alam and Seema Alavi, introduction to Alam and Alavi, trans., *A European Experience of the Mughal Orient: The I'jāz-i Arsalānī (Persian Letters, 1773–1779) of Antoine-Louis Henri Polier* (New Delhi, 2001); Phillip B. Wagoner, "Precolonial Intellectuals and the Production of Colonial Knowledge,"

they have afforded of layered, cross-cutting intellectual and political currents has presented a challenge to historical synthesis. Recent erudite attempts to remap the terrain of Kopf, Cohn, and Bayly have eschewed broad conclusions at the risk of lapsing into a diffident microhistory.[59] These attempts have succeeded in complicating or deconstructing old narratives. This book builds upon them to offer a distinctly new narrative.

* * * * *

To introduce the main argument of the chapters that follow, a good point of departure can be found in the preface to Ramkamal Sen's *A Dictionary in English and Bengalee* (1834). There the Calcutta entrepreneur and litterateur related the following anecdote. Many years ago, an East India Company ship sailed for the first time from the Bay of Bengal up the Hooghly River and anchored near the villages that would one day grow to become the city of Calcutta. The captain of the vessel sent ashore to the local magnates and requested the services of a "dubash." This word, on the coast and elsewhere in India, referred to a middleman of some learning and standing who facilitated trade. In riverine Bengal, however, the utterance more readily called to mind a *dhoba*, or washerman. Accordingly, the magnates selected one such man and deputed him to tender his services to the Company. The *dhoba* boarded the East Indiaman bearing the customary gifts – only to be received in a most uncustomary manner. The captain and officers saluted the *dhoba*, honored him with

Comparative Studies in Society and History 45 (2003); Kapil Raj, "Mapping Knowledge Go-Betweens in Calcutta, 1770–1820," in Simon Schaffer et al., eds., *The Brokered World: Go-Betweens and Global Intelligence, 1770–1820* (Sagamore Beach, MA, 2009); Simon Schaffer, "The Asiatic Enlightenments of British Astronomy," in ibid.; Savithri Preetha Nair, *Raja Serfoji II: Science, Medicine and Enlightenment in Tanjore* (New Delhi, 2012); Robert Travers, "The Connected Worlds of Haji Mustapha (c. 1730–91): A Eurasian Cosmopolitan in Eighteenth-Century Bengal," *Indian Economic and Social History Review* 52 (2015).

[59] For example, Sanjay Subrahmanyam, *Europe's India: Words, People, Empires, 1500–1800* (Cambridge, MA, 2017); James Watt, *British Orientalisms, 1759–1835* (Cambridge, 2019).

ceremonies, and discharged him with bags not of laundry but "of gold and other precious articles." The *dhoba*-dubash soon took to his new employment. He learned the English language and became "one of the principal native servants of the Company." In Ramkamal's words, "He may be considered the first English scholar among the natives of Calcutta."[60]

The tale of the *dhoba*-dubash, though evidently in common circulation, had a special significance for Ramkamal.[61] As he related elsewhere in the preface to his dictionary, he too had risen from humble village origins to become a leading "English scholar" and "native servant" of the Company. The story contrasted sharply and purposely, however, with the account Ramkamal proceeded to give of his own literary fortunes, the thrust of which was that he had suffered years of setbacks and losses owing to a lack of patronage. A dictionary was the very "key of knowledge," Ramkamal observed, and in the past, the Company had favored such works with "encouragement and assistance." The scanty patronage it now offered, however, "will not exempt me from loss in printing, nor ... in employing writers, pundits, &c." What accounted for the change? The way that Ramkamal now advertised his dictionary offered some clues. Rather than dwell upon the scholarly merits of his work, like earlier lexicographers, he framed it as a practical aid to "native education." He maintained this stance in a dedication on behalf of the "Native public" to the Company's governor-general, to whom he must have thought it would appeal.[62] Thus, in the course of his preface, Ramkamal provided readers with a striking series of contrasts. First, while harking back to a past in which the Company had patronized scholars, he alluded to a present in which it espoused the cause of education. Second, while recalling

---

[60] [Ramkamal Sen] Ram Comul Sen, *A Dictionary in English and Bengalee*, 2 vols. (Serampore, 1834), vol. I, pp. 16–17.

[61] For another version of the tale, see C. R. Wilson, "Introductory Account of the Early History of the English in Bengal," in Wilson, ed., *The Early Annals of the English in Bengal*, 3 vols. (Calcutta, 1895–1917), vol. I, p. 59.

[62] [Ramkamal Sen], *Dictionary*, vol. I, pp. 3–8.

that it had once wooed learned men, he implied that it now sought favor with a broader "native public." Finally, while portraying the Company of old as a body of traders, he addressed the Company of his day as a powerful sovereign. With this set of juxtapositions, Ramkamal anticipated the argument of this book.

From almost its founding in 1600, the Company sponsored learning in connection with its activities. In the 1770s, when it began to directly govern large territories, this sponsorship assumed an ideological aspect. Warren Hastings, the first governor-general of Bengal, advanced what he called a "system of conciliation." He argued that the beleaguered Company would gain allies at home and abroad by patronizing European scholar-officials and Indian learned elites. The idea of conciliation befitted both merchant and sovereign and was rooted in both British and Indian political thought. It remained a mainstay of Company ideology throughout much of the next six decades. Not only did this idea survive the impeachment of Hastings, it flourished and spread, including to the Company's Court of Directors. Lord Wellesley's governor-generalship posed a greater challenge: He used knowledge not to defend but to attack the Company state. After Wellesley's departure, scholar-officials and learned elites struggled to find favor with wary Company leaders. At the same time, the Company's trade dwindled, while its territory expanded dramatically. By the 1820s, it was "paramount" in India; its ideas about knowledge began to change accordingly. Rather than conciliate a few elites, officials increasingly sought to convince wider publics of the Company's good government. Now, more and more, the idea of conciliation competed with one of mass education. By the late 1830s, the latter had supplanted the former at the heart of the Company's ideology.

This is a new account in many respects, owing to its focus on ideas about knowledge. It reveals that these ideas were integral to the Company state and reconstructs the debates they animated. It shows that, far from a cultural-structural phenomenon comprehensible only to modern scholars, the politics of knowledge is a subject on which

⌣historical actors themselves have been highly articulate. The histories of the Company, Britain, and India look different when contemporary ideas about knowledge are foregrounded. To trace the career
of these ideas is to cast an illuminating light on the decades around
1800. Familiar narratives – the rise and fall of an Orientalist cultural
formation, the consolidation of colonial knowledge, the reshaping of
the information order – find few echoes in the knowledge debates
of the period. On the contrary, these debates, inasmuch as they per-
tained to the Company, revolved around its hybrid constitution and
that constitution's legitimacy.

A word should be said about the scope and terminology of the
book. It treats the "Company state": the East India Company in its
dual character. It understands the Company not as a unitary body
but, rather, as a far-flung constellation of individuals and institutions.[63] It centers on the Company's capitals, London and Calcutta,
but ranges across a "Greater India" from the Red Sea to the Pearl
River Delta. It examines the "high thought" of leaders of or involved
with the Company but also the "medium thought" of its rank-and-
file agents and interlocutors.[64] European scholar-officials and Indian
scholar-collaborators figure prominently – among the latter, "learned
elites" in particular.[65] More will be said about this category. For now,
suffice it to say that it reflects the Company's view, and not a neutral
view, of Indian society. A similar caveat applies to the category of
"knowledge," which the book treats not as an objective category but
rather as a contested one. *The East India Company and the Politics of
Knowledge* is concerned with what contemporaries called knowledge

---

[63] On the Company's decentralized structure, see Emily Erikson, *Between Monopoly
and Free Trade: The English East India Company, 1600–1757* (Princeton, 2014).

[64] For the distinction, see Emma Rothschild, "Language and Empire, c.1800," *Historical
Research* 78 (2005), p. 210.

[65] "Scholar-officials" seems preferable to "scholar-administrators" because the category
might include not only civil servants but also army officers and surgeons. For an
important reminder about the scholarly activities of the Company's military personnel, see Douglas M. Peers, "Colonial Knowledge and the Military in India, 1780–1860,"
Journal of Imperial and Commonwealth History 33 (2005). "Scholar-collaborators,"
meanwhile, seems preferable to the more passive "native informants."

and does not assign greater or lesser relevance to any of its branches or forms. It should be stipulated, however, that the book is about "knowledge" not in the very broadest sense but rather in connection with learning and scholarship. It was knowledge in this sense that became a fixture in the politics of the Company – just as it seems to be becoming a fixture in today's politics.

I   Warren Hastings and the Idea of Conciliation

"It is new," wrote Samuel Johnson to Warren Hastings in 1781, "for a Governour of Bengal to patronise learning."[1] In this opinion, Johnson was hardly alone among contemporary intellectuals. Sir William Jones praised Hastings as "the first liberal promoter of useful knowledge in Bengal"; John Gilchrist held that an "era of Oriental literature dawned" with his administration.[2] What accounted for such statements? The East India Company, like other European trading companies, had long patronized learning to facilitate its operations and to burnish its image.[3] Since the seventeenth century, the Company's leaders in Bengal and elsewhere had encouraged pursuits including the collection of natural objects and the study of Asian languages. Undeniably, however, Hastings as governor (1772–4) and governor-general (1774–85) patronized learning on a larger scale than any of his predecessors. He founded a madrasa (Islamic college), ordered the compilation and translation of Hindu and Islamic laws, commissioned expeditions to Bhutan and Tibet, and backed dozens of other humanistic and scientific ventures. Hitherto no Company official had done any of these things. It has often been asked why Hastings did.

---

[1] Johnson to Hastings, 29 Jan. 1781, in *The Letters of Samuel Johnson*, ed. Bruce Redford, 5 vols. (Princeton, 1992–4), vol. III, p. 324.

[2] [William Jones], "The Introduction," *Asiatick Researches* 1 (Calcutta, 1788), p. vii; John Gilchrist, *Dictionary, English and Hindoostanee*, 2 vols. (Calcutta, 1787–98), vol. I, p. i.

[3] Anna Winterbottom, *Hybrid Knowledge in the Early East India Company World* (Basingstoke, 2016). For points of comparison, see Steven J. Harris, "Long-Distance Corporations, Big Sciences, and the Geography of Knowledge," *Configurations* 6 (1998); Harold J. Cook, *Matters of Exchange: Commerce, Medicine, and Science in the Dutch Golden Age* (New Haven, 2007); Ted Binnema, *"Enlightened Zeal": The Hudson's Bay Company and Scientific Networks, 1670–1870* (Toronto, 2014).

Historians have offered several explanations. One is that Hastings was stirred by intellectual curiosity. He had excelled at Westminster School and remained a dabbler in subjects ranging from agriculture to classical poetry. Another explanation is that he felt a sense of duty to encourage such curiosity in others; this he wrote to Johnson.[4] Meanwhile, most of the projects he sponsored had, or could be seen to have, practical benefits for the Company's trade or administration. And yet few readers of Hastings have been satisfied with these explanations alone.[5] Several have detected in his writings evidence of an enlightened cosmopolitan program to "reconcile" Britons and Indians. They have suggested on this basis that he was a committed Indophile or cultural relativist.[6] But while "reconciliation" – or, more accurately, "conciliation" – was indeed a key idea for Hastings, these readers have misconstrued it and hence missed its political implications. First, any appearance in Hastings of relativism must be weighed against his stated conviction that Europe's learning had surpassed that of "the rest of the world."[7] Second, he was a canny and changeable politician whose commitment to any cultural stance should not be overstated. Finally, he did not have the luxury to indulge in fantasies: To find a place on his agenda, scholarly patronage would have had to serve vital interests. And indeed, it did.

The main ideological challenge Hastings faced was to square the Company's growing political footprint with its hybrid constitution.

---

[4] Hastings to Johnson, 7 Aug. 1775, in *MWH*, vol. II, p. 18.

[5] For the above explanations and their insufficiency, see P. J. Marshall, "Warren Hastings as Scholar and Patron," in Anne Whiteman, J. S. Bromley, and P. G. M. Dickson, eds., *Statesmen, Scholars and Merchants: Essays in Eighteenth-Century History Presented to Dame Lucy Sutherland* (Oxford, 1973), pp. 243–6, 252–6.

[6] Ibid., pp. 256–62; J. L. Brockington, "Warren Hastings and Orientalism," in Geoffrey Carnall and Colin Nicholson, eds., *The Impeachment of Warren Hastings: Papers from a Bicentenary Commemoration* (Edinburgh, 1989), p. 91; Lynn Zastoupil and Martin Moir, introduction to *GIED*, pp. 2–4; Michael J. Franklin, "'The Hastings Circle': Writers and Writing in Calcutta in the Last Quarter of the Eighteenth Century," in Emma J. Clery, Caroline Franklin, and Peter D. Garside, eds., *Authorship, Commerce and the Public: Scenes of Writing, 1750–1850* (Basingstoke, 2002), p. 186.

[7] [Warren Hastings], *A Proposal for Establishing a Professorship of the Persian Language in the University of Oxford* [c. 1766], p. 9.

This was no abstract concern. The British government and Indian powerholders alike threatened the Company's very existence. Its conquest of the province of Bengal from mid-century had stirred up arguments that a body of merchants could not or should not rule vast and populous territories. Hastings sympathized with such arguments, but he was bound by duty and circumstances to oppose them. "Conciliation" offered him a means to do so. This idea, derived from both European and Mughal sources, denoted a commercial style of politics based on accommodation and negotiation. In the context of scholarly patronage, it tapped into widespread positive associations between commerce and knowledge. Hastings maintained that patronizing European scholar-officials and Indian learned elites would conciliate opinion toward the Company state. If this hybrid entity was to last, he suggested, it must traffic not only in material goods but also in intellectual ones.

HASTINGS AND THE COMPANY STATE

What were the origins of Hastings' idea of conciliation? Why did he nearly always invoke it in connection with scholarly patronage? Answering these questions requires revisiting the foundations of the Company's regime in Bengal, in the construction of which Hastings played a central role. Hastings has long been seen to embody the Company's apparently abrupt transition from merchant to ruler in the second half of the eighteenth century. He himself did much to cultivate this reputation by espousing an ideal of strong, uncommercial sovereignty. In reality, however, he was forced to uphold the Company's hybrid constitution, even in the face of mounting criticism in Britain and India. It was the search for a mode of politics that made the best of this reality, and that might assuage the Company's critics, that led Hastings to conciliation via scholarly patronage.

From his early days in India, Hastings often voiced disapproval of the Company's conflation of politics and trade. He began his career with the Company in the 1750s handling textiles, and for some time insisted that such alone was its proper domain. Accordingly, after joining the ruling council in Calcutta in 1761, he urged it to submit to the "lawful authority" of the nawab of Bengal. "Instead of erecting themselves into lords and oppressors of the country," he urged, Company officials should "confine themselves to an honest and fair trade."[8] But if this argument was tenuous given the Company's creeping domination of the province, then it became untenable upon its assumption of the diwani (the right to collect the land revenue). With this development in 1765, Hastings acknowledged, the Company had "undergone a total change. From a merely Commercial Body, they are grown up into a Military & Territorial Power, to w[hi]ch their Commerce is but a Secondary concern."[9] Hastings continued to express this opinion after the Court of Directors appointed him governor of Bengal in 1772. The Company's constitution, he wrote the directors in one dispatch, consisted of "charters ... framed for the jurisdiction of your trading settlements, the sales of your exports, and the provision of your annual investment. I need not observe how incompetent these must prove for the government of a great kingdom."[10] Hastings did not reserve these sentiments for the directors alone. To the prime minister, he likewise argued that the Company's "mercantile concerns" must be subordinated to its political ones. As he now put it, "the details of commerce are not fit objects of attention to the supreme administration of a state."[11]

These objections bespoke an ideal of a robust sovereignty unbounded by the Company's commercial lineage. This ideal took several forms. At times, Hastings suggested that a body of merchants was unfit to rule and that the Company's political authority should be transferred to the Crown.[12] At others, he portrayed himself as a loyal

---

[8] Hastings, Minute (1 Mar. 1763), in *Original Papers Relative to the Disturbances in Bengal: Containing Every Material Transaction from 1759 to 1764*, 2 vols. (London, 1765), vol. II, p. 53.

[9] Hastings to [Earl of Shelburne], 16 July 1771, BL, Add. MS 29126, f. 74v.

[10] Hastings to Directors, 11 Nov. 1773, in *MWH*, vol. I, p. 368.

[11] Hastings to Lord North, 2 Apr. 1775, in *MWH*, vol. I, pp. 534, 539.

[12] Neil Sen, "Warren Hastings and British Sovereign Authority in Bengal, 1774–80," *Journal of Imperial and Commonwealth History* 25 (1997).

servant of the Company who merely sought to bring its constitution
in line with its altered situation.[13] Finally, whether under the Crown's
or the Company's auspices, he spoke of establishing an "oriental despotism" ostensibly on the model of the Mughal emperors.[14] Hastings
never settled on a coherent political program, much less philosophy.
He was constantly adapting his message to different audiences and circumstances. Yet, for all of the ambiguities and contradictions in his
thinking, he expressed a consistent desire – at least while in office – to
render the Company less of a company and more of a state.

There is a distinction to be observed, however, between
Hastings' grand projections and the practicalities of the system in
which he operated. His calls for an uncommercial politics after 1765
were no more realistic than his calls for an unpolitical commerce formerly. Declaring "the details of commerce" below the dignity of his
government meant little when most officials – sometimes including
Hastings – were engaged in trade. These officials intended to make a
private fortune and used their public positions to do so.[15] Something
similar was true of the Company at large. The assumption of the
diwani had shifted the main source of its profits without diminishing their primacy.[16] In this broad sense, "commerce" had hardly
become, as Hastings would have it, "a secondary concern." To quote
one report, the Company remained fixated on keeping "in motion the
great machine of [its] commerce," notwithstanding its "accession ...

[13] In 1771, for instance, Hastings railed against a Crown commission whose "purpose
was apparently to invade the Rights of the Co[mpany]." He claimed that "though I
have read the History of England more t[ha]n once I do not remember such an Invasion
of ... a great Commercial body." Hastings to Randolph Marriott, 26 Mar. 1771, BL,
Add. MS 29126, f. 62r; Hastings to [Shelburne], 16 July 1771, f. 76v. For Hastings'
alternate appeals to the Company and to the ministry, see Ben Joseph Gilding, "British
Politics, Imperial Ideology, and East India Company Reform, 1773–1784" (PhD dissertation, University of Cambridge, 2019), ch. 5.

[14] Robert Travers, *Ideology and Empire in Eighteenth-Century India: The British in
Bengal* (Cambridge, 2007), pp. 106–7, 139–40.

[15] P. J. Marshall, *East Indian Fortunes: The British in Bengal in the Eighteenth Century*
(Oxford, 1976).

[16] P. J. Marshall, *Bengal: The British Bridgehead: Eastern India 1740–1828* (Cambridge,
1987), p. 133.

to the Government of the Country."[17] The Company as merchant bought goods using the revenue the Company as ruler collected and drove down their cost using its political leverage.[18] Even to put things in this way may be to draw too neat a distinction between two sides of the Company that remained bound together in its constitution.

Hastings understood this reality only too well as an official whose commission was to exercise sovereignty for profit. Hitherto, governors of Bengal, first appointed in 1758, had played a minor role in actually governing the province. Upon the Company's assumption of the diwani, Robert Clive had delegated most of its new functions to the naib nazim (nawab's deputy), Muhammad Reza Khan. As Hastings put it, the governor had "contrived to enjoy all the Emoluments of it [power] with[ou]t Responsibility."[19] But by the early 1770s, Clive's system of "double government" had broken down completely. Commentators blamed it for low revenue from the diwani lands and, in part, for a famine that threw markets and trade into disarray. It must now be admitted that, to quote the surveyor James Rennell, "In a Countrey void of civil Polity these Accidents are not easily remedied."[20] Thus it was that the directors appointed Hastings to "stand forth as Duan [diwan]" and to rescue the Company's troubled finances.[21] They expected him to largely fund the Company's debts, its trading settlements, and its "investment" (the goods it bought in India to sell in London).[22] Many of Hastings' reforms, later seen as laying the foundations of the Raj, were ad hoc, desperate fundraising measures. So too were his aggressive attempts to extract

---

[17] Report (6 Aug. 1789), cited in Rajat Datta, "The Commercial Economy of Eastern India under Early British Rule," in H. V. Bowen, Elizabeth Mancke, and John G. Reid, eds., Britain's Oceanic Empire: Atlantic and Indian Ocean Worlds, c. 1550–1850 (Oxford, 2012), p. 343.

[18] Marshall, Bengal, p. 115; Om Prakash, "The English East India Company and India," in H. V. Bowen, Margarette Lincoln, and Nigel Rigby, eds., The Worlds of the East India Company (Woodbridge, UK, 2002).

[19] Hastings to [Shelburne], 16 July 1771, f. 74v.

[20] Rennell to Gilbert Burrington, 1 Sept. 1770, BL, IOR H/765, p. 208.

[21] Fort William – India House Correspondence, 21 vols. (Delhi, 1949–85), vol. VI, p. 123.

[22] See Travers, Ideology and Empire, pp. 101–2.

"casual and extraordinary resources" from zamindars (landholders) and neighboring rulers.[23] Hastings, in other words, largely complied with the directors' expectations. Between occasional calls to abolish the Company state, he was toiling on its behalf.

Hastings resented the Company's hybrid constitution but was ultimately compelled to uphold it. He aspired to wield a strong sovereignty, uncompromised by commercial imperatives, but was forced to work within the existing system.[24] In his early months in office, Hastings was preoccupied with averting a fiscal crisis and imparting a semblance of order to his administration. No sooner had he begun to entertain grander ambitions than he became mired in a series of conflicts. While the long-awaited Regulating Act of 1773 made him "governor-general" and granted him authority over all of the Company's Indian territories, it also established local counterweights to his authority in the form of a "Supreme Council" and a "Supreme Court." Bitter wrangling ensued in Calcutta. Having "formed great designs," Hastings now found himself "curbed, and prevented from carrying" them "into execution."[25] Nor did he obtain much support from the Court of Directors or the ministry in Britain, both of which were also paralyzed by disagreement.[26] Finally, to effect any great change required negotiating with Indian powerholders, who could seldom be corralled. For all of these reasons, Hastings was forced to compromise his leviathanic vision. Whatever the dictates of his conscience, judgment, or ego, he had no choice but to prioritize the Company's finances. It was thus in vain, according to Hastings' councilor and rival Philip Francis, that he should pretend

---

[23] *Fort William – India House Correspondence*, vol. VIII, p. 421. See P. J. Marshall, *The Impeachment of Warren Hastings* (Oxford, 1965), p. 108; Michael H. Fisher, *A Clash of Cultures: Awadh, the British, and the Mughals* (New Delhi, 1987), pp. 81–5.

[24] See P. J. Marshall, "The Shaping of the New Colonial Regime in Bengal," in Mahmudul Huque, ed., *Bangladesh: History, Politics, Economy, Society and Culture* (Dhaka, 2016).

[25] Hastings to [Robert] Palk, undated, in *MWH*, vol. I, p. 477; Hastings, cited in Keith Feiling, *Warren Hastings* (London, 1954), p. 100.

[26] See Lucy S. Sutherland, *The East India Company in Eighteenth-Century Politics*, corr. edn (Oxford, 1962), pp. 291–317; Gilding, "British Politics," ch. 5.

"to reconcile ... justice" in his "administration, with injustice in its fundamental principle – I mean that of uniting the character of Sovereign and merchant, and exercising the power of the first for the benefit of the second."[27] Hastings scarcely disagreed. He himself perceived a "radical and incurable" contradiction between the "primary exigencies" of the Company and "those which in all States ought to take [the] place of every other concern, the interests of the people." His conclusion was revealing: "All that the wisest institutions can effect in such a system can only be to improve the advantages of a temporary possession, and to protract that decay, which sooner or later must end it."[28] In his own sober estimation, then, Hastings was not the builder of a sturdy edifice but the carpenter of one ultimately beyond repair. The Company's constitution contained "the seeds of death in it." But as long as it remained, he must do what he could to preserve it.[29]

In fact, there was much that Hastings could do, thanks to the limitations of contemporary criticism. In Britain, the Company state was controversial but not yet anomalous: Concepts of public and private, political and economic were only just beginning to diverge. Hence, while the jurist William Blackstone espoused an influential unitary view of sovereignty, a composite view amenable to corporate sovereignty remained the norm.[30] And while the philosopher Adam Smith helped to shape political economy into a distinct discipline, he identified neither an "economy" independent of the polity nor an "economics" independent of politics.[31] Smith did demonstrate a growing tendency among British critics to trace the Company's ills to its hybrid constitution. In holding in *The Wealth*

---

[27] Philip Francis, *Letter from Mr. Francis to Lord North, Late Earl of Guildford* [17 Sept. 1777] (London [1793]), p. 13.

[28] Hastings to Alexander Elliot, 10 Feb. 1777, in *MWH*, vol. II, pp. 149–50.

[29] Hastings to Laurence Sulivan, 18 Apr. 1779, in *MWH*, vol. II, p. 275.

[30] Alison L. LaCroix, *The Ideological Origins of American Federalism* (Cambridge, MA, 2010), pp. 15–20.

[31] Emma Rothschild, *Economic Sentiments: Adam Smith, Condorcet, and the Enlightenment* (Cambridge, MA, 2001).

of Nations (1776) that "a company of merchants are ... incapable of considering themselves as sovereigns," he invoked an increasingly popular premise.[32] For every commentator who insisted that "the greatest evil arises when traders become princes," however, there was another ready to point out:

> Is not our own legislature composed principally of merchants
> and of mercantile men? And are not the mercantile concerns of
> this, and of most countries now-a-days, so intimately connected
> with their prosperity and well-being, that the great concern of
> governments is to put them on a right and respectable footing?[33]

Some of the most outspoken detractors of the Company state advocated reforming it rather than abolishing it outright. This indeed was what the British government sought to do in the Regulating Act of 1773 and again in Pitt's India Act of 1784. The coalition ministry of 1783 advocated a more radical intervention, which would have involved appointing separate commissions to oversee the Company's government and trade. Yet even this plan, which was thwarted by the king, would have kept much of the Company's existing structure intact. Indeed, according to its prime mover, Edmund Burke, one of its key objects was to "restore the Company." There was nothing inherently wrong, Burke assured the Commons, with placing "extensive political powers in the hands of a company of merchants.... I have known merchants with the sentiments and the abilities of great statesmen; and I have seen persons in the rank of statesmen, with the conceptions and character of pedlars."[34]

---

[32] Adam Smith, *An Inquiry into the Nature and Causes of the Wealth of Nations*, 2 vols. (London, 1776), vol. I, p. 251. For the work most responsible for popularizing this premise, see William Bolts, *Considerations on India Affairs*, 2 vols. (London, 1772–5), vol. I, pp. vi, 222.

[33] Archibald Keir, *Thoughts on the Affairs of Bengal* (London, 1772), p. 5; Thomas Pownall, *The Right, Interest, and Duty, of the State, as Concerned in the Affairs of the East Indies* (London, 1773), pp. 43–4.

[34] Edmund Burke, "Speech on Fox's India Bill" (1 Dec. 1783), in Burke, *The Writings and Speeches of Edmund Burke*, ed. Paul Langford, 9 vols. (Oxford, 1981–2015), vol. V, pp. 386–7, 433.

So much for British opinion, but what of its Indian counter-part? Could Indian subjects and rulers tolerate the sovereignty of the Company? Some Britons assumed not. "Brought up under regal government," wrote one London newspaper contributor, "the Indians place a confidence in the promises of princes, which they never bestow upon commercial bodies."[35] Indian "princes" too, according to another commentator, were "humiliated and galled with the thought of being under the sway of a company of merchants."[36] Such arguments projected British ideas onto Indian minds. But there is reason to think that some of these ideas reached India and found a receptive audience. A vast network of news-writers translated and circulated foreign publications for the consumption of the literate and "literacy aware."[37] The free merchant Joseph Price, who had lived in Bombay and Calcutta, went so far as to argue that "newspapers are as much read in Asia as in London." Indians, he advised the statesman Charles James Fox, were familiar with his views and those of other Company critics, and quoted his "speeches against the Company, in as many modes and ways, as you could and have done yourself."[38] If Price is to be credited, then politically active Indians took an early interest in metropolitan debates surrounding the Company.[39] Whatever they learned of these debates from newspapers and other sources likely served to reinforce locally inspired

---

[35] Creon [pseud.], "The State of Asiatic Affairs, as Represented by a Writer Well Acquainted with the Concerns of Government," *Gentleman's Magazine* 39 (Aug. 1769), p. 375.

[36] *Thoughts on Improving the Government of the British Territorial Possessions in the East Indies* (London, 1780), p. 15.

[37] On these news-writers and their audiences, see Michael H. Fisher, "The Office of Akhbār Nawīs: The Transition from Mughal to British Forms," *Modern Asian Studies* 27 (1993); C. A. Bayly, *Empire and Information: Intelligence Gathering and Social Communication in India, 1780–1870* (Cambridge, 1996), pp. 36–44, 69–73, 199–207.

[38] Joseph Price, *A Short Commercial and Political Letter from Mr. Joseph Price to the Right Honourable Charles James Fox* (London, 1783), pp. 15–16.

[39] Others corroborated his account. One Calcutta observer in 1782 remarked at "the translating into persian, & circulating throughout India, the disputes in council at Calcutta, & angry paragraphs in general letters from home." Alexander Macaulay to Charles Francis Greville, 5 Dec. 1782, BL, Mss Eur E309/1/4.

critiques. Among the Mughal elite in eastern India, in particular, it had long been a common charge that the Company behaved like an irresponsible merchant.[40] According to the courtier Karam Ali, for instance, though the Company had become "supreme in economic and political affairs," it was still "caught in the snare of greed."[41]

Yet, this was not to say that the Company was constitutionally incapable of good government. The commercialization of politics, in parts of India at least, made it possible to countenance the rule of a mercantile body. Hence, most panegyrists of the *ancien régime* in Bengal sought not to delegitimize their new rulers, however short they fell of the ideal, but to counsel them and to assert the indispensability of such counsel. This was certainly the intention of the nobleman Ghulam Husain Khan Tabataba'i in his great *Tarikh* (history) *Siyar al-Muta'akhkhirin* (c. 1781–5).[42] Writing a quarter-century after Plassey, Ghulam Husain saw "nothing strange in those Merchants having found the means of becoming masters of this country." In his understanding, merchants in general and the Company, in particular, had already acquired in Britain a power to rival that of parliament or the king. While the Company now behaved in arrogant and exclusive ways, it seemed to have come from a system, like the Mughal one, in which sovereignty was parcellated and negotiated. Ghulam Husain suggested that to become a virtuous sovereign, or even a competent one, the Company must renew the reciprocal relations on which such a system was based. European notions of commercial sociability found an analog in his call for open "gates of communication and intercourse" between rulers and ruled.[43] It was fitting, therefore, that

---

[40] See Rajat Kanta Ray, "Colonial Penetration and the Initial Resistance: The Mughal Ruling Class, the English East India Company and the Struggle for Bengal 1756–1800," *Indian Historical Review* 12 (1988), pp. 98–102; Kumkum Chatterjee, *The Cultures of History in Early Modern India: Persianization and Mughal Culture in Bengal* (New Delhi, 2009), pp. 175–8.

[41] Karam Ali, *Muzaffarnama* [c. 1772–3] (Patna, 1992), p. 483.

[42] See Robert Travers, *Empires of Complaints: Mughal Law and the Making of British India, 1765–1793* (Cambridge, 2022), ch. 5.

[43] [Ghulam Husain Khan Tabataba'i] Seid-Gholam-Hossein-Khan, *A Translation of the Seir Mutaqharin; or, View of Modern Times*, trans. Nota Manus [Haji Mustafa], 4 vols.

in the English translation of *Siyar al-Muta'akhkhirin* (1789–90), various Indo-British interactions (*mulaqat, musahabat*) were rendered simply as "commerce."[44]

Faced with audiences in Britain and India that were critical of the Company state but perhaps not inveterately so, Hastings needed means to legitimize it. Within months of taking office in 1772, he located one in the idea of conciliation. Hastings announced that a major task of his administration would be to "conciliate the affection and confidence of the people."[45] Soon, he was defending his conduct on the ground of "the effect which it has produced ... in conciliating the minds of the natives."[46] He also wrote of "conciliating" Britons. So, what did conciliation mean? It is evident that it was, to quote Hastings, a "mode" of politics, and that he had embraced it because, to quote his biographer, "his powers were limited."[47] But there is more to be said on the subject. As Samuel Johnson's *Dictionary* (1755) indicated, "conciliation" carried a double meaning: It could refer either to "the act of gaining" or to the act of "reconciling."[48] The term might thus describe the sovereign art of condescension or the merchant art of concession; it might connote dominance or deference. Furthermore, by combining these things in speech, it could lend itself to combining them in policy. In a celebrated parliamentary address of 1775, Burke urged "conciliation" with the restive American colonies. "All government," he reasoned, "is founded on compromise and barter," especially governments of large

---

(Calcutta, 1789–90), vol. II, pp. 544–5, vol. III, pp. 331–2. Coeval Indian observers seem to have broadly shared Ghulam Husain's impression of the Company's standing vis-à-vis parliament and the king. See Gulfishan Khan, *Indian Muslim Perceptions of the West during the Eighteenth Century* (Karachi, 1998), p. 54.

[44] [Ghulam Husain], Seir, vol. II, p. 598; Ghulam Husain Khan Tabataba'i, *Siyar al-Muta'akhkhirin*, 2 vols. (Calcutta, 1833), vol. I, p. 417.

[45] Warren Hastings, "Regulations Proposed for the Government of Bengal" [c. 1772], in M. E. Monckton Jones, ed., *Warren Hastings in Bengal, 1772–4* (Oxford, 1918), p. 160.

[46] *Fort William – India House Correspondence*, vol. VII, p. 527.

[47] *An Authentic Copy of the Correspondence in India between the Country Powers and the Honourable the East India Company's Servants*, 6 vols. (London, 1787), vol. IV, p. 273; MWH, vol. I, p. 407.

[48] "Conciliate," in Samuel Johnson, *A Dictionary of the English Language* (London, 1755). See similarly George Crabb, *English Synonyms Explained: in Alphabetical Order, with Copious Illustrations and Examples Drawn from the Best Writers* (London, 1816), p. 257.

empires, where "despotism itself is forced to truck and huckster."[49] Burke's argument adapted the language and logic of commerce to the management of a transmarine political community that was understood as composite rather than unitary.[50] Conciliation was not egalitarian: The aim was to retain the colonies "in a profitable and subordinate connexion with us."[51] But Burke's usage conveyed the notion that even such a connection could and should involve reciprocity.

Conciliation in this sense had echoes in Indian political thought, especially in the idea of *sulh-i kull*. The term has been variously translated, and had multiple meanings even for the Mughal emperor Akbar, with whom it has been closely associated.[52] In general, however, it referred to mediation among different groups within a polity or across polities.[53] This idea still enjoyed a wide circulation in Hastings' day, owing in part to the fame of the courtier Abu al-Fazl's *Ain-i Akbari* (c. 1595–8). Hastings made attempts to get this work translated, eventually with success, and praised it as a guide to Akbar's "magnificent machine."[54] In addition, he could have encountered the idea in any one of a number of later texts.[55] It is probable, therefore, that Hastings' idea of conciliation drew on this Indian

[49] Edmund Burke, "Speech on Conciliation with America" (22 Mar. 1775), in Burke, *Writings and Speeches*, vol. III, pp. 125, 157.
[50] Richard Bourke, *Empire and Revolution: The Political Life of Edmund Burke* (Princeton, 2015), pp. 476–87. See also J. G. A. Pocock, "Empire, State and Confederation: The War of American Independence as a Crisis of Multiple Monarchy," in John Robertson, ed., *A Union for Empire: Political Thought and the Union of 1707* (Cambridge, 1995).
[51] Burke, "Speech on Conciliation," p. 118.
[52] On the various origins of *sulh-i kull*, and for other points of comparison, see A. Azfar Moin, ed., "Sulh-i Kull as an Oath of Peace: Mughal Political Theology in History, Theory, and Comparison," special issue of *MAS* 56 (2022).
[53] Rajeev Kinra, "Revisiting the History and Historiography of Mughal Pluralism," *ReOrient* 5 (2020).
[54] Hastings to Earl of Moira, 12 Nov. 1812, Mount Stuart, HA/10. On these attempts, see [Abu al-Fazl], *Ayeen Akbery: Or, The Institutes of the Emperor Akber*, trans. Francis Gladwin, 3 vols. (Calcutta, 1783–6), vol. I, pp. iii, ix–x; Mouluvee Khyr ood Deen [Maulvi Khair ud-Din Ilahabadi] to William Sleeman [c. Mar. 1820], PCFW, vol. 566, pp. 90–1.
[55] On the post-Akbar career of *sulh-i kull*, see Rajeev Kinra, "Handling Diversity with Absolute Civility: The Global Historical Legacy of Mughal Ṣulḥ-i Kull," *Medieval History Journal* 16 (2013); Kinra, "Revisiting," pp. 160–71.

example as well as on British and European ones. Not for nothing did contemporary writers translate *sulh-i kull* as "conciliation" and portray Hastings as a latter-day Akbar.[56] To be sure, such analogies were superficial. Nowhere does Hastings seem to have grappled seriously with the ethical or spiritual dimensions of Akbar's philosophy. Nor was there much textual basis for tying *sulh-i kull* to commerce in the manner of Burke's "conciliation" or the language of Ghulam Husain. Still, in at least one respect, Hastings' idea bore an unmistakable resemblance to that of Akbar and Abu al-Fazl. Just as these men had figured scholarly patronage as central to *sulh-i kull*, so Hastings figured it as central to what he called his "system" of conciliation.[57]

The workings of this system can be gleaned from several of the governor-general's writings. In a minute of 1778, he held that in its "present state and constitution," the Company should consider it a duty "to encourage the efforts of genius."[58] He expanded on this argument in two texts of 1784: a letter to his London agent and an accompanying address to the chairman of the directors. The address solicited the directors' patronage of Charles Wilkins' translation of the *Bhagavad Gita* (1785), and would serve as an introduction to the printed work. Hastings described it to his agent as "part of a system, which I long since laid down & supported, for reconciling the People of England to the Natives of Hindostan, & the Company to their Serv[an]ts."[59] The address explained this system in greater detail:

---

[56] Philip Francis, Minute (22 Jan. 1776), in *Minutes of Evidence Taken at the Trial of Warren Hastings*, 11 vols. (London, 1788–95), vol. X, p. 1728; William Robertson, *An Historical Disquisition Concerning the Knowledge Which the Ancients Had of India* (London, 1791), p. 273; Charles Grant, *Observations on the State of Society among the Asiatic Subjects of Great-Britain* (London, 1797), pp. 76–7. See also Justin Biel, "Edge of Enlightenment: The Akbar Tradition and 'Universal Toleration' in British Bengal," *MAS* 53 (2019), pp. 11–25.

[57] On the connection between *sulh-i kull* and scholarly patronage, see Rajeev Kinra, *Writing Self, Writing Empire: Chandar Bhan Brahman and the Cultural World of the Indo-Persian State Secretary* (Berkeley, 2015), ch. 5.

[58] Warren Hastings, Minute (20 Feb. 1778), in R. B. Ramsbotham, ed., "Pages from the Past: Extracts from the Records of the Government of India," *Bengal Past and Present* 29 (1925), p. 213.

[59] Hastings to John Scott, 2 to 9 Dec. 1784, BL, Add. MS 29129, f. 275r.

> Every accumulation of knowledge, and especially such as is
> obtained by social communication with people over whom we
> exercise a dominion founded on the right of conquest, is useful
> to the state: it is the gain of humanity: in the specific instance
> which I have stated, it attracts and conciliates distant affections;
> it lessens the weight of the chain by which the natives are held in
> subjection; and it imprints on the hearts of our own countrymen
> the sense and obligation of benevolence.[60]

This passage has become famous, in the wake of Michel Foucault and Edward Said, as an acknowledgment of the relationship between power and knowledge. Little, if any, attention has been paid, however, to the commercial language in which Hastings figured that relationship. Unnoticed has been the way in which each phrase in the passage refers to the idea of conciliation at its heart: "Knowledge ... is useful to the state" and "is the gain of humanity" *because* "it attracts and conciliates distant affections." Hastings thus signaled that his idea of conciliation was to be realized through a system involving scholarly patronage. He also signaled that there were two branches to this system, corresponding to its two audiences, British and Indian.

CONCILIATING BRITAIN

Contemporary British political opinion tended toward criticism of the Company and anyone connected with it. Company officials, in particular, were widely regarded as grasping, uncultivated "nabobs." Still, the negative views of commerce that underpinned such criticism coexisted with positive ones. Hastings sought to mobilize the latter through a policy of scholarly patronage. In a lofty vein, he played to Enlightenment associations between knowledge and commerce. In a prosaic one, he asserted that importing knowledge was part of the Company's business. This dual approach was on display in his two most ambitious scholarly projects: to compile and translate

---

[60] Hastings to Nathaniel Smith, 4 Oct. 1784, in Charles Wilkins, trans., *The Bhăgvăt Geetă* (London, 1785), p. 13.

Hindu and Islamic laws, and to survey Bhutan and Tibet. Yet while these projects yielded opportunities for conciliating Britain, they also pointed up the distinct challenge of conciliating India.

Hastings had good reason to devote one branch of his "system" to the metropole. There, he observed, Company officials had been vilified and Indians likened to savages.[61] Both sets of prejudices could be traced to the Company's rise to power in Bengal and to some extent in the Carnatic, and to the "nabob controversy" that had erupted in Britain as a result.[62] As officials returned home, some swollen with ill-gotten wealth, the "nabob" (from nawab) became a stock character in plays, pamphlets, and parliamentary speeches. Modeled largely on Robert Clive, the nabob of popular repute was a man of mercantile origins and attitudes who threatened the socio-political order. He embodied old anxieties about foreign commerce and new ones about foreign conquest. And if his avarice and corruption made him reprehensible, then so too did his ignorance and philistinism.[63] As the Company critic William Bolts put it, there was no reason to expect advancements in knowledge from "one whose great object, [in] going to India, is the acquisition of wealth."[64] The nabob was, in the words of another writer, "equally hostile to literature and freedom."[65] Meanwhile, any knowledge the nabob had picked up was liable to be tainted by Asiatic despotism and superstition. Such was the rhetoric that continually circulated in Britain and obtruded upon Hastings in India. No wonder that he concluded that "the English World"

---

[61] Hastings to Scott, 2 to 9 Dec. 1784, f. 270r; Hastings to Smith, 4 Oct. 1784, p. 13.

[62] The following discussion draws upon Philip Lawson and Jim Phillips, "'Our Execrable Banditti': Perceptions of Nabobs in Mid-Eighteenth Century Britain," *Albion* 16 (1984); James Raven, *Judging New Wealth: Popular Publishing and Responses to Commerce in England, 1750–1800* (Oxford, 1992); Tillman W. Nechtman, *Nabobs: Empire and Identity in Eighteenth-Century Britain* (Cambridge, 2010); James Watt, *British Orientalisms, 1759–1835* (Cambridge, 2019), ch. 2.

[63] The latter point has gone largely unrecognized in studies of the nabob controversy. But for a discussion of how the cultural tastes of nabobs came under suspicion, see Nechtman, *Nabobs*.

[64] Bolts, *Considerations*, vol. I, p. 5.

[65] Thomas Maurice, *Indian Antiquities*, 7 vols. (London [1793]–1800), vol. I (1794 edn), p. 57.

distrusted everything to do with "the Indian World."[66] Conciliating Britain, for Hastings, would entail rehabilitating the Company – its servants, subjects, leaders, and of course himself.

Luckily for Hastings, the Enlightened commercial imagination furnished equipment for such an undertaking. In seventeenth- and eighteenth-century Europe, criticism of merchants had often been mitigated by the notion that trade and learning flourished together. Francis Bacon had seen a link between "the opennesse and through-passage of the world, and the encrease of knowledge."[67] Montesquieu had submitted that "commerce has spread knowledge of the mores of all nations everywhere."[68] Hastings would have been exposed to such ideas at school, in books, and during a sojourn in England in the late 1760s.[69] It was at this time that he wrote "of the advantages which might be derived to every branch of knowledge, from an acquaintance with ... the most remote nations."[70] He was calling here for the creation of a Persian professorship at the University of Oxford. But the same thinking could inspire more grandiose proposals. Jacques-Pierre Brissot, for instance, conceived of a global network of learned societies that would exchange knowledge by means of the Company's ships.[71] Less *grand philosophe* than Grub Street hack, Brissot was echoing ideas coming from both sides of the English Channel.[72] In 1774, Samuel Johnson sent Hastings a copy of William Jones' *A Grammar of the Persian Language* (1771), which foresaw that, thanks to "the flourishing state of our commerce ...

---

[66] Hastings to John Scott, 15 Apr. 1782, BL, Add. MS 29129, f. 41r.

[67] Francis Bacon, *The Advancement of Learning* (1605), ed. Michael Kiernan (Oxford, 2000), p. 71.

[68] Montesquieu, *The Spirit of the Laws* (1748), ed. and trans. Anne M. Cohler, Basia C. Miller, and Harold S. Stone (Cambridge, 1989), p. 338.

[69] Hastings also implied in at least one letter that he was familiar with Montesquieu's writings. See Hastings to John Purling, 22 Feb. 1772, BL, Add. MS 29126, f. 128r.

[70] [Hastings], *Proposal*, p. 5.

[71] Jacques-Pierre Brissot, *London Literary Lyceum; or, an Assembly and Correspondence Established at London* (London, 1783), p. 9.

[72] See Robert Darnton, "The Grub Street Style of Revolution: J.-P. Brissot, Police Spy," *Journal of Modern History* 40 (1968).

the eastern nations will be perfectly known."[73] Johnson put the
matter directly to Hastings in an accompanying letter: With his
"attention and patronage," those regions that supplied Europe with
luxuries might also inform it on "many subjects" on which it was
ignorant.[74] There was more than a passing resemblance between
Johnson's appeal and Hastings' own claim that works like the *Gita*
translation "may open a new and most extensive Range for the
human mind."[75] What made this claim political was the identity of
the translation's patron. Hastings made his argument explicit in the
preface: Because the Company was the greatest "commercial body"
in history, it offered Britain unequalled access to the "field of fruitful
knowledge."[76]

Johnson and Jones were two sources for this argument, but
Hastings would also have encountered it in India. After all, other
Company officials were similarly exercised by metropolitan attacks
on nabobery. As one noted, the "pernicious" character of a government composed of men fixated on "private Emolument … is now the
only theme instilld in us."[77] If a recent attribution is correct, then this
official was none other than Richard Johnson.[78] After being recalled
from Lucknow in 1782 for amassing a fortune by dubious means,
Johnson insisted to Hastings that he was actually "very indifferent"
when it came to wealth. He requested to stay in northern India for
intellectual reasons: "My mind is bent upon compleating some literary objects in the Sa[n]skrit and Persian, and these can only be effected
at Luc[k]now or Delhi or Benares."[79] Perhaps Johnson was not being
entirely disingenuous. In his private notes, he outlined a plan to give

---

[73] William Jones, *A Grammar of the Persian Language* (London, 1771), pp. xi–xiii.

[74] Johnson to Hastings, 30 Mar. 1774, in Johnson, *Letters*, vol. II, p. 136.

[75] Hastings, Minute, 9 Dec. 1783, BL, IOR H/207, p. 172.

[76] Hastings to Smith, 4 Oct. 1784, pp. 5, 13.

[77] [Richard Johnson], Journal (undated), Ames Library, Mss B 114, no. 6.

[78] For the attribution, see Anna Clark and Aaron Windel, "The Early Roots of Liberal
Imperialism: 'The Science of a Legislator' in Eighteenth-Century India," *Journal of
Colonialism and Colonial History* 14 (2013).

[79] Johnson to Hastings, 15 Jul. 1782, BL, Add. MS 29155, f. 102r.

"up all my advantages and Prospects in pursuit of my Studies."[80] This plan never materialized. And yet, thanks in part to his reputation for learning, Johnson eventually obtained a prestigious, if only modestly paid, appointment as the Company's resident at Hyderabad.[81]

Johnson was not the only scholar-official who reaped the benefit of Enlightened associations between commerce and knowledge. Another was the Bengal administrator and favorite of Hastings, David Anderson. In 1772, Anderson wrote to his old Edinburgh schoolmaster, enclosing an astrolabe and an account of the arts and sciences of Asia.[82] This scholarly turn, the schoolmaster replied, "surprises and pleases me not a Little," since Europeans in Asia were typically obsessed with lucre. The schoolmaster expected that Anderson's "greater Thirst after knowledge and Wisdom than after the Golden Calf so generally worshiped" would spare him from "the Reproachfull Epithet of Nabob" upon his return. He also hoped that Anderson, by following the trail of an earlier India merchant, might supply his home country with a much sought-after article of knowledge:

Lord Monboddo relates and believes that a swede named Koeping[,] Lieutennant aboard of a dutch East India Ship of force, saw on the Island Nicobar in the Gulf of Bengal a race of men with Taills like those of Catts which they moved in the same manner .... [T]hey were Canniballs, for says the swede they devoured five of the Crew .... Now as a tradition of these human Cats ... may yet Remain in the memory of some old inhabitant on the Coast of that Gulf, it would not be pains or Labour Lost to Enquire into the truth of ... an ugly Tail with which his Lordship is disgracefully painted in this Island.[83]

[80] [Richard Johnson], Notes (undated), John Rylands Library, GB 133 Eng MS 194, no. 14.
[81] See P. J. Marshall, "Johnson, Richard, (1753–1807)," Oxford Dictionary of National Biography (2004), https://doi.org/10.1093/ref:odnb/63514.
[82] Anderson to Alexander Mackenzie, 11 Sept. 1772, BL, Add. MS 45438, ff. 70r–73v.
[83] Alexander Mackenzie to Anderson, 5 Jun. 1773, BL, Add. MS 45430, ff. 282v–284v. An assistant surgeon in the Company's service later did investigate the subject, while on a visit to the Nicobar Islands, and concluded that "this supposed tail, may have

Whether or not Anderson ever looked into Monboddo's "ugly Tail," or shared with Hastings the contents of the schoolmaster's letter, this exchange showed how the governor-general might exploit associations between commerce and knowledge to rescue the nabob and the Company.

But if Hastings entertained lofty views, then he also emphasized prosaic ones. He presented the Company as an importer of knowledge that would be useful as well as curious to his British audience. He remitted plant and animal specimens with an eye to introducing new commodities to the metropole.[84] Even the *Gita* preface and translation he told his London agent to defend as "Business" and not "Levities."[85] Hastings clearly anticipated the charge that his scholarly projects were fanciful indulgences. Accordingly, he entrusted them to scholar-officials who combined "capacity for business" with "liberal knowledge"; men like Nathaniel Brassey Halhed, "who with a Genius adapted equally to the first Compositions of Judgment and Imagination, could ... unravel the Intricacies of a Salt Account, or ... study the Reports of a Com[mitt]ee of the H[ous]e of Commons." There was a further reason that Hastings appreciated such men of "universal talents": Critics of the Company like Bolts often staked their own credibility on their varied expertise.[86] In *A Grammar of the Bengal Language* (1778), a work proposed and patronized by Hastings, Halhed dismissed Bolts' linguistic and typographic abilities. Whereas, according to Halhed, Bolts had a questionable grasp of Bengali and had "egregiously failed" to produce a set of types in the language, Hastings' protégé Wilkins had succeeded in this task beyond "every expectation."[87] Thus, the practical held political

been the stripe of cloth hanging down from their [the human inhabitants'] posteriors." Nicolas Fontana, "On the Nicobar Isles and the Fruit of the Mellori," *Asiatick Researches* 3 (Calcutta, 1792), pp. 151–2 n. †.

[84] Marshall, "Warren Hastings," pp. 251–3.

[85] Hastings to Scott, 2 to 9 Dec. 1784, ff. 270v, 275r.

[86] Hastings to Halhed, 2 Nov. 1783, BL, Add. MS 29129, f. 194v; Hastings to Smith, 4 Oct. 1784, p. 12; Hastings, Minute (14 Oct. 1776), NLS, MS.1072, f. 92r.

[87] Nathaniel Brassey Halhed, *A Grammar of the Bengal Language* (Hoog[h]ly, 1778), p. xxiii.

significance for Hastings and coexisted with the profound in many of his scholarly ventures. Certainly, it did so in his two greatest ones.

Two projects dominated the British branch of Hastings' system of conciliation. One was the compilation and translation of Hindu and Islamic laws. With this project, Hastings sought to facilitate the business of the courts set up by his administration and by the Regulating Act, but also to improve British opinion of the "Indian World." Hence, in one letter on the subject, he wrote of freeing Indians "from the reproach of ignorance and barbarism"; in another, he avowed a zealous regard for the "credit and interest" of the directors; on many occasions, he praised the scholar-officials involved in the work; and finally, he admitted the further aim of obtaining "public credit" for himself.[88] The project yielded several publications, which were fulsome in their praise of Hastings, in particular, and which he ensured would reach prominent jurists, scholars, and politicians at the metropole.[89] One reader who responded in what must have been the desired manner was the historian Robert Orme. In 1775, Orme wrote to Hastings after perusing the manuscript of Halhed's *A Code of Gentoo Laws* (1776):

> The educated world have received with the greatest satisfaction
> the portion you have sent of the laws of Bengal, and earnestly wish
> the continuation and accomplishment of a work, which does you
> so much honour. I always thought that such a work must be the
> basis of any reasonable government exercised by us; but always
> despaired of its execution, knowing to what other views and objects
> the abilities of Europeans have hitherto been directed in Indostan.
> The silent step of philosophy is gaining ground every day; and your
> name will not be forgot amongst the foremost of her disciples, for
> the valuable present you are making to learning and reason.[90]

[88] Hastings to Johnson, 7 Aug. 1775, p. 18; Hastings to Lord Mansfield, 20 Jan. 1776, in *MWH*, vol. II, p. 22; Hastings to Directors, 21 Feb. 1784, in *MWH*, vol. III, p. 160.

[89] Nathaniel Brassey Halhed, trans., *A Code of Gentoo Laws, or, Ordinations of the Pundits* (London, 1776), pp. vi–vii; Charles Hamilton, trans., *The Hedaya, or Guide; A Commentary on the Mussulman Laws*, 4 vols. (London, 1791), vol. I, pp. i–ii.

[90] Orme to Hastings, 14 Jan. 1775, in Robert Orme, *Historical Fragments of the Mogul Empire* (London, 1805), p. xxxvi.

What Orme expressed privately others did so before a wide audience. Several leading magazines carried favorable notices and extracts of Halhed's *Code*. Hastings' larger system even received visual endorsement, in James Rennell's map *Hindoostan* (1782), to which he had also leant his support. The cartouche of the map, between marginal illustrations of war and commerce, depicted a group of pandits (Hindu learned elites) entrusting to Britannia their *shastras* (laws).[91] It thus bid the observer to regard the Company state as devoted – centrally no less – to the cause of knowledge.

Hastings' other major project to conciliate Britain comprised two expeditions to Bhutan and Tibet. In 1774 and again in 1783, he dispatched envoys to these secluded countries northeast of Bengal. One purpose was political: to establish diplomatic relations. Another was commercial: to evaluate the prospects of trade and of a land route to China. But the "intercourse with distant nations" that Hastings hoped to stimulate had an intellectual component as well.[92] Hastings instructed his first envoy, George Bogle, to correspond regularly on the trade, government, history, religion, and topography of the places he visited.[93] Bogle must also keep a diary, inserting information on "the people, the country, the climate, or the road, their manners, customs, buildings, cookery &c." Finally, he must obtain specimens of "useful" or "remarkably curious" animals; of "curious or valuable seeds or plants"; and of "natural productions, manufactures, paintings, or what else may be acceptable to persons of taste in England."[94] Hastings expected that he and Bogle "should both acquire reputation" from the mission's success, but even a failure might be compensated by additions to European knowledge. "Do not return," he instructed him, "without something to show where you have been, though it be but a contraband walnut, a pilfered slip

---

[91] James Rennell, *Memoir of a Map of Hindoostan* (London, 1783), frontispiece.

[92] Hastings to Bogle, 10 Aug. 1774, in Alastair Lamb, ed., *Bhutan and Tibet: The Travels of George Bogle and Alexander Hamilton, 1774–1777* (Hertingfordbury, UK, 2002), p. 120.

[93] Hastings to Bogle, 13 May 1774, in ibid., pp. 46–7; Hastings, Memorandum (1774), in ibid., pp. 52–5.

[94] Hastings to Bogle, 16 May 1774, in ibid., pp. 47–8.

of sweet briar, or the seeds of a Bhutanese turnip."[95] The commerce that Hastings envisioned with Bhutan and Tibet was, in large part, a commerce of knowledge.

After all, in Hastings' view, it was the intellectual component of the expedition that would serve to conciliate Britain. As he wrote to Bogle,

> I feel myself more interested in the success of your mission than in reason perhaps I ought to be; but there are thousands of men in England whose good-will is worth seeking, and who will listen to the story of such enterprises in search of knowledge with ten times more avidity than they would read accounts that brought crores [tens of millions] to the national credit, or descriptions of victories that slaughtered thousands of the national enemies.[96]

For this reason, upon Bogle's return to Calcutta in 1775, Hastings sought to have his bulging journal edited and published with the aid of Samuel Johnson.[97] Unfortunately, according to the testimony of Bogle's brother, "the Doctor died before it came home."[98] In 1777, however, Hastings had his agent John Stewart draw up an account of the young envoy's discoveries to read before the Royal Society. Stewart's account likewise served a conciliatory purpose: It praised Hastings for seizing "every opportunity which could ... tend to the advancement of natural knowledge."[99] Meanwhile, after plans for a second embassy were suspended, Hastings continued to ask Bogle

---

[95] Hastings to Bogle, 10 Aug. 1774, in ibid. pp. 118–19.
[96] Hastings to Bogle, 8 Sept. 1774, in ibid. p. 122.
[97] Hastings to Johnson, 7 Aug. 1775, pp. 19–20.
[98] Robert Bogle to Henry Dundas, 23 Aug. 1799, Cleveland Public Library, 091.92 B634L. This is surprising, for Johnson did not die until 1784, but perhaps the journal was misplaced or delayed in transit.
[99] John Stewart, "An Account of the Kingdom of Thibet. In a Letter from John Stewart, Esquire, F. R. S. to Sir John Pringle, Bart. P. R. S.," *Philosophical Transactions of the Royal Society of London* 47 (1777), p. 469. The same purpose would seem to have been served by a painting of Bogle's first meeting with the Panchen Lama that was commissioned by Hastings and presented to George III. Kate Teltscher, *The High Road to China: George Bogle, the Panchen Lama and the First British Expedition to Tibet* (London, 2006), p. 176.

to procure botanical specimens through intermediaries. Placing an order for some Bhutanese cinnamon in 1780, he foreshadowed his later remark on the "business" achieved by the *Gita* translation and preface: "You w[oul]d wonder that I could write to you on such Trifles, if you knew what weighty concerns pressed upon my Mind. But I do not think this altogether a Trifle."[100] By the time a second embassy materialized three years later, Bogle had died. Hastings renewed his instructions to his replacement, Samuel Turner: "extend your enquiries to every subject which a scene so new may afford ... for at least it will be no Discredit to you to have added to the store of Knowledge."[101]

Yet while Hastings fancied that his vision of an intellectual commerce would be embraced at the courts of Bhutan and Tibet, his envoys continually found themselves suspected of harboring sinister motives. On one occasion, Bogle learned that the shah (king) of neighboring Nepal sought to bar the Company from bringing to Tibet scientific objects like telescopes and clocks. Might he suspect the Company of importing arms, Bogle wondered, or of trying to outshine his own emissaries in Lhasa? On another occasion, the Panchen Lama proffered Bogle "a map of Tibet from Ladakh to the frontier of China," which included tantalizing details missing from European maps. Tempted as Bogle was by this "splendid" present, which "would reflect much lustre on my commission," he was forced to turn it down, lest he increase "that jealousy, which had ... thwarted me in all my negotiations." It seemed that such incidents, and such "jealousy," were imputable to the growing notoriety of the Company. Bogle learned that the vakil (ambassador) of Raja Chait Singh of Benares had "described the English as a people designing and ambitious; who, insinuating themselves into a country on pretence

---

[100] Hastings to Bogle, 1 Mar. 1780, Glasgow City Archives, TD1681/74.

[101] NAI, Bengal Public Consultations (13 Mar. 1783), no. 10. Hastings told another correspondent that "Turner's Embassy ... will at least satisfy curiosity." Hastings to John Macpherson [Apr. to May 1783], in *Warren Hastings' Letters to Sir John Macpherson,* ed. Henry Dodwell (London, 1927), p. 189.

of trade, became acquainted with its situation and inhabitants, and afterwards endeavoured to becomes masters of it." The vakil denied the charge and implicated the agent of another grandee instead. But the source of these remarks was almost beside the point: As the Panchen Lama told Bogle, "many people" had warned him against dealing with the Company.[102] The suspicion that commerce, including the commerce of knowledge, was but an accessory to conquest threatened to undermine Hastings' policy.

Hastings worried that, were his embassies to fail, his larger scheme to conciliate Britain would suffer.[103] Even were they to succeed, it boded ill that grievances against the Company had reached this remote aerie. In the long term, suspicion of British designs on Tibet would profoundly shape Chinese policy toward the Company.[104] More immediately, in 1781, the rebellion of Chait Singh spread across northern India and nearly cost Hastings his life. Had the rebellion succeeded, Hastings and others believed, the Company might have been driven out of India for good. To conciliate Britain was one matter; to conciliate India another.

CONCILIATING INDIA

Indian opinion was as much a concern for Hastings as its British counterpart. He perceived that the grip of the Company in Bengal was tenuous and that powerholders in the region must be conciliated. One way to do this, it appeared to him, was to patronize "respectable" Indian scholars. According to his sources, such scholars had long been key participants in the "commerce" between Indian rulers and political classes. Some were themselves aristocrats, zamindars, or other individuals of status and authority. Others, especially maulvis (Muslim learned elites) and pandits, were believed to exercise influence with such individuals. Hastings' attempt to conciliate India, therefore, was essentially an

---

[102] Bogle, Journal, in Lamb, ed., *Bhutan and Tibet*, pp. 212, 216–17, 239–40, 243.

[103] See Hastings to Bogle, 10 Aug. 1774, p. 118.

[104] Mathew Mosca, *From Frontier Policy to Foreign Policy: The Question of India and the Transformation of Geopolitics in Qing China* (Stanford, 2013).

attempt to cultivate Indian elites. But if the exigencies of the Company state presented opportunities for this strategy, then they also presented obstacles. At the same time, some of Hastings' most ambitious ventures raised the prospect of an altogether different form of conciliation.

When Hastings wrote in the *Gita* preface of conciliating "distant affections," he referred to those of the Indian world as well as the British world. And when he called for lightening "the chain by which the natives are held in subjection," he invoked a political imperative as well as a moral one. Writing shortly after Hastings' departure, Haji Mustafa, the translator of Ghulam Husain's *Siyar al-Muta'akhkhirin*, censured the Company for seeing Indians as "a dead stock, that may be worked upon without much consideration." He enjoined it to treat them with "a more watchful eye" but especially with "a more winning deportment, and a more caressing hand." Finally, he warned that there persisted across the Company's territories "a subterraneous vein of national resentment," which, until Chait Singh's rebellion, had been known to only "eight or ten" Company officials. One of these men would have been Mustafa's longtime friend and patron, Hastings.[105] Indeed, Hastings was well aware of the precariousness of the Company in India. He acknowledged that "this government subsists more by the influence of public opinion than by its real power or resources."[106] Like other officials, he denied that the Company was accountable to an Indian "public," yet he grasped that it could not maintain its position through domination alone.[107] The Company needed Indian allies; men who would not be "dead stock" but instead participants in an active "commerce." Ghulam Husain and other authorities recommended one sort of ally in particular.

According to these sources, Indian rulers had long endeared themselves to their subjects by patronizing learned individuals.

---

[105] Nota Manus [Haji Mustafa], preface [2 Nov. 1786] to [Ghulam Husain], *Seir*, vol. I, pp. 21, 22, 27, 31.

[106] Hastings to the Earl of Shelburne, 12 Dec. 1782, in *MWH*, vol. III, p. 23.

[107] See P. J. Marshall, *The Making and Unmaking of Empires: Britain, India, and America c. 1750–1783* (Oxford, 2005), pp. 256–70.

Ghulam Husain praised earlier nawabs of Bengal for gathering scholars at court, conversing with them, and showering them with rewards.[108] Mustafa held that "learning is the sure road to honour" in India: "Men of eminent learning are treated as equals by the Princes of the country."[109] Salim Allah made much the same point in his *Tarikh-i Bangala* (c. 1760–4), as did Alexander Dow in his *History of Hindostan* (1768–72).[110] "No princes in the world," Dow averred, "patronised men of letters with more generosity and respect, than the Mahommedan Emperors of Hindostan." Scholars stood in such high credit, he claimed, that "literary genius was ... an infallible road for rising to the first offices of the state."[111] The message of Dow, Ghulam Husain, Salim Allah, Mustafa, and other interpreters of the Mughal inheritance was that this policy must be emulated by the new rulers if they were to replicate the success of the old ones.

This expectation helps to explain the crisis that Hastings triggered, in 1772, when he arrested the *naib nazim* Muhammad Reza Khan. The nawab's deputy in name, Reza Khan, as Hastings recognized, was "in real authority more than the Nâzim."[112] The charges against the Khan were dubious, but Hastings dutifully pressed them at the behest of the directors.[113] Four months later, he complained that "Reza Cawn's influence still prevailed generally throughout the country."[114] Hastings (and the directors) had misjudged not only the extent

---

[108] [Ghulam Husain], *Seir*, vol. I, pp. 20–21, 685–716, vol. II, pp. 197–9, 462–3, 536.

[109] [Mustafa], in ibid., vol. I, p. 264 n. 211. See also ibid., vol. II, p. 305 n. 141.

[110] Salim Allah, *Tarikh-i Bangala* (c. 1760–4), trans. Francis Gladwin, as *A Narrative of the Transactions in Bengal* (Calcutta, 1788), pp. 24, 115–18.

[111] Alexander Dow, *The History of Hindostan*, 2 vols. (London, 1768–72), vol. I, p. x.

[112] Hastings to Secret Committee, 1 Sept. 1772, in *MWH*, vol. 1, p. 247. Edmund Burke would later describe Reza Khan as uniting "the character of First Lord of the Treasury, the character of chief Justice, the character of Lord High Chancellor and the character of Archbishop of Canterbury." Edmund Burke, "Speech on Sixth Article: Presents" (21 Apr. 1789), in Burke, *Writings and Speeches*, vol. VII, p. 45.

[113] Abdul Majed Khan, *The Transition in Bengal, 1756–1775: A Study of Saiyid Muhammad Reza Khan* (Cambridge, 1969), pp. 294–349.

[114] Hastings to Secret Committee, 1 Sept. 1772, p. 250.

but also the basis of the Khan's support. He was a canny operator, true, but he also embodied the Mughal ideal of the learned bureaucrat:

> He has a very good Understanding, improved first by Education, and afterwards by long Practice in publick Affairs. His Learning ... is ... greater than can often be found in Bengal, even among professed Scholars. He seems to have an extensive Acquaintance not only with Persian but Arabian Authours, has obtained, from Arabick Translations of Greek Books, some Knowledge of the Philosophy and even of the Politicks of ancient Greece, and has been thereby ... enabled to understand so well as he does ... our Constitution and Government.[115]

So wrote one supporter of the Khan, the Calcutta Supreme Court judge Robert Chambers. Even Ghulam Husain, a rival as well as a discerning critic, could not deny the Khan's intellect.[116] For friends and enemies alike, the ruination of this "fountain of knowledge" over "a few lakh [hundred thousand] rupees" reinforced existing criticisms of the Company.[117] So too did Hastings' reduction of the nawab Mubarak ud-Daula's stipend within weeks of the arrest.[118] Apart from the nawab and his dependents, the stipend supported "a number of deserving persons," among them scholars, "to whom attention had always been paid."[119] As Hastings himself acknowledged, it represented the only provision for hundreds "of the ancient nobility of the Country, excluded under our government from almost all employments."[120] But if Hastings anticipated a backlash, then

---

[115] Chambers to Charles Jenkinson, 25 Mar. 1778, BL, Add. MS 38401, ff. 94r–v. On this ideal, see Rajeev Kinra, "The Learned Ideal of the Mughal *Wazīr*: The Life and Intellectual World of Prime Minister Afzal Khan Shirazi (d. 1639)," in Paul M. Dover, ed., *Secretaries and Statecraft in the Early Modern World* (Edinburgh, 2016).

[116] [Ghulam Husain], *Seir*, vol. II, p. 539.

[117] Karam Ali, *Muzaffarnama*, pp. 383, 482.

[118] Khan, *Transition*, pp. 327–9.

[119] [Ghulam Husain], *Seir*, vol. II, p. 426.

[120] Secret Letter from Bengal, 10 Nov. 1772, in Monckton Jones, *Warren Hastings*, p. 191. See also John Stewart, "A Letter from John Stewart, Secretary and Judge Advocate of Bengal, 1773," ed. L. S. Sutherland, *Indian Archives* 10 (1956), p. 6.

he may not have appreciated its scale until Reza Khan was exonerated in 1774. Not only was the Khan now at liberty to oppose the Company but he warned that other Indians "of consequence" would do so too.[121]

Hastings' plans to conciliate India thus took shape around an urgent need to patronize Indian learned elites. The business of the Company threw up opportunities in this regard but also obstacles. One channel of patronage was the legal system created by Hastings and by the Regulating Act in the early 1770s. Hastings sought out the "most respectable" pandits and maulvis from "every part of Bengal" to staff the new courts and to compile and translate Hindu and Islamic laws. When his protégé Nathaniel Brassey Halhed claimed that such efforts would "conciliate ... the Natives," he was alluding mainly to these learned elites and their powerful connections.[122] Several maulvis and pandits declined or resigned employment with the Company, apparently because of its political connotations.[123] Those who accepted and remained understood that they were lending their names in support of it. Hence, Maulvi Majd ud-Din, who had been a courtier of the nawab of Awadh, could demand treatment befitting his value.[124] Hence, too, the eleven pandits and four maulvis who helped to compile and translate the laws accepted it as part of their duty to write in praise of their employer.[125] As the news and fruits of Hastings' patronage circulated among India's political

[121] Charles Goring to Philip Francis, Dec. 1774, cited in Khan, *Transition*, p. 346.

[122] Halhed, trans., *Code*, pp. ix–x. By "Gentoos" Halhed seems to have meant elite Brahmans. See Sushil Srivastava, "Constructing the Hindu Identity: European Moral and Intellectual Adventurism in 18th Century India," *Economic and Political Weekly* 33 (1998), p. 1185.

[123] See *Calendar of Persian Correspondence*, 11 vols. (Calcutta and Delhi, 1911–69), vol. V, pp. 194–5; Rosane Rocher, "The Career of Rādhākānta Tarkavāgīśa, an Eighteenth-Century Pandit in British Employ," *Journal of the American Oriental Society* 109 (1989), pp. 628, 633.

[124] See John Hyde, Notes (12 Jul. 1782), Victoria Memorial Hall, Hyde Notebooks; William Jones, Notebook, Beinecke Library, MS Osborn c400, p. [3].

[125] Halhed, trans., *Code*, pp. 3–5; Hamilton, trans., *Hedaya*, vol. I, pp. ix–xii. See also Charles Rieu, *Catalogue of the Persian Manuscripts in the British Museum*, 3 vols. (London, 1879), vol. I, pp. 63–4; Rocher, "Career of Rādhākānta," p. 628.

classes, so too would his good reputation and that of the Company. Or, at least, so he imagined.

In March 1777, Hastings was vexed to discover on two *mahzarnamas* (memorials) "intended to vilify my character" the signature of one of his favorite maulvis:

> Of the little weight that Gratitude bears in the Scale of Indian Policy, both Lists afford a remarkable Instance in Golam Yahyah Cawn whose name appears in both. He was without Employment and little known, but as a Man of Learning I employed him to translate the Mahomedan Laws from the Arabic into the Persian Language with other Molavies to assist him, with monthly salaries ... during three years to an Amount which I am ashamed to mention. He was afterwards appointed by me to the Cauzy ul Cazaut or head Cauzee [judge] of the Province, which Office he since holds under Mahomed Reza Cawn. He has been taxed with having been privy to this Affair and has solemnly denied it.[126]

The two *mahzarnamas* raised numerous questions for Hastings. Had one been composed by Afaz ud-Din Husaini, a maulvi under Reza Khan's control? Was the Khan himself involved, notwithstanding his denials? Who else had seen the documents? Were the signatures even genuine? Whatever the answers, Hastings expressed confidence that the *mahzarnamas* would do him little harm either in India or in Britain. His perturbation stemmed instead from the fact that so many "Nobles and Worthies" – not least his client Ghulam Yahya Khan – had ostensibly affixed their names.[127] One possible lesson from this affair was that loyalty could not always be bought, that Reza Khan still commanded a greater share than

---

[126] Hastings to John Graham and Lauchlin Macleane, 5 Mar. 1777, BL, Add. MS 29128, ff. 45v–46r. On *mahzarnamas*, see Nandini Chatterjee, "*Mahzar-nama*s in the Mughal and British Empires: The Uses of an Indo-Islamic Legal Form," *Contemporary Studies in Society and History* 58 (2016).

[127] Hastings to Graham and Macleane, 5 Mar. 1777, ff. 44r–46v; Hastings to George Vansittart, 5 to 28 Mar. 1777, BL, Add. MS 48370, ff. 41r–43v, 47r–54v.

Hastings of elite affection. Another was that, for many elites, siding with the Khan still appeared to be a better bet. In 1775, the council majority restored Reza Khan to the office of *naib nazim*, from which Hastings would be able to oust him again only temporarily. Ghulam Yahya's response to this second ouster suggested that he may well have had flexible or divided loyalties. Mere months after eulogizing Hastings in the translator's preface to the law tract *Hidaya-i Farsi*, Ghulam Yahya resigned his position as *qazi ul-quzat*, reportedly in solidarity with the dismissed Khan.[128] When he died in 1784, having reassumed this position, Hastings made sure that a more dependable ally – Ahmad, the brother of Majd ud-Din – succeeded him.[129]

Hastings fared better with another jurist, the Mughal aristocrat Ali Ibrahim Khan. Distinguished also as a poet and historian, and well-connected, Ali Ibrahim was the kind of learned elite that Hastings sought to cultivate. His opportunity came when a dispute with Reza Khan resulted in Ali Ibrahim's dismissal from the court of the nawab. Hastings invited the nobleman, who had been reduced to living "at his own house in obscurity and retirement," to accompany him on a tour upcountry. Not only did Hastings' overture earn the approval of Ghulam Husain, who dubbed him "a connoisseur of the first rate," but it proved decisive in forging an alliance with Ali Ibrahim.[130] For it was during the visit of Hastings' suite to Benares in August 1781 that tensions with Chait Singh came to a head and northern India erupted in rebellion. Presenting himself as a victim of the Company's aggression, Chait Singh mounted a campaign to draw rulers and grandees across the region to his standard. Yet Ali Ibrahim, steeped in the establishmentarian politics of the Mughal court, saw the "raja" as merely a zamindar who had forgotten his place. The triumph of this view among the regional aristocracy was, in large part,

[128] *Calendar of Persian Correspondence*, vol. V, pp. 120, 194–5, 197.
[129] Ibid., vol. VI, pp. 368, 372, 393.
[130] [Ghulam Husain], *Seir*, vol. II, pp. 469–73, vol. III, p. 330.

what prevented the rebellion from getting out of hand.[131] And here, Ali Ibrahim may have contributed decisively. While Hastings framed a justification of his actions toward Chait Singh in English, Ali Ibrahim drew up a complementary narrative in Persian.[132] Declaring himself a "well-wisher" and "intermediary" of the Company, Ali Ibrahim dwelt upon Hastings' reasonableness and fidelity as compared with Chait Singh's "evil ways."[133] That autumn, with the uprising quelled and Benares annexed to the Company, Hastings repaid Ali Ibrahim's loyalty by appointing him chief magistrate. "It is chiefly from the reliance which I have in him personally," Hastings wrote, "that I have ventured to delegate a degree of authority to him, which it would perhaps be unsafe to vest in a person of a less established character."[134] This judgment would prove well founded: Ali Ibrahim maintained the esteem of the city's leading figures and of the Company until his death in 1793.

Hastings also had notable success enlisting Indian learned elites as vakils (ambassadors). His greatest prize in this category was the remarkable Tafazzul Husain Khan. Born to a prominent family of Mughal administrators, Tafazzul studied rational sciences in the Greco-Arabic tradition before serving as a tutor to the second son of the nawab of Awadh. Finding himself on the wrong side of a dynastic struggle in 1776, Tafazzul was forced to flee the court and, during a period of exile, was drawn into the orbit of the Company.

[131] G. F. Grand, *The Narrative of the Life of a Gentleman Long Resident in India* (1814), ed. Walter K. Firminger (Calcutta, 1910), p. 110.
[132] Ali Ibrahim Khan, *Tarikh-i Chait Singh*, BL, Or. 1865, ff. 36r–40v; Warren Hastings, *A Narrative of the Insurrection Which Happened in the Zemeedary of Banaris* (Calcutta, 1782). See Shayesta Khan, *A Biography of Ali Ibrahim Khan (circa 1740–1793): A Mughal Noble in the Administrative Service of the British East India Company* (Patna, 1992), pp. 155–9; Nandini Chatterjee, "Hindu City and Just Empire: Banaras and India in Ali Ibrahim Khan's Legal Imagination," *Journal of Colonialism and Colonial History* 15 (2014). Hastings also commissioned another Indian poet to compose an epic work on the occasion. James White, "On the Road: The Life and Verse of Mir Zeyn al-Din 'Eshq, a Forgotten Eighteenth-Century Poet," *Iranian Studies* 53 (2020), pp. 797–803.
[133] Ali Ibrahim, *Tarikh-i Chait Singh*, ff. 36r, 36v, 38r.
[134] Hastings to Supreme Council, 1 Nov. 1781, in Hastings, *Narrative*, Appendix, p. 22.

After befriending the officials William Palmer and David Anderson, he was sent by Hastings to help the one to negotiate with the *rana* of Gohad and the other to conclude a treaty with the maharaja of Gwalior. By this time, Hastings was on personal terms with Tafazzul and appreciated the political value of his reputation "throughout the country for ... integrity and knowledge."[135] Upon sending Palmer to Gohad in 1781, he assured him that "Tofuzzal Hussein Cawn is already fully informed .... I have much reliance on his abilities."[136] Meanwhile, having arrived before Palmer, Tafazzul apprised the governor-general that "I am diligently employed in enquiring into every particular of the State of this Quarter." Within days, Tafazzul had succeeded not only in making the *rana* "truly & Sincerely attached to him [Hastings]" but also in forging friendly relations with "learned Men," other "Men of Distinction[,] & Rajahs."[137] Palmer would soon confirm Tafazzul's achievements, writing to Hastings, "He is the most able & faithful adherent which you could have given me & his services have been inestimable."[138] In Anderson's later recollection, Tafazzul was no less a boon to the negotiations in Gwalior the following year. "As he wrote the Persian language with uncommon elegance," it was Tafazzul who penned Anderson's letters of introduction to the maharaja and other Maratha leaders. As he was a skillful and erudite speaker, he far outclassed his opponent in the ensuing negotiations. "In all my intercourse with the natives of India," Anderson summarized, "I never knew any man who combined, in so eminent a degree, great talents for public business, profound learning, and the liberal ideas and manners of a gentleman."[139] At the time of Hastings' departure, Tafazzul had not yet begun the project for which he would be most remembered:

[135] Hastings to Supreme Council, 25 Nov. 1781, in Hastings, *Narrative*, p. 57.

[136] Hastings to Palmer [1781], John Rylands Library, GB 1313 Eng MS 173, no. 24.

[137] Tafazzul to brother [Rahmatullah Khan], 13 to 23 Feb. [1781], BL, Add. MS 29123, ff. 103r, 106r, 108r.

[138] Palmer to Hastings, 21 Mar. 1781, BL, Add. MS 29148, f. 151r.

[139] Anderson, cited in "An Account of the Life and Character of Tofuzzel Hussein Khan," *Asiatic Annual Register* [5] (1804), "Characters," pp. 2–4.

a translation of Sir Isaac Newton's *Principia* (1687). But Hastings commissioned him to procure, and apparently to produce, scientific manuscripts and leant early support to his collaborator, the mathematician Reuben Burrow.[140] Tafazzul likely figured in a project of Burrow's to establish an observatory, which Hastings approved shortly before leaving India.[141] This was one of several projects that suggested that Hastings' plans for conciliating India went beyond individual patronage.

Two other such projects were a Hindu college that Hastings pledged to build in Benares, also shortly before his departure, and a madrasa that he did in fact build in Calcutta. Like the observatory, these institutions were rooted in patronage and yet pointed toward greater conciliatory possibilities. The Hindu college seems to have been inspired at least in part by the example of Raja Krishnachandra, the influential zamindar or little king of Nadia. Krishnachandra owed his preeminent status among Hindus in Bengal to his reputation as a scholar and patron of scholars. He stocked his court with leading poets, astronomers, philosophers, and physicians.[142] He developed Nadia's colleges into "the most frequented as well as the most learned university in the east."[143] No wonder that Hastings contacted Krishnachandra on learned matters and inquired into how the Company could support his "university."[144] Yet an alliance was not to be. Krishnachandra was in debt to the Company, whose officials

[140] Hastings to Charles Wilkins, 7 Apr. 1809, cited in Peter Gordon, *The Oriental Repository at the India House* [London, 1835], p. 3; *Calendar of Persian Correspondence*, vol. VI, pp. 296, 397. On the activities of Tafazzul and Burrow, see Simon Schaffer, "The Asiatic Enlightenments of British Astronomy," in Schaffer et al., eds., *The Brokered World: Go-Betweens and Global Intelligence, 1770–1820* (Sagamore Beach, MA, 2009).

[141] R. H. Phillimore, *Historical Records of the Survey of India* (Dehra Dun, 1945), vol. I, pp. 162–3.

[142] Bharatchandra Ray, *In Praise of Annada* (1752), trans. France Bhattacharya, 2 vols. (Cambridge, MA, 2017–20), vol. I, pp. 41–51.

[143] "Particular Account of the Nuddeah University," *Calcutta Monthly Register and India Repository* (Jan. 1791), p. 137.

[144] Joshua Ehrlich, "New Lights on Raja Krishnachandra and Early Hindu-European Intellectual Exchange," *JRAS* 3rd ser. 31 (2021).

considered him untrustworthy.[145] Hastings must also have seen more advantage in making his own reputation for learning than in elevating that of the raja. He lured several pandits from Krishnachandra's court to work on the *Code of Gentoo Laws*.[146] Rather than restore a former grant to the colleges of Nadia, he formed plans to establish a college of his own in Benares.[147] The new institution would be a font of patronage for pandits, especially Kasinath Sarma, who reportedly conceived of it in the first place and sought Hastings' support.[148] The pandits could be expected to sway other elites in favor of the Company. But Hastings seems to have been pursuing a still wider constituency. Since Benares was a holy city for Hindus, he wrote, attentions to it served to "conciliat[e] a great People to a Dominion which they see with envy and bear with reluctance."[149]

A similar dual logic, patronizing learned elites while grasping toward a broader mode of politics, informed Hastings' founding of the Calcutta Madrasa. The institution also appears to have originated under similar circumstances. In 1774, Hastings restored a former grant to the maulvi Amsa ud-Din for the maintenance of his madrasa in the Burdwan district. One zamindar after another refused to honor the agreement and Hastings allowed it to lapse.[150] Again, however, he proved willing to exert himself when given the chance to establish a college in the Company's name. Such an opportunity arose

---

[145] David L. Curley, "Maharaja Krisnacandra, Hinduism, and Kingship in the Contact Zone of Bengal," in Richard B. Barnett, ed., *Rethinking Early Modern India* (New Delhi, 2002), p. 223; Ratan Dasgupta, "Maharaja Krishnachandra: Religion, Caste and Polity in Eighteenth Century Bengal," *Indian Historical Review* 38 (2011), pp. 227–30.

[146] Michael S. Dodson, *Orientalism, Empire, and National Culture: India, 1770–1870* (Basingstoke, 2007), p. 49.

[147] Ehrlich, "New Lights," p. 162.

[148] Kasinath, Petition (1801), trans. in Surendranath Sen and Umesha Mishra, introduction to Sen and Mishra, eds., *Sanskrit Documents: Being Sanskrit Letters and Other Documents Preserved in the Oriental Collection at the National Archives of India* (Allahabad, 1951), p. 58. After the college was established in 1791, Kasinath served as its first principal.

[149] Hastings, cited in Feiling, *Warren Hastings*, p. 236.

[150] Chambers to Jenkinson, 25 Mar. 1778, f. 96r; *Calendar of Persian Correspondence*, vol. VIII, pp. 70–72.

six years later, when "Mussulmen of Credit and Learning" petitioned him to build a madrasa for the maulvi Majd ud-Din. According to Hastings, the petition reflected "the Belief which generally prevailed that Men so accomplished usually met with a distinguished Reception from myself." And he implied that this was a belief that he intended to perpetuate. At one level, therefore, in founding the madrasa Hastings was bidding for the allegiance of Majd ud-Din and his supporters. At another, however, he was bidding for the allegiance of the institution's future students and scholars, and even of a class of Indian society. Since the Company's assumption of the diwani, Hastings observed, most of the Muslim revenue officials favored by the old regime had been replaced by Hindus and Europeans. At the same time, the decline of the Mughal Empire had led to "the Decline of Learning" in towns and cities across India. Hence, the madrasa was meant to qualify "the once respectable, but now decayed and impoverished Mahometan families" for work in the Company's courts and police. It was also meant to promote "the Growth and Extension of liberal Knowledge" even beyond the Company's borders. Hastings boasted that in its early months, still operating on a limited basis, the institution was already drawing students from Kashmir, Gujarat, and the Carnatic.[151] In 1784, he apprised the directors that "it has contributed to extend the credit of the Company's name, and to soften the prejudices excited by the rapid growth of the British dominions."[152]

While Hastings' plans for the colleges in Benares and Calcutta coupled elite patronage with larger ambitions, another of his statements on conciliation eschewed such "commerce" altogether in favor of a bolder political vision. This statement, engraved on a marble monument that was erected in Bhagalpur in 1784, read as follows:

---

[151] Warren Hastings, Minute (17 Apr. 1781), in *GIED*, pp. 73–4; Warren Hastings, Minute [1784], in S. C. Sanial, "History of the Calcutta Madrassa," *Bengal Past and Present* 8 (1914), pp. 109–10.

[152] Hastings to Directors, 21 Feb. 1784, p. 159.

To the memory of Augustus Cleveland, Esq.
Late collector of the districts of Bhaugulpore and Rájamahall,
Who, without bloodshed or the terrors of authority,
Employing only the means of conciliation, confidence, and benevolence,
Attempted and accomplished
The entire subjection of the lawless and savage inhabitants of the
jungleterry of Rájamahall,
Who had long infested the neighbouring lands by their predatory incursions,
Inspired them with a taste for the arts of civilized life,
And attached them to the British Government by a conquest over their minds;
The most permanent, as the most rational, mode of dominion.[153]

Cleveland's alleged feat, before he died at sea, was to convince several hill tribes to give up a life of raiding for one of agriculture and trade. He had offered material incentives, recruited a local militia, established bazaars, introduced husbandry and manufactures, and even laid the foundations of a school. These measures comprised a very different program, adapted to a very different situation, than those of Hastings in lower Bengal or in India at large. Nonetheless, as Hastings wrote elsewhere, he found much to admire in Cleveland's "system of conciliation" and had favored it with "public support and private encouragement."[154] There was nothing of the enlightened cosmopolitan or cultural relativist in the lines he composed for Cleveland's epitaph, nor, for that matter, of the Company man resigned to a commercial mode of politics. These lines approached far nearer to conciliation as "the act of gaining," to use Johnson's terms, than to conciliation as the "act of reconciling." And yet, like the blustery paeans to conquest that appeared on other Anglo-Indian monuments, they bore little

[153] Cited in Thomas Shaw, "On the Inhabitants of the Hills Near Rájamahall," *Asiatick Researches* 4 (Calcutta, 1795), p. 106 [emphasis removed]. See also the derivative epitaph composed for another monument to Cleveland in Calcutta. [John Hawkesworth], *Asiaticus: In Two Parts* (Calcutta, 1803), Part Two, p. 19.
[154] Warren Hastings, *Memoirs Relative to the State of India* (1786), in Hastings, *Selections from the State Papers of the Governors-General of India: Warren Hastings*, ed. G. W. Forrest, 2 vols. (Oxford, 1910), vol. II, p. 79.

resemblance to reality.[155] As his own system of conciliation demonstrated, Hastings seldom made policy in the heroic mood. He seldom got the chance.

CONCLUSION

In early 1785, Hastings resigned from the governor-generalship and sailed for England. He had been threatening to do so for the past two years, in response to renewed opposition from the ministry, the directors, and his council. Only the hope that parliament would finally grant him the increased powers he had sought induced him to stay as long as he did.[156] But he was to be disappointed. Of the bill drawn up by Prime Minister William Pitt and passed in 1784 he complained, "An Act more injurious to ... my Character and Authority ... could not have been devised."[157] On the return voyage, Hastings set about penning a memoir of his years in office. It was in this period that the Company, whose "first existence was commercial," had come to possess a "political character." It was now "impossible to retrace the perilous and wonderful paths by which they have attained their present elevation, and to redescend to the humble and undreaded character of trading adventurers." Still, Hastings lamented revealingly, "we have not been able ... to change our ideas with our situation."[158]

Hastings had been prevented from realizing his ideal of a robust, uncommercial sovereignty. Enjoying only "intervals of accidental authority," he had been forced to accept the Company's priorities and to adopt a commercial style of politics.[159] Accordingly,

---

[155] Rebecca M. Brown, "Inscribing Colonial Monumentality: A Case Study of the 1763 Patna Massacre Memorial," *Journal of Asian Studies* 65 (2006); Robert Travers, "Death and the Nabob: Imperialism and Commemoration in Eighteenth-Century India," *Past and Present* 196 (2007).

[156] C. C. Davies, "Warren Hastings and the Younger Pitt," *English Historical Review* 70 (1955).

[157] Hastings to Marian Hastings, 29 Dec. 1784, in Hastings, *The Letters of Warren Hastings to His Wife*, ed. Sydney C. Grier (London, 1905), p. 413.

[158] Hastings, *Memoirs*, pp. 60–61, 85.

[159] Hastings to David Anderson, 13 Sept. 1786, in *MWH*, vol. III, p. 303.

he had devised strategies to "conciliate" British and Indian political classes. These strategies differed in some respects. Whereas the British one entailed rehabilitating the nabob and the "Indian World" this figure had come to represent, the Indian one entailed forging alliances with scholars from or close to powerful groups in Indian society. The two strategies also posed different challenges. Whereas the former demanded that Hastings frame the Company's commerce of knowledge in both exalted and mundane terms, the latter demanded that he identify "respectable" Indian scholars and engage them in such commerce. Nonetheless, the two strategies overlapped. Both centered on the use of scholarly patronage to pacify the Company state's discontents, paper over its contradictions, and protract its tenuous existence. What was more, projects undertaken as part of one strategy often implicated the other. The compilation and translation of Hindu and Islamic laws, for instance, was meant largely to win over opinion in Britain but also presented opportunities to cultivate Indian scholars. And the reverse seems to have been true of the founding of the Calcutta Madrasa, which Hastings announced in a dispatch tailored for general metropolitan consumption.

If Hastings' designs spanned oceans, however, then so too did those of his adversaries. The irksome *mahzarnama*s were apparently intended to reach authorities in Britain and convince them that he had alienated respectable Indians. A similar motive seems to have inspired several letters from the Calcutta judge Robert Chambers to the statesman Charles Jenkinson. In one, Chambers ascribed the decline of "Mahommedan Learning throughout Bengal" to Hastings' disdain for knowledge:

> It is said that ... in this Country, the Study of Law and of every other Kind of Learning is neglected because it is no longer honourable. The Observation is true and the Cause is evident: Much of the Dignity of Knowledge depends on the Power it is supposed to have of introducing its Possessour to the Society of

his Superiours; and the Knowledge of a conquered People must lose its Rank and Importance if it neither excites the Curiosity nor ministers to the Passions of the Conqueror.[160]

For Chambers, Hastings was a nabob; a representative of "the Old Indian System" whose only "object is to enrich the company's servants."[161] The persecutor of Reza Khan, he implied, could hardly be credited with success in cultivating learned men. Chambers expressed these views in the late 1770s. Perhaps they informed Hastings' decision to found the Calcutta Madrasa. But while doing so may have propitiated the scholarly judge, it provided fodder for another, more steadfast enemy.[162] In 1786, Philip Francis printed Hastings' dispatch on the madrasa as part of a campaign to have him impeached in parliament. Francis ridiculed Hastings for claiming to be "the promoter of learning and patron of men of letters," considering his wars and "all the havock he has made." And yet, Francis continued, "absurdity is not incompatible with cunning." He asserted that the founding of the madrasa had been a piece of financial chicanery.[163] Francis made the case – a disturbing one for Hastings and his supporters – that Hastings' system of conciliation was a system of corruption instead.

Other developments augured better for this system. Sir William Jones had lately arrived in Bengal and was now presiding over the Asiatic Society. Hastings' acting successor, John Macpherson, was a son of the Scottish Enlightenment who pledged to follow his example in everything.[164] And while Hastings' system could not be said to be similarly entrenched at the other presidencies, the Madras

---

[160] Chambers to Jenkinson, 25 Mar. 1778, ff. 96r–v.

[161] Chambers to Jenkinson, 29 Dec. 1779, BL, Add. MS 38403, f. 315v.

[162] Chambers' biographer has noted that his opposition to Hastings softened in the early 1780s and that the two bonded over intellectual pursuits. Thomas M. Curley, *Sir Robert Chambers: Law, Literature, and Empire in the Age of Johnson* (Madison, 1998), pp. 414–15, 422.

[163] [Philip Francis], *A Letter from Warren Hastings, Esq., Dated 21st of February, 1784, with Remarks and Authentic Documents* (London, 1786), pp. 26, 29.

[164] Hastings to Marian Hastings, 10 Jan. 1785, in *MWH*, vol. III, p. 218.

government had appointed a naturalist and was soon to build an observatory. Even the Court of Directors, which had figured doubly in this system as a body that must be both defended and persuaded, now seemed positively well disposed toward it. True, the directors were sometimes unresponsive to requests for scholarly patronage, leading one London critic to write that "the genius of a Hastings does not shine in ... Leadenhall-street."[165] But they had agreed to most such requests from Hastings, encouraged their servants in learned pursuits, and appointed a hydrographer and a historiographer.[166] Doubts about the directors' interest in knowledge lingered. In 1778, James Rennell, for whom Hastings had sought a pension, wrote from London that "any sum you had fixed would be beat down here by men accustomed to drive Bargains."[167] After initially reducing the award, however, the directors soon restored it.[168] Accordingly, the geographer performed a volte-face. "Whatever charges may be imputable to the Managers for the Company," Rennell declared in 1785, "the neglect of useful Science ... is not among the number." This was proof for him that "a body of subjects may accomplish, what the State itself despairs even to attempt."[169] In other words, the Company's attention to knowledge was due not to its emergence as a state but rather to its endurance as a mercantile company. Hastings would have been loath to draw such a conclusion. Still, he had done much to support it.

[165] Review of Halhed, *Grammar*, in *English Review* (Jan. 1783), p. 13; Miles Ogborn, *Indian Ink: Script and Print in the Making of the English East India Company* (Chicago, 2007), p. 225.

[166] H. V. Bowen, *The Business of Empire: The East India Company and Imperial Britain, 1756–1833* (Cambridge, 2006), pp. 174–6.

[167] Hastings to Richard Becher, 25 Mar. 1777, BL, Add. MS 29128, ff. 50r–51r; Rennell to Hastings, 1 May 1778, BL, Add. MS 29140, f. 343r.

[168] Clements R. Markham, *Major James Rennell and the Rise of Modern English Geography* (London, 1895), p. 61.

[169] James Rennell, *Memoir of a Map of Hindoostan; or the Mogul Empire*, 2nd edn (London, 1785), pp. iv–v n.

2   Conciliation after Hastings

One tomb rises above the others in Kolkata's South Park Street Cemetery. At the time it was built, in 1794, it would have dominated the marshy landscape for miles around. This was fitting. For the tomb's occupant, Sir William Jones, had enjoyed a similar prominence in Calcutta's intellectual topography. As the leading light of the Supreme Court and the Asiatic Society, Jones put the Company and its capital firmly on the Enlightenment map. And yet his tomb nearly had a rival. Had Lord Cornwallis died in Calcutta, an imposing monument like that built for him in Ghazipur instead would have graced a plot nearby.[1] Cornwallis served as governor-general for most of Jones' decade in India. He overhauled the Company's administration in Bengal and expanded its territory around Madras. Most importantly, he helped the Company to recover from its greatest scandal, the impeachment of Warren Hastings, by conveying to its British audience the appearance of probity. Just as Jones embodied the intellectual ferment of the era, so Cornwallis embodied its reformist politics. How the two figures, and the two phenomena, related to each other is the issue at the heart of this chapter.

Historians have tended to see in the age of Jones an expansion of Hastings' program, and in the age of Cornwallis a turn away from it.[2]

---

[1] The Earl Cornwallis, as he was styled when he took up the governor-generalship, was created the Marquess Cornwallis in 1792.

[2] On Jones, see Garland Cannon, *The Life and Mind of Oriental Jones: Sir William Jones, the Father of Modern Linguistics* (Cambridge, 1990); Michael J. Franklin, *Orientalist Jones: Sir William Jones, Poet, Lawyer, and Linguist, 1746–1794* (Oxford, 2011). On Cornwallis, see Franklin Wickwire and Mary Wickwire, *Cornwallis: The Imperial Years* (Chapel Hill, 1980); Robert Travers, *Ideology and Empire in Eighteenth-Century India: The British in Bengal* (Cambridge, 2007), ch. 6; Jon E. Wilson, *The Domination of Strangers: Modern Governance in Eastern India, 1780–1835* (Basingstoke, 2008), ch. 3; Robert Travers, *Empires of Complaints: Mughal Law and the Making of British India, 1765–1793* (Cambridge, 2022), ch. 6.

This Janus-faced perspective on the decade, paradoxical though it is, is not without basis. Shortly after arriving in Calcutta in late 1783, Jones hailed Hastings as a kindred spirit, a fellow voyager on "the sea of knowledge."[3] He befriended many of the same Indian learned elites and European scholar-officials, involved them in the Asiatic Society, and asked Hastings to be its first president. He also took up Hastings' plan to compile and translate Hindu and Islamic laws and shared his aim to save the "Indian World" from metropolitan disdain. Meanwhile, and in as many ways, Cornwallis distanced himself from the former governor-general. Upon arriving in 1786, he set about discarding Hastings' connections and policies in the name of purifying the Company state. No wonder that Jones and Cornwallis have often appeared as opposites, or as masters of separate domains. But were their views really so antithetical, their spheres of activity – knowledge and politics – so discrete? Not according to Jones, who figured Cornwallis as the Justinian to his Tribonian; nor according to Cornwallis, who praised Jones for bringing "the greatest Honour upon our Administration."[4] For all of their differences, the two men were bound together. They were useful to each other. What made them so was the evolving relevance of the idea of conciliation.

In these years, Hastings' idea of conciliation, of patronizing scholars to attract support for the Company state, encountered new and formidable opposition. Hastings relied on the idea in his defense against impeachment charges, but his principal accuser, Edmund Burke, identified it with corruption. Conciliation also acquired a bad name in India, where Hastings' acting replacement, John Macpherson, made it the watchword of his scandalous administration. Hence, it fell to Cornwallis to rid the idea of its unsavoriness, as part of his

[3] Jones to Hastings [early Feb. 1784], in *LWJ*, vol. II, p. 629.
[4] See Governor-General in Council to Jones, 19 Mar. 1788, in *LWJ*, vol. II, p. 801 n. 3; Bernard S. Cohn, "Law and the Colonial State," in Cohn, *Colonialism and Its Forms of Knowledge: The British in India* (Princeton, 1996), p. 70. Justinian was the emperor who sponsored, and Tribonian the jurist who oversaw, the codification of Roman law in the sixth century.

attempt to restore metropolitan faith in the Company state. His alliance with Jones helped in this regard. And in the 1790s, pressure on the Company state and on the idea of conciliation abated. Yet this was to be a temporary reprieve. Soon, both would be challenged afresh by the governor-generalship of Lord Wellesley.

KNOWLEDGE ON TRIAL

Looming over the era of Jones and Cornwallis was the impeachment of Warren Hastings. Few individuals, institutions, or ideas linked to the Company were unaffected by this development. The relevant contemporary publications take up one-eighth of a definitive bibliography comprehending the entire history of the Company.[5] For its part, modern coverage has ranged from minute investigations of the charges against Hastings to broad homilies on the sins of imperialism.[6] Recent works have added a salient reminder that it was the Company state that was on trial as much as the former governor-general.[7] Still, the role of knowledge in the proceedings has gone unstudied, despite its evident importance to his administration. Hastings had patronized learned elites and scholar-officials in service of what he called his system of conciliation. He now enlisted their aid to vindicate this system before parliament and the British public. Emphasizing his connections with such individuals, however, proved to be a risky strategy. It allowed his main prosecutor Edmund Burke to identify conciliation with corruption.

In February 1787, months after his return to England, Hastings appealed to his friend John Shore and his agent George Thompson in Calcutta. The charges Burke had brought against him in the Commons the previous year now seemed certain to result in a trial in the Lords

---

[5] Catherine Pickett, *Bibliography of the East India Company*, 2 vols. (London, 2011–15), vol. II, p. vii.

[6] P. J. Marshall, *The Impeachment of Warren Hastings* (Oxford, 1965); Nicholas B. Dirks, *The Scandal of Empire: India and the Creation of Imperial Britain* (Cambridge, MA, 2006).

[7] For example, Richard Bourke, *Empire and Revolution: The Political Life of Edmund Burke* (Princeton, 2015), pp. 635–7, 647–56, 827.

in which his "lasting reputation" would be at stake. Since he was accused of "having sacrificed every duty to the views of interest," he solicited "testimonials of the most respectable" Indians as to his "more positive merit." Among the several questions he hoped they would address was, "Whether I have shown a disregard to science; or whether I have not, on the contrary ... given effectual encouragement to it."[8] Nor would he be disappointed. Of the fifty testimonials, or *razinamas*, Hastings later received and submitted into evidence most emphasized his scholarly patronage. Of the thousands of signatories, many were "learned men" and most of the rest were the kinds of "Persons of Family and Rank" whom he had sought to conciliate by patronizing them. According to one document signed by hundreds of "Pundits and Bramins" from the district of Nadia, "the whole body of the learned" sang in Hastings' praise. According to another graced by the seals of the nawab of Bengal and his household, "Thousands, reaping the Benefit" of the Calcutta Madrasa, prayed "for the Success of the Company." Similar statements, likewise echoing Hastings' conciliatory logic, issued from prominent constituencies across India. They chimed with another submission: a parting address from Calcutta's British residents, which held that by patronizing "Arts" Hastings had fostered "Communication" with "the Natives."[9]

Hastings mobilized scholars not only as passive witnesses but also as active campaigners on his behalf. In the letter of February 1787, he instructed Shore and Thompson to employ several Indian learned elites in the collection of the *razinamas*. These included the maulvi Majd ud-Din, the mufti (Islamic legal scholar) Ahmad, the magistrate Ali Ibrahim Khan, and the mathematician Tafazzul Husain Khan.[10] Hastings later acknowledged that he was "much indebted"

---

[8] Hastings to John Shore, 19 Feb. 1787, in *MWH*, vol. III, pp. 321–3.

[9] *Minutes of Evidence Taken at the Trial of Warren Hastings*, 11 vols. (London, 1788–95), vol. V, pp. 2333–432, vol. VI, pp. 2433–74. Hastings' agent John Scott also printed the Indian and British testimonials in [John Scott, ed.], *Copies of the Several Testimonials Transmitted from Bengal by the Governor and Council, Relating to Warren Hastings, Esq. Late Governor General of Bengal* (London, 1789).

[10] Hastings to Shore, 19 Feb. 1787, p. 323.

to the last two for their efforts; "You will not meet with Characters of more Faith or worth," he wrote to a friend.[11] European scholar-officials likewise lent their names and talents to Hastings' cause. Charles Wilkins and Jonathan Scott translated some of the *razina-mas*; David Anderson and Nathaniel Brassey Halhed helped to prepare Hastings' defense, testified on his behalf, and battled his accusers in the pamphlet press.[12] Haji Mustafa tried to afford Hastings "some timely assistance" by publishing his translation of *Siyar al-Muta'akhkhirin*. He dedicated the work to Hastings and praised him in the preface, in addition to rendering in English the plaudits of the author, Ghulam Husain Khan.[13]

While Hastings' connections with scholars would seem to have been an asset, however, they threatened to become a liability. By adver-tising his successes in cultivating such individuals, Hastings risked drawing attention to his failures. Notably absent from the Burdwan *razinama* were any signatures of scholars, or, for that matter, any ref-erence to Hastings' scholarly patronage. For critics of Hastings, there would have been a ready explanation: Rather than tend the district's once-famed madrasas, he had built a new one in Calcutta.[14] More awkward still was the absence from the Murshidabad *razinama* of the signature of Muhammad Reza Khan, with whom Hastings had frequently sparred. Thompson reported that he had felt obliged to mention the address to the Khan's agent but that, when the Khan equivocated about signing it, he had declined to respond. "In truth," Thompson explained,

[11] Hastings to David Anderson, 15 Jul. 1788 and 1 Oct. 1790, BL, Add. MS 45418, ff. 21r, 39r.
[12] Hastings to David Anderson, 5 Aug. 1788, ibid., f. 24r; [Scott, ed.], *Copies*, p. 177; Rosane Rocher, *Orientalism, Poetry, and the Millennium: The Checkered Life of Nathaniel Brassey Halhed, 1751–1830* (Delhi, 1983), pp. 131–55; T. H. Bowyer, "Anderson, David (1751–1825)," Oxford Dictionary of National Biography (2004), https://doi.org/10.1093/ref:odnb/63498.
[13] [Ghulam Husain Khan Tabataba'i] Seid-Gholam-Hossein-Khan], *A Translation of the Seir Mutaqharin*, trans. Nota Manus [Haji Mustafa], 4 vols. (Calcutta, 1789–90), vol. I, dedication, pp. 3–4, 13.
[14] See Robert Chambers to Charles Jenkinson, 25 Mar. 1778, BL, Add. MS 38401, f. 96r; [Philip Francis], *A Letter from Warren Hastings, Esq., Dated 21st of February, 1784, with Remarks and Authentic Documents* (London, 1786), pp. 28–9.

I knew how far he had committed himself in conjunction with [Hastings' enemy Philip] Francis, and was not sorry that he did not seek to sign the address for he is certainly a double dealer, and would probably ... have written to Francis that he did it either from fear or favour and have thus furnished that viper with an increase of poison.[15]

Some scholar-officials who had once been close to Hastings now distanced themselves from him; they too endangered his cause. Jonathan Duncan, the Company's resident at Benares, refused to involve himself with the *razinama*s on the ground that they had "no Connection with the Business of the Company."[16] This reaction must have surprised Hastings: He had not only advanced Duncan's career and encouraged his intellectual pursuits but also counted him as a friend.[17] It was proximity to Hastings that compelled officials like Duncan to refuse him aid. If they remained loyal, scholars or not, they too risked being branded as nabobs.

In the trial before the Lords, which began in 1788, Burke made an issue of Hastings' various enmities and intimacies with scholars. There was irony in this. For Burke was a friend to letters and commerce, and most likely a source for Hastings' idea of conciliation. He had once been well disposed toward the Company. He never advocated its liquidation or even the uncoupling of its dual functions.[18] But by the 1780s, he was arguing that officials, especially Hastings, had corrupted its virtuous "mercantile constitution."[19] For Burke, the problem was not that Hastings had behaved like a merchant but

---

[15] Thompson to Hastings, 12 Feb. 1788, in "The Nesbitt-Thompson Papers," *Bengal Past and Present* 8–23 (1914–21), vol. XVIII, p. 183.

[16] Duncan to Ali Ibrahim Khan, trans. in *Minutes of Evidence*, vol. V, p. 2334.

[17] See Thompson to Hastings, 12 Feb. 1788, p. 182; Hastings to Anderson, 15 Jul. 1788, f. 21r; V. A. Narain, *Jonathan Duncan and Varanasi* (Calcutta, 1959), pp. 16–17.

[18] Gregory M. Collins, "The Limits of Mercantile Administration: Adam Smith and Edmund Burke on Britain's East India Company," *Journal of the History of Economic Thought* 41 (2019).

[19] Edmund Burke, "Speech on Opening of Impeachment" (15 to 19 Feb. 1788), in Burke, *The Writings and Speeches of Edmund Burke*, gen. ed. Paul Langford, 9 vols. (Oxford, 1981–2015), vol. VI, p. 295.

rather that he had behaved like an unprincipled one. As a corollary, any scholar or scholarly undertaking Hastings had patronized was inherently suspect. Thus,

> We find and trace him through the whole of his conduct, following a great variety of mercantile employments, and when he comes to you, you would imagine that he had been bred in the sublime sciences, who never knew any act any further than as it made a part in the business of the sublime matters he was engaged in, that he had been engaged in writing a poem, an Iliad, or sometime to revive fallen literature. And yet you find this man dealing in accounts contriving to make up a good account for himself.[20]

In Burke's telling, Hastings was a "swindling M[aec]enas," who, despite affecting "the honour and glory of a Patron," had duped scholars or made them his accomplices.[21] To the extent that his patronage had conciliated – more often it had injured – it was under false pretenses.

Burke offered three examples. First, there was the patronage of Ali Ibrahim. Burke claimed that Hastings had taken bribes from the Khan, employed him in dark dealings, and used his supposed rank and learning to distract from his own crimes. As Burke put it, "Mr. Hastings has covered all his injustice and all his violences ... by proving what good he had done at Benares by taking Ali Ibrahim Khan with him."[22] Then, there was the codification of Hindu and Islamic laws. Burke saw merit in the project but accused Hastings, with Halhed's connivance, of cheating the financier Raja Nabakrishna to pay for it. In his words, Hastings had "obtained a false credit with the Public for an Act of liberality which he did not perform, for the production of Laws for

---

[20] Edmund Burke, "Speech in Reply" (28 May to 16 Jun. 1794), in ibid., vol. VII, pp. 620–21.

[21] Ibid., p. 285. Gaius Maecenas was the patron of Horace and Virgil (and not known to be a swindler).

[22] Ibid., pp. 454–6. See also Edmund Burke, "Articles of Impeachment" (14 to 28 May 1787), in Burke, Writings and Speeches, vol. VI, p. 244.

which he forced other people contrary to all Laws to pay."[23] Finally, there was the founding of the Calcutta Madrasa. Burke alleged that Hastings had defrauded not only Nabakrishna but also the Company, and that he had appointed a disreputable principal in Majd ud-Din. Contrasting Hastings' praises for the maulvi with recent complaints against him, Burke maintained that the two men had conspired in "fraud, injury and peculation," and even in the training of "Robbers and House breakers." According to Burke, the fact that several of the *razinamas* lauded Hastings on account of the madrasa merely proved that the documents were spurious.[24] It was one of his assumptions that all of Hastings' "learned" and "respectable" Indian allies had been bribed or coerced.

Burke's message was that Hastings' system of conciliation was a system of corruption instead. This was also a warning. His objective in prosecuting Hastings was to make a public example of him. Burke's sharpest comments on scholarly patronage came late in the trial, but they would have been long anticipated, and not only because his ally Francis had foreshadowed them.[25] Since his earliest writings, Burke had maintained that knowledge was only good insofar as it served to promote social order and virtue.[26] His *Reflections on the Revolution in France* (1790) warned of what could happen when men of letters colluded with men of commerce in political intrigues.[27] Burke's case against Hastings may have been tenuous, his rhetoric overblown; but his basic insistence on oversight appealed to his British audience. Pending the outcome of the trial, the Company's scholarly patronage would be under intense scrutiny. If Hastings' system of conciliation was to endure, then it must be carefully delimited.

[23] Burke, "Speech in Reply," pp. 262, 265, 268, 273, 285. For the transaction to which Burke was referring, see P. J. Marshall, "Nobkissen versus Hastings," in Marshall, *Trade and Conquest: Studies on the Rise of British Dominance in India* (Aldershot, 1993).
[24] Burke, "Speech in Reply," pp. 650–2, 665–9.
[25] See [Francis], *Letter from Warren Hastings*, pp. 26–34.
[26] Bourke, *Empire and Revolution*, p. 80.
[27] Edmund Burke, *Reflections on the Revolution in France* (London, 1790), in Burke, *Writings and Speeches*, vol. VIII, pp. 160–2; Paul Keen, *The Crisis of Literature in the 1790s: Print Culture and the Public Sphere* (Cambridge, 2004), pp. 42–53.

MACPHERSON AND CONCILIATION

Burke's attack on Hastings' system of conciliation drew additional force from the record of the latter's acting replacement. Though it has been neglected by historians, the nineteen-month administration of John Macpherson did much to shape those that followed. Macpherson was a son of the Scottish Enlightenment who advocated a lofty commercial politics. Rather than turn to conciliation out of necessity, he keenly took up and developed the idea. He described conciliation as a natural impulse underlying all of the principles that guided his conduct. Like Hastings, he understood conciliation in close connection with scholarly patronage. Macpherson succeeded in forging alliances with scholar-officials like Jones and with learned elites like Majd ud-Din. He even nurtured the Company's reputation as a global broker of knowledge. And yet his elevated visions coincided with an evident streak of corruption. This did much to tarnish them in the eyes of contemporaries, including his successor, Cornwallis.

Macpherson nowhere seems to have set down a "system" of conciliation in the manner of Hastings and yet he evidently envisioned something of the kind. He used the term "conciliate" often – nearly a dozen times in one defense of his administration.[28] And like Hastings, he used it to refer to a mode of politics in line with the Company's hybrid constitution. Unlike Hastings, he championed this mode and this constitution: Sound policy dictated preserving the Company's "old System," which entailed "conciliating the Native Population."[29] Nonetheless, Macpherson likewise sought to do this through scholarly patronage, which he described as "natural" to his disposition.[30]

---

[28] *The Case of Sir John Macpherson, Baronet, Late Governor-General of India, Containing a Summary Review of his Administration and Services Prepared by Friends from Authentic Documents* (London, 1808). The work must have been prepared either by Macpherson or with substantial input from him.

[29] Macpherson to Charles Grant, 31 Jul. 1807, BL, Mss Eur F291/57, f. 38r. For earlier praise of the Company's constitution, see Macpherson to James Macpherson, 27 Jul. 1782 and 1 Nov. 1783, BL, Mss Eur F291/129, ff. 18r-v, 91r.

[30] Macpherson to John Gilchrist [1785], in John Gilchrist, *Dictionary, English and Hindoostanee*, 2 vols. (Calcutta, 1787–98), vol. I, p. vii n.

In 1781, soon after being appointed to Hastings' council, Macpherson signed, and likely authored, a statement praising his attentions to Ali Ibrahim and the "colleges" of Benares. These measures were important "in a political view"; they would earn the respect of "leading" Indians, and of Europeans, who were starting to investigate Eastern "antiquities" and "sciences."[31] As governor-general too, Macpherson made the case for conciliation in terms reminiscent of his predecessor. In a minute meant for the eyes of the directors, he recommended Joseph Champion's The Poems of Ferdosi (1785) on the ground that it was "political in a Government like ours to encourage" such writings.[32] And yet Macpherson's system of conciliation, such as it was, was more intuitive and idealistic than that of Hastings. It intersected with what he called "my two great Principles of action" in India: building alliances and establishing public credit.[33]

Macpherson's principle of building alliances took shape through a series of commercial, political, and literary entanglements and conducted him to a system of conciliation rooted in his own experience. Macpherson was born to a minister on the Isle of Skye. A polite education prepared him to earn his "bread by embarking in the world."[34] In the 1760s, he attended the University of Edinburgh, where he began a lifelong friendship with his tutor, Adam Ferguson, and mixed with other literati. He considered using these connections to try to obtain a chair at the university.[35] As it was, he long

---

[31] Supreme Council to Governor-General, 3 Dec. 1781, in George W. Forrest, ed., Selections from the Letters, Despatches, and Other State Papers Preserved in the Foreign Department of the Government of India, 1772–1785, 3 vols. (Calcutta, 1899), vol. III, p. 38.

[32] NAI, Bengal Public Consultations (19 Dec. 1785), no. 26.

[33] Macpherson to unknown, 6 May 1800, Edinburgh University Library, Dc.1.77, no. 64B.

[34] This, at least, was what he later implied in a letter on the curriculum to be adopted at a proposed Highland academy. Macpherson to Provost Mackintosh, 23 Mar. 1789, in Charles Fraser-Mackintosh, ed., Letters of Two Centuries, Chiefly Connected with Inverness and the Highlands, from 1616 to 1815 (Inverness, 1890), p. 314.

[35] James Noel Mackenzie Maclean, "The Early Political Careers of James 'Fingal' Macpherson (1736–1796) and Sir John Macpherson, Bart. (1744–1821)" (PhD dissertation, University of Edinburgh, 1967), pp. 104–12.

anticipated spending his retirement among this illustrious set.[36] "Though we have lost you for a while," read a typical letter to him from Hugh Blair, "this will find you acting in a much wider and more purposeful sphere .... [W]hen we meet, your health is drunk, and much conversation carried on about all that you are to do in India."[37] Macpherson's first voyage east, as a ship's purser in 1767, landed him at Madras, where he promptly put both his learning and his charm to use. After obtaining an audience by demonstrating "some Electrical experiments," he convinced the nawab of Arcot to appoint him as his London agent.[38] In this lucrative capacity, Macpherson renewed his acquaintance with James Macpherson, with whom he shared more than a Highland clan affiliation. Among other things, both men had already used "literature as a means of raising capital: James with the poems of Ossian, and John with his father's work on customs and antiquities."[39] Together, the Macphersons wrote a flattering sketch of the nawab, coaxed Alexander Dow to insert it in his *History of Hindostan*, and, finally, sent the section to ministers and puffed it in the press.[40] No wonder that Macpherson took to Hastings' idea of conciliation upon encountering it in the 1780s: Building alliances through commerce, politics, and letters was something he had long done already.

Accordingly, rather than merely continue Hastings' system of conciliation, Macpherson made it his own. This could be observed in his distinctive approach to patronizing learned elites. Macpherson not only kept up ties with friends of Hastings like Ali Ibrahim but also traded "philosophical observations" with his enemy

---

[36] Macpherson to James Macpherson, 20 Nov. 1783, BL, Mss Eur F291/129, f. 94v.

[37] Blair to Macpherson, 28 Nov. 1781, BL, Mss Eur F291/83, ff. 25r–v.

[38] Robert Harland to Earl of Rochford, 10 Sept. 1772, in Maclean, "Early Political Careers," p. 114.

[39] Maclean, "Early Political Careers," p. 120.

[40] George McElroy, "Ossianic Imagination and the History of India: James and John Macpherson as Propagandists and Intriguers," in Jennifer J. Carter and Joan H. Pittock, eds., *Aberdeen and the Enlightenment: Proceedings of a Conference Held at the University of Aberdeen* (Aberdeen, 1987), p. 365. See Alexander Dow, *The History of Hindostan*, 2nd edn, 3 vols. (London, 1770–72), vol. II, pp. 396–8.

Reza Khan.[41] He showed singular tact in resolving a crisis at the Calcutta Madrasa that had threatened to turn a friend into an enemy. According to several petitions, Majd ud-Din was withholding the allowances of the madrasa's students as well as demanding excessive rent from the tenants of its endowed lands. The maulvi implored Macpherson not to "give ear to the unjust complaints which are raised against him."[42] An entry in Macpherson's notes, however, suggests his own conclusion: "The Mulovie of the Mudrussa seems to be going mad with avarice & ignorance & if a remedy is not speedily applied, this Honourable ... Institution will soon go to ruin altogether."[43] The problem with simply removing Majd ud-Din was that he wielded influence with leading Muslims in Calcutta and beyond – perhaps as far away as his home of Awadh. Macpherson's solution was to tell the maulvi's discontents one thing and the maulvi himself another. Replying to the students, Macpherson declared that he had heard their complaints and that Majd ud-Din would be brought under his supervision.[44] Replying to Majd ud-Din, he dismissed these complaints as interested fabrications and expressed undiminished confidence in him.[45] Macpherson ultimately issued a *sanad* (edict) appointing the official William Chambers as *amin* (monitor) of the institution.[46] At the same time, he took pains to reassure Majd ud-Din, telling him that Chambers was "a sensible man fit for the business."[47]

Macpherson proved no less adept at building alliances with European scholar-officials. John Gilchrist praised him as a "gentleman and scholar" who "did all in his power to forward" his views.[48]

---

[41] Allan Macpherson, Notes (12 Dec. [1785]), Cambridge South Asian Archive, Macpherson Family Papers, f. 2869; Ali Ibrahim to Macpherson, received 19 Oct. 1786, trans., BL, Mss Eur F291/6, p. 50.

[42] Abstract [of Majd ud-Din to Macpherson], undated, Cambridge South Asian Archive, Macpherson Family Papers, ff. 2607–8.

[43] Note, ibid., ff. 2647–8.

[44] Macpherson to [students], undated, trans., ibid., f. 5.

[45] Macpherson to [Majd ud-Din], undated, trans., ibid., f. 1282.

[46] Macpherson, Sanad, trans., ibid., ff. 2814–15.

[47] Macpherson to [Majd ud-Din], undated, trans., ibid., f. 2813.

[48] Gilchrist, *Dictionary*, vol. I, p. vii.

Chambers no doubt was equally grateful for his appointment as *amin* at the madrasa. Still, it was a third orientalist whose friendship most interested Macpherson. Chambers was the interpreter at the Supreme Court and the brother of one of its judges, as well as a member of the Asiatic Society. Hence, he was doubly known to William Jones, who applauded his selection as *amin* and may have suggested it to Macpherson in the first place.[49] Macpherson found other ways to cultivate Jones. He lent him letters from Ferguson, obtained for him Samuel Turner's account of Bhutan and Tibet, and made known to him his shared fondness for the naturalist Johann Koenig.[50] Moreover, at Jones' behest, he met with the poet Zain ud-Din 'Ishqi and with the pandit Ramalocana Kanthavarna.[51] Jones, in turn, flattered Macpherson that "your mind can grasp the whole field of literature ... as well as that of politics, and ... in the manner of ancient rulers in Asia, particularly Cicero, the governor of Cilicia, you unite the character of the statesman and the scholar."[52] This endorsement was valuable in Britain, where Jones had acquired a name already and was becoming famous anew for his Indian studies. Macpherson and his supporters would trot out Jones' lines for decades to come; they would even appear in his epitaph.[53] Still, there seems to have been more to Macpherson's adoption of the motto than vanity: It accorded not only with the principle of building alliances but also with that of establishing public credit.

[49] Jones to Macpherson, 17 and 26 May 1785, in *LWJ*, vol. II, pp. 673, 675–6; Jones to Macpherson, 22 May 1785, in Joshua Ehrlich, "Empire and Enlightenment in Three Letters from Sir William Jones to Governor-General John Macpherson," *Historical Journal* 62 (2019), p. 548; *Proceedings of the Asiatic Society*, 4 vols. (Calcutta, 1980–2000), vol. I, p. 54.

[50] Jones to Macpherson, 6 May and Nov. 1786, in *LWJ*, vol. II, pp. 698, 727; Jones to Patrick Russell, 28 Sept. 1786, in *LWJ*, vol. II, p. 707.

[51] Jones to Macpherson, May 1785, in *LWJ*, vol. II, pp. 674–5; Jones to Macpherson [1785], in Ehrlich, "Empire and Enlightenment," p. 551; Jones to Allan Macpherson, 6 Jan. 1786, in W. C. Macpherson, ed., *Soldiering in India, 1764–1787* (Edinburgh, 1928), p. 345.

[52] Jones to Macpherson, 17 May 1785, in *LWJ*, vol. II, p. 672.

[53] *Case of Sir John Macpherson*, p. 99 n *; William Essington Hughes, ed., *Monumental Inscriptions and Extracts from Registers of Births, Marriages, and Deaths, at St. Anne's Church, Soho* (London, 1905), p. 17.

Whereas Macpherson's first "great principle" of building alliances was early in evidence, his second one of establishing public credit marked a late apostasy. Before he became governor-general, Macpherson was apt to concur with his tutor Ferguson that state borrowing was among the evils of modern commercial society.[54] But, as he later put it, "Judge what a Disciple of Ferguson ... must have learned when he sat on the Throne of Timur, without a rupee in his Treasury, with an immense army a year in arrears, & when Bills on England could not raise a shilling."[55] Faced with these circumstances, Macpherson sought to cut costs, increase the circulation of specie, and in general set the "credit of the Company on the firmest basis."[56] His understanding of public credit, however, went beyond simply a government's borrowing of money. Macpherson wrote that the rise of "commerce and modern finance" had made public credit "the grand heart-spring which ... keeps up the ... progress of civilisation."[57] He perceived the emergence of a global system of interaction and called for a politics attuned to it. Macpherson had once described India, in a Fergusonian key, as a field "too great for the narrow and interested Politics of a commercial society."[58] As governor-general, however, he espoused a politics based on "the reciprocal advantages of Commercial Intercourse."[59] "A solid foundation for the Power of the Company," Macpherson asserted, must rest "on a Commercial connection" – and not on extended territory.[60] His retrenchments and encouragements to trade marked only the first

---

[54] For Ferguson's view, see Iain McDaniel, *Adam Ferguson in the Scottish Enlightenment: The Roman Past and Europe's Future* (Cambridge, MA, 2013), p. 116.

[55] Macpherson to Alexander Carlyle, 12 Jan. 1797, Edinburgh University Library, Dc.4.41, no. 40.

[56] [John Macpherson], *Documents Explanatory of the Case of Sir John Macpherson, Baronet, as Governor General of Bengal* [London, 1800], p. 28.

[57] Macpherson, cited in *Annual Register, or a View of the History, Politics, and Literature for the Year 1797* (London, 1800), p. 176; Macpherson, cited in John Sinclair, *Memoirs of the Life and Works of Sir John Sinclair, Bart.*, 2 vols. (Edinburgh, 1837), vol. II, p. 266.

[58] Sallust [John Macpherson] to ed., *Public Advertiser* (16 Aug. 1769), cited in McElroy, "Ossianic Imagination," p. 365.

[59] Macpherson to Vicomte de Souillac, 26 Jan. 1786, BL, Add. MS 38409, f. 47v.

[60] Macpherson to Directors, 11 Jan. 1786, TNA, PRO 30/8/362, f. 116v.

steps in "the opening of a system" that would ultimately "embrace the Commerce of the Globe."[61] Macpherson wrote in these terms to the directors and the prime minister, to rulers across India, and even to the French Compagnie des Indes.[62] His furthest-reaching statements, however, were reserved for men of letters back in Britain.

In a missive to Ferguson of 1786, the various strands of Macpherson's thought on commerce, politics, and knowledge came together. Here, it became clear how building alliances and establishing public credit figured in a project to conciliate India, Britain, and the wider world. Macpherson first wrote of the benefits that "may flow from the practical operation of the commercial and political systems I have opened." He expressed a desire to foster "the happy communications of all the inhabitants of the globe ... till the east and the west are united." He boasted:

> I have at this moment at Calcutta ambassadors from Tidore, in the eastern seas, from Thibet, from all the states of India, and from Timur Shaw, who is crossing the Attock; and as Manilla is opening her trade, I hope to hear direct from Lima before I leave India, and to make the Incas of Peru acquainted with the Brahmin Rajas on the banks of the Ganges.

After developing the theme of "commerce" in a political as well as in an economic sense, Macpherson turned to its role in disseminating knowledge: "Curious are, besides, the treasures in literature and the oblivious history of nations that are drawing upon us from the researches of Sir William Jones and others." As the Company's commerce placed more "useful and elegant information" into the hands of scholars, so their studies would yield even greater treasures.[63] In

---

[61] Macpherson to William Pitt, 12 Jul. 1786, ibid., ff. 136r–136v.

[62] For Macpherson's attempt to broker a trade agreement with the Compagnie, see John Shovlin, *Trading with the Enemy: Britain, France, and the 18th-Century Quest for a Peaceful World Order* (New Haven, 2021), p. 267.

[63] Macpherson to Ferguson, 12 Jan. 1786, in *The Correspondence of Adam Ferguson*, ed. Vincenzo Merolle, 2 vols. (London, 1995); vol. II, pp. 315–16.

the tradition of Montesquieu – and of Hastings, but without his reservations – Macpherson envisioned a global exchange of ideas that
would reconcile differences and stimulate progress.

Whatever the merits of this exalted vision, its fate would soon
be thrown into doubt by the arrival of Cornwallis. In the new
governor-general's estimation, Macpherson was thoroughly corrupt, and lucky not to have been impeached alongside Hastings.[64]
Certainly, in his dealings with scholars, Macpherson was liable
to mix considerations of public and private utility. He offered the
management of the prospective Calcutta Botanic Garden to a crony,
who replied that he might accept "if the thing were made worth my
while."[65] Still, Macpherson's "philosophical politics" and its reso-
nance with contemporaries cannot be entirely dismissed.[66] Years
later, removed from office and no longer ambitious to return, he continued to entertain his old designs. As he told the historian Edward
Gibbon in 1791, "I too have long been forming general ideas upon
the … consequences, which letters … and commerce are likely to
introduce." He expected that "the fruits of knowledge, which were
originally so poisonous will mellow into useful Ripeness." He also
hoped to draw Gibbon's "eye to the Indian Scene" and recommended
William Robertson's *Historical Disquisition* (1791) as a model.[67]
That work lauded Alexander and Akbar for stimulating intellectual
and material exchange, and placed Hastings in the same line of commercial sovereigns.[68] "By tracing the progress of the trade of Europe
with India," Robertson later acknowledged, he had meant to "suggest

[64] Cornwallis to Henry Dundas, 1 Nov. 1788, 8 Aug. and 1 Nov. 1789, in Marquis
Cornwallis, *Correspondence of Charles, First Marquis of Cornwallis*, ed. Charles
Ross, 2nd edn, 3 vols. (London, 1859), vol. I, pp. 383, 430, 454.

[65] Archibald Keir to Allan Macpherson, 10 Jul. 1786, Cambridge South Asian Archive,
Macpherson Family Papers, f. 1809.

[66] For the description, see James Macpherson to Macpherson, 17 Jun. 1783, BL, F291/125,
f. 14v.

[67] Macpherson to Gibbon, 1 Nov. 1791 and 4 Dec. 1792, BL, Add. MS 34886, ff. 227v,
229r–229v, 231v–232r, 319r [emphasis removed].

[68] William Robertson, *An Historical Disquisition Concerning the Knowledge Which the
Ancients Had of India* (London, 1791), pp. 12–13, 22–5, 272–5, 336, 347–9.

some hints to an intelligent ... Statesman."[69] Indeed, he did more than just hint: He urged the Company to appoint someone to perform the "important" task of "investigating ... Indian philosophy."[70] Surely, Macpherson would have leapt at the chance to gratify his important friend and to advance his own designs. His replacement, Cornwallis, however, did not.

CORNWALLIS AND CONCILIATION

Hastings and Macpherson provided cautionary examples for Cornwallis. The one was on trial in parliament and the other, he believed, ought to be. And yet, his conclusion was not that the Company state was fundamentally flawed but rather that it must be purified and rehabilitated. This conclusion had important consequences for the idea of conciliation and for the attendant policy of scholarly patronage. Both were to be preserved, indeed protected, but at the cost of some of their former amplitude. They must be purged of corruption, brought in line with Cornwallis' regulatory politics. Certain learned elites and scholar-officials would fall from grace but others would adapt and benefit. One of the latter was Jones, who, despite his former closeness with Hastings and Macpherson, adjusted to the new dispensation. He and his Asiatic Society served to give the appearance of a more detached, less corruptible relationship between knowledge and the Company state.

Cornwallis has often been seen as a transformative governor-general, but in at least one crucial respect he was a conservative one. Although – or perhaps because – he was an outsider with no Indian experience, he was inclined to preserve the Company state. This was also his directive. His reforms were underpinned by Pitt's India Act,

---

[69] Robertson to Henry Dundas, 6 Jul. 1791, cited in Stewart J. Brown, "William Robertson, Early Orientalism and the *Historical Disquisition* on India of 1791," *Scottish Historical Review* 88 (2009), p. 303. Robertson also had his son, one of two in the Company's service, present a copy of the *Historical Disquisition* to Cornwallis. Robertson to Cornwallis, 17 Dec. 1791, TNA, PRO 30/11/270, ff. 70r–71r.

[70] Robertson, *Historical Disquisition*, p. 311.

which, in the words of the eponymous prime minister, was intended to remodel the Company's "old constitution ... rather than make a new one." The act was drawn up with the directors' "concurrence"; it served to "connect" the Company with the government rather than absorb it into it. For, Pitt held, "commercial companies could ... govern empires" if their servants behaved with "purity and abstinence."[71] This, accordingly, was what the "Cornwallis system," as it would come to be known, sought to ensure. It sought to close off avenues of corruption by stamping out profiteering, regulating diplomacy, and curbing the power of Indian intermediaries.[72] These reforms came mainly from within the Company: They were worked out by Cornwallis' advisers.[73] They were also in keeping with its ideology. In the words of Pitt, "Commerce was our object, and with a view to its extension, a pacific system should prevail, and a system of defence and conciliation."[74] Like Hastings, Cornwallis would undermine such claims by indulging in war and conquest. And like Hastings, he would rely all the more for that reason on the idea of conciliation.

While Cornwallis adopted this idea for the same general reason – to legitimize the Company state – he did so under new conditions and in service of a new agenda. Conciliation, now associated with corruption, must be brought in line with his regulatory politics. This could be seen in Cornwallis' treatment of Indian learned elites, whom he continued to patronize but on more restrictive terms than his predecessors. Unlike Hastings or Macpherson, Cornwallis refused to smooth over accusations against Majd ud-Din, the head maulvi of the Calcutta Madrasa. Following new reports of peculation

---

[71] William Pitt, Speech in HC Deb (6 Jul. 1784), in *The Parliamentary History of England, from the Earliest Period to the Year 1803*, 36 vols. (London, 1806–20), vol. XXIV, cols. 1089, 1091, 1099.

[72] The Cornwallis moment was an important one, especially in Britain and its empire, for the emergence of the modern understanding of corruption as the abuse of office. See Mark Knights, *Trust and Distrust: Corruption in Office in Britain and Its Empire, 1600–1850* (Oxford, 2021).

[73] Lilian M. Penson, "The Bengal Administrative System, 1786–1818," in *The Cambridge History of India*, 6 vols. (Cambridge 1922–37), vol. V, pp. 434–7.

[74] Pitt, Speech (6 Jul. 1784), col. 1095.

and permissiveness – those cited by Burke at Hastings' trial – the Supreme Council finally removed the maulvi from his post.[75] At the same time, other learned elites benefited from Cornwallis' high-mindedness. The successor to Majd ud-Din, Muhammad Israel, was chosen as much "for the purity of his moral Character as for his literary attainments."[76] Cornwallis' scruples also worked in favor of Ali Ibrahim Khan, whom the prince of Wales, in 1789, sought to have removed as chief magistrate of Benares.[77] There is little doubt that Macpherson, at least, would have sacrificed his friendship with the Khan for the sake of one with the prince. (In fact, he befriended the latter after returning to Britain.) Cornwallis, however, responded to the prince firmly in the negative. "The great and truly respectable character of" Ali Ibrahim, he wrote, "would have rendered it a very difficult and unpopular measure" to have replaced him with the prince's protégé.[78] Nor was this all. As Cornwallis informed his brother, he was duty-bound to refuse such an "infamous and unjustifiable job."[79] The idea of conciliation thus aligned with Cornwallis' principles to keep Ali Ibrahim where he was.

Cornwallis patronized a number of other learned elites. To do so may have been all the more important at a time when Indians were vanishing from the upper ranks of the Company's service.[80] On different occasions, he proposed to appoint as resident at Hyderabad the writer Mirza Abu Talib Khan and the mathematician Tafazzul Husain Khan.[81] Neither man ultimately filled the post, perhaps because, as

---

[75] West Bengal State Archives, Bengal Revenue Proceedings (23 Jan. 1788), no. 1; ibid. (18 Mar. 1791), no. 9.

[76] Ibid. (18 Mar. 1791), no. 9.

[77] Prince of Wales to Cornwallis, 30 May 1789, in Cornwallis, *Correspondence*, vol. II, p. 29.

[78] Cornwallis to Prince of Wales, 14 Aug. 1790, in ibid., vol. II, p. 35.

[79] Cornwallis to Bishop of Lichfield and Coventry, 16 Nov. 1790, in ibid., vol. II, p. 52.

[80] On the displacement of Indians by Britons as a gradual process that Cornwallis concluded rather than began, see P. J. Marshall, "Indian Officials under the East India Company in Eighteenth-Century Bengal," in Marshall, *Trade and Conquest*.

[81] Tafazzul to David Anderson, undated, trans. and cited in "An Account of the Life and Character of Tofuzzel Hussein Khan," *Asiatic Annual Register* [5] (1804), "Characters," p. 5; Richard Johnson to [Henry Dundas], 8 Feb. 1800, BL, IOR H/435, p. 189.

one official put it, "the spirit of the times made it necessary to find an English Gentleman."[82] Still, Abu Talib credited Cornwallis with helping him on other occasions; and Tafazzul wrote that he "treats me with favour" and has "encouraged me to hold my connection with public affairs."[83] The "integrity" and "honor" of these men now did much to recommend them, but, as in the past, so did their "erudition."[84] If Cornwallis demonstrated a new concern with the morals of learned elites patronized by the Company, then he did not lose sight of the reason for patronizing them. Thus, in 1788, he readily agreed to enlist the support of the pandit Jagannatha Tarkapanchanan for a project to compile and translate Hindu laws. Since "his Opinion, Learning and Abilities are held in the highest Veneration," Cornwallis wrote, "the Work will Derive infinite Credit ... from the Annexation of his Name."[85] This was the kind of statement Hastings himself might have made were he still governor-general. It showed that his idea of conciliation continued to resonate.

Nowhere was this continuity clearer than at the Benares Sanskrit College, plans for which had begun under Hastings. After Hastings' departure, the pandit Kasinath Sarma reportedly brought these plans to the resident Jonathan Duncan, who, in turn, took them up with Cornwallis.[86] That Cornwallis would establish the institution was by no means a foregone conclusion. Given the history of the Calcutta Madrasa, he might have foreseen the troubles that would plague its Hindu counterpart. But Duncan had earned his confidence as

---

[82] Johnson to [Dundas], 8 Feb. 1800, p. 189. See also "Mirza Abu Taleb Khan," *Asiatic Annual Register* [3] (1802), "Miscellaneous Tracts," pp. 100–1.

[83] Tafazzul to David Anderson, undated, p. 6; Mirza Abu Taleb Khan, *The Travels of Mirza Abu Taleb Khan*, trans. Charles Stewart, 2 vols. (London, 1810), vol. I, pp. 15–16, 112.

[84] Lord Teignmouth to ed., undated, cited in "An Account of the Life and Character of Tofuzzel Hussein Khan," p. 8.

[85] Cornwallis, Minute (22 Aug. 1788), cited in *LWJ*, vol. II, p. 803 n. 1.

[86] Kasinath, Petition (1801), trans. in Surendranath Sen and Umesha Mishra, introduction to Sen and Mishra, eds., *Sanskrit Documents: Being Sanskrit Letters and Other Documents Preserved in the Oriental Collection at the National Archives of India* (Allahabad, 1951), p. 58.

"the first Resident who has done any thing but plunder the Country."[87] Moreover, he made a compelling argument that the college would endear "our Government to the native Hindus."[88] Cornwallis reprised this argument in a letter to the directors, explicitly invoking the idea of conciliation. "An Institution founded expressly to promote the study of Laws and Religion," he wrote, "must be extremely flattering to their [Hindus'] prejudices, and tend greatly to conciliate" them.[89] It was clear that the Hindus whom Duncan and Cornwallis had most in mind were Brahmans and other elites who reputedly venerated them. Preferences for Brahmans and Brahmanical learning were built into the college's rules and curriculum, and its professorships all initially went to Brahman pandits.[90] It was also clear, however, that the founders of the college, like Hastings before them, entertained notions of popular engagement. Duncan's inaugural visit in 1791 included a procession through the streets, and proclamations in the square outside.[91] Finally, the college may have figured in Cornwallis' designs to strengthen the zamindar class, on which he believed the social order in India rested.[92] Just as Hastings had founded the madrasa partly to provide tutors for declining Muslim families, so perhaps Cornwallis sought to do the same for their Hindu analogs.

Like Hastings too, if not to an even greater extent, Cornwallis sought to conciliate metropolitan opinion by patronizing scholar-officials. Like Majd ud-Din, however, some of these officials fell afoul

---

[87] Cornwallis to John Shore, 6 Nov. 1789, TNA, PRO 30/11/165, f. 72r.

[88] Duncan to Cornwallis, 1791, cited in George Nicholls, *Sketch of the Rise and Progress of the Benares Patshalla or Sanskrit College* (Allahabad, 1907), p. 1.

[89] Governor-General in Council to Directors, 10 Mar. 1792, cited in Narain, *Jonathan Duncan*, p. 173.

[90] Nicholls, *Sketch*, pp. 2–4; Sen and Mishra, introduction, pp. 53–4; Michael S. Dodson, *Orientalism, Empire, and National Culture: India, 1770–1870* (Basingstoke, 2007), pp. 51–2.

[91] "Extract of a Letter from Benares, dated 17th November 1791," in *Selections from the Calcutta Gazettes*, 5 vols. (Calcutta, 1864–8), vol. II, pp. 310–11.

[92] Elsewhere, Cornwallis advocated enabling zamindars "to give a liberal education to their children." Cornwallis to Directors, 2 Aug. 1788, in Cornwallis, *Correspondence*, vol. I, p. 554. See Ranajit Guha, *A Rule of Property for Bengal: An Essay on the Idea of Permanent Settlement*, 3rd edn (Ranikhet, 2016), pp. 223–5.

of the new governor-general's stricter standards of behavior. In 1786, Cornwallis approved the officer Robert Kyd's proposal to establish the Calcutta Botanic Garden. Not only were the reasons of science, commerce, and sustenance worthy in themselves but in combination, they served to justify the Company state.[93] Cornwallis and Kyd thus would seem to have had a mutual interest in the success of the garden. But tensions grew over the former's refusal to let the latter gather specimens in China or salt on the Maratha frontier. Kyd grumbled to Hastings about Cornwallis' "Ignorance (I further apprehend a contempt) of every thing relating to the Institution."[94] Given Cornwallis' claim that the garden "has proved of much General Utility," it seems likelier that he, as Kyd sensed, suspected him of pursuing his "personal interest."[95] Kyd was not the only discontent. Another was the Persianist and factotum Francis Gladwin, who similarly wrote to Hastings to complain: "Under your patronage, oriental Learning was cultivated with success, but his Lordship, despising every branch of Science, there is not the smallest encouragement for publication so that my literary labours have ... ceased to be of any value."[96] This charge does not hold up either. Cornwallis agreed to subscribe to Gladwin's proposed history of the emperor Aurangzeb and asked an adviser how many copies "would be right."[97] What seems to have irked Gladwin was that he would not intercede personally – as indeed Hastings might have done – to help with his mounting debts.[98]

---

[93] See Richard Drayton, *Nature's Government: Science, Imperial Britain, and the "Improvement" of the World* (New Haven, 2000), pp. 117–19; Adrian P. Thomas, "The Establishment of the Calcutta Botanic Garden: Plant Transfer, Science and the East India Company, 1786–1806," *JRAS* 3rd ser. 16 (2006).

[94] Kyd to Hastings, 20 Jul. 1789, BL, Add. MS 29171, f. 332r.

[95] Kyd to unknown, 6 Mar. 1788, BL, IOR H/799, ff. 95v–96r; Governor-General to Governor of Madras, 5 Jul. 1793, cited in Tim Robinson, *William Roxburgh: The Founding Father of Indian Botany* (Chichester, 2008), p. 42.

[96] Gladwin to Hastings, 15 Feb. 1790, BL, Add. MS 29172, f. 47v.

[97] Cornwallis to Shore, 29 Aug. 1787, TNA, PRO 30/11/28, f. 18v.

[98] See Gladwin to Cornwallis, 9 Aug. 1787, TNA, PRO 30/11/18, ff. 82r–v; Gladwin to Cornwallis [Sept. 1787], TNA, PRO 30/11/19, ff. 98r–99v; Gladwin to Cornwallis, 19 May 1789, TNA, PRO 30/11/30, ff. 96r–v; Reginald Craufuird Sterndale, *An Historical Account of "The Calcutta Collectorate,"* 2nd edn (Alipore, 1958), p. 23.

The picture of Cornwallis that emerges from his interactions with Kyd and Gladwin is of an opponent not of knowledge but of clientelism. He would have been especially wary of officials like these who had formed close relations with his predecessors. Hastings' agent Thompson informed him that Cornwallis "stands aloof from the men who were most honored by your patronage and confidence."[99] His longtime secretary William Palmer went further, claiming that Cornwallis' style was "too circumscribed & distant to conciliate general attachment."[100] Yet Cornwallis did aim to conciliate, and by the same means of scholarly patronage. He simply maintained that, if this policy was to succeed, then it must be separated from personal interests. This was among the ends that he sought by raising officials' salaries while barring them from engaging in private trade. A greater number of Company servants now would enjoy the means and leisure to undertake their studies independently.[101] Cornwallis' ideal scholar-official pursued letters as a recreation. He combined learning and integrity. Most importantly, he impressed the political classes in Britain on both accounts. All of this could be said of Alexander Hamilton, who learned Sanskrit while serving as Cornwallis' private secretary.[102] The standard-bearer of the new ethos, however, was William Jones.

Jones helped to give the impression of a new relationship between knowledge and the Company that was more distant and hence less corruptible. Despite having been a friend and associate of Hastings and Macpherson, Jones quickly fell in with the new order. As early as 1787, he could speculate that Cornwallis and his chief adviser John Shore were "the most virtuous governors in the world."[103] He could claim, moreover, that "I live in perfect friendship

---

[99] Thompson to Hastings, 14 Nov. 1786, in "Nesbitt-Thompson Papers," vol. XVII, p. 92.

[100] Palmer to Hastings, 18 Feb. 1787, BL, Add. MS 29170, f. 381r.

[101] Holden Furber, *John Company at Work: A Study of European Expansion in India in the Late Eighteenth Century* (Cambridge, MA, 1948), p. 340.

[102] Rosane Rocher, *Alexander Hamilton (1762–1824): A Chapter in the Early History of Sanskrit Philology* (New Haven, 1968), pp. 7–9. For further evidence of this employment, see "Proceedings of Societies," *AJ* new ser. 23 (1837), p. 74.

[103] Jones to John Eardley-Wilmot, 3 Oct. 1787, in *LWJ*, vol. II, p. 781.

with both, but in as perfect independence of them; never asking patronage even for those whom I wish to serve."[104] Jones' image of "perfect independence" was plausible thanks to his reputation, his appointment, and his salary. It also carried over to his leadership of the Asiatic Society. Upon forming the society in 1784, Jones had offered its presidency to Hastings, only to accept it himself after Hastings demurred. The governor-general cited as his reasons lack of time and ability but likely sought to shield the society from the mounting campaign against him in Britain. Perhaps this was the significance of his remark that he feared becoming an "incumbrance" on Jones and the other members.[105] In any case, with Jones as its president and the governor-general as its patron – a ceremonial role – the society could redound to the Company's credit while appearing to be free of its control. This arrangement evidently suited Cornwallis, who attended meetings of the society but withheld material support.[106] It also suited Jones, who, in the preface to the society's transactions, claimed that though its members were officials they pursued their studies in a personal capacity.[107]

There was one matter that tested the Jones-Cornwallis alliance but ultimately contributed to its success. This was Jones' project to compile a "Digest of Hindu and Mohammedan laws." The project followed from earlier efforts commissioned by Hastings, but whereas Hastings had framed such efforts as a means to patronize and conciliate learned elites, Jones framed them in addition as a means to keep these allies honest. With the aid of the digest, he claimed, judges would no longer "be led astray by the Pandits or Maulavi's [sic], who would hardly venture to impose on us, when their impositions might so easily be detected." This was but one of a number of ways in which

---

[104] Jones to the Second Earl Spencer, 1 Sept. 1787, in *LWJ*, vol. II, p. 764.

[105] Hastings to Jones et al., 30 Jan. 1784, in [William Jones], "The Introduction," *Asiatick Researches* 1 (Calcutta, 1788), p. vii.

[106] S. N. Mukherjee, *Sir William Jones: A Study in Eighteenth-Century British Attitudes to India* (Cambridge, 1968), p. 80; O. P. Kejariwal, *The Asiatic Society of Bengal and the Discovery of India's Past* (Delhi, 1988), p. 58.

[107] [Jones], "The Introduction," p. iii.

Jones signaled to Cornwallis that he shared his upright principles. Jones disclaimed any "personal interest" in the project, pledged to work on it only when he found time away from his duties, declined additional pay, and proposed that the governor-general select his assistants. He suggested that only "the most learned" maulvis and pandits be employed in this capacity, that they be paid a modest salary, and that it cease after three years lest they "protract their work."[108] In other words, Jones thoroughly guarded against the kind of accusations being leveled against Hastings in connection with scholarly patronage. Accordingly, Cornwallis fully approved the proposal within the day; he even let Jones select his own assistants. Cornwallis' statement on the occasion, that the project "would reflect the greatest Honour upon our Administration," fell somewhat short of the grandest pronouncements of Hastings or Macpherson.[109] All the same, it was not out of keeping with their spirit.

CONCILIATION AFTER CORNWALLIS

In the 1790s, metropolitan censure of the Company state abated and, with it, wariness about the idea of conciliation. In Bengal, Hastings' system was restored by the new governor-general, Sir John Shore, while in Britain, it was praised and taken up by a wider range of actors. Not only Hastings but also the directors, and the president of the Board of Control, now sought to demonstrate their enlightened support of knowledge. Britain's political classes appeared more receptive to such demonstrations than ever before.

The Company was one of the great beneficiaries of a sea change in British opinion at the end of the eighteenth century. For various reasons, not least the popularity of Cornwallis, widespread qualms about empire were giving way to widespread support.[110] Company

---

[108] Jones to Cornwallis, 19 Mar. 1788, in *LWJ*, vol II, pp. 794–800.

[109] Governor-General in Council to Jones, 19 Mar. 1788, pp. 801–2 n. 3.

[110] P. J. Marshall, "'A Free Though Conquering People': Britain and Asia in the Eighteenth Century," in Marshall, *"A Free Though Conquering People": Eighteenth-Century Britain and Its Empire* (Aldershot, 2003).

servants now were less likely to be depicted as predatory nabobs than as virtuous professionals.[111] Cornwallis' campaign against Tipu Sultan of Mysore, unlike previous wars of conquest, was greeted with acclaim by parliament and the public.[112] When the Company's charter came up for discussion in 1792–3, it was renewed with few changes and "a quietness unexampled in the annals of Parliament."[113] And Burke and his fellow prosecutors of Hastings, who had enjoyed success at first, now faced enmity in the press and almost certain defeat in the Lords.[114] All of this served to vindicate the restrictive regime of Cornwallis but, at the same time, to lessen the need for it. Hence, by the time Cornwallis left India in 1793, the idea of conciliation could be safely restored to its former amplitude.

Something like a return to the status quo ante was evident in the approach to scholarly patronage of Cornwallis' successor, Shore. For him, "the grand Object of our Government … should be to conciliate … the Natives," and Hastings had been "wise" to do so by "encouraging the pursuits of literature."[115] By all accounts, Shore imitated the guarded stance of Cornwallis while serving as his lieutenant. But a sojourn in England in 1790–92 seems to have convinced him that this was no longer necessary. Whereas Cornwallis had maintained a distance from Jones and the Asiatic Society, Shore voiced his "affection" – nay "reverence" – for the one and took an active part in the other.[116] He even broke with precedent and accepted the presidency of the society upon Jones' death in 1794. Meanwhile, Shore involved himself personally in the affairs of learned elites. He provided relief

---

[111] Ibid., pp. 16–19.

[112] P. J. Marshall, "'Cornwallis Triumphant': War in India and the British Public in the Late Eighteenth Century," in Marshall, *Trade and Conquest*.

[113] William Pitt, Speech in HC Deb (24 May 1793), in *Parliamentary History*, vol. XXX, col. 944.

[114] P. J. Marshall, introduction to vol. 7 of Burke, *Writings and Speeches*, pp. 3–6.

[115] Shore, Minute (18 May 1785), in *Minutes of Evidence*, vol. III, p. 1277; Lord Teignmouth, *Memoirs of the Life, Writings, and Correspondence, of Sir William Jones* (London, 1804), pp. 237–9, 260 n. Shore was created Baron Teignmouth in 1798.

[116] John Shore, *The Literary History of the Late Sir William Jones, in a Discourse* (London, 1795), pp. 3–4; Kejariwal, *Asiatic Society*, p. 93.

to the ailing Benares pandit Kanhardas and advanced the career of his onetime private pandit Radhakanta Tarkavagisa.[117] It is hard to imagine Cornwallis bestowing such kindnesses. It is also hard to imagine him imposing on Tafazzul Husain Khan as Shore did in 1797. Keen to leverage Tafazzul's reputation, and heedless of propriety, Shore pressed him into accepting an appointment as deputy of the nawab of Awadh.[118] Though ostensibly an honor, the post was perilous given the level of infighting and suspicion at the nawab's court – not to mention the unpopularity of the encroaching Company. Relating the matter to Hastings, William Palmer confided that "I tremble for the peace & Reputation of my Friend."[119] His premonitions proved correct. Tafazzul would last but a few harrowing months in Lucknow before fleeing to Calcutta, where he died in 1800.

If the 1790s saw a return to Hastings' system of conciliation in Bengal, then they also saw a fuller and wider adoption of it in Britain. Hastings himself played a role in this development, expounding his system not only at trial but also upon his acquittal in 1795. He prepared and circulated a volume containing the *razinama*s along with new addresses that praised him for, among other things, "establishing colleges" and "promoting science."[120] Meanwhile, the Court of Directors too was beginning to see advantage in portraying the Company as an enlightened broker of knowledge. In a report to a Crown committee of 1792, the directors claimed to have used "every Endeavour to extend ... Trade" and "to cultivate Knowledge and Science." They boasted of having put the historian

---

[117] Kanhardas, Petitions, trans. in Sen and Mishra, eds., *Sanskrit Documents*, pp. 81–8; Rosane Rocher, "The Career of Rādhākānta Tarkavāgīśa, an Eighteenth-Century Pandit in British Employ," *Journal of the American Oriental Society* 109 (1989), p. 632.

[118] Arif Abid, "A Poisoned Chalice," 3 Quarks Daily (2006), https://3quarksdaily .com/3quarksdaily/2006/03/nawab_tafazzul_.html. The author of this paper kindly provided a version with citations.

[119] Palmer to Hastings, 15 Apr. 1797, BL, Add. MS 29175, f. 88r.

[120] [Warren Hastings, ed.], *Debates of the House of Lords, on the Evidence Delivered in the Trial of Warren Hastings in Consequence of His Acquittal* (London, 1797), p. 820. See Hastings to David Anderson, 23 Nov. 1796 to 22 Jan. 1799, BL, Add. MS 45418, 74r-95v.

Robert Orme, the geographer James Rennell, and the hydrographer Alexander Dalrymple on their payroll. They also played up their role in "the Establishment of Botanical Gardens in Calcutta, Madras, and St. Helena" for scientific and commercial purposes. They even took credit for the founding of the Asiatic Society, which, they noted, embraced not only "Literature and Science" but also "Arts, Manufactures, and Commerce."[121] The message was clear: The Company's combined politico-economic power enabled it to contribute to British knowledge, and any attempt to curtail the one would have a corresponding effect on the other.

The directors buttressed their case in 1798 by announcing the founding of an "Oriental Repository" at their London headquarters. This institution, which would come to be known as the India Museum and Oriental Library, followed in a long line of collections meant to advertise the fruits of the Company's trade.[122] If in the past these fruits had been material, then the directors now insisted that they were intellectual as well. The announcement stressed their "disposition for the encouragement of Indian literature" and their desire to assist in the "exportation" of its "Stores."[123] For that matter, in a plan drawn up for the institution, Charles Wilkins envisioned that its "objects of commerce" would contribute to "the cause of science."[124] And in letters supporting Wilkins' bid to serve as its curator, Hastings beheld "a new system for ingrafting the knowledge of India on the commercial p[u]rsuits of the Company."[125] Of course, all

[121] *First, Second, and Third Reports of the Select Committee, Appointed by the Court of Directors of the East India Company, to Take into Consideration the Export Trade from Great Britain to the East Indies* (London, 1793), pp. 37–8.

[122] Memorandum [c. 1838–58], BL, Mss Eur F303/54; Arthur MacGregor, *Company Curiosities: Nature, Culture and the East India Company, 1600–1874* (London, 2018), pp. 168–9.

[123] Public Despatch to Bengal (25 May 1798), cited in A. J. Arberry, *The Library of the India Office: A Historical Sketch* (London, 1938), p. 10.

[124] Charles Wilkins, "Sketch of a Plan for an Oriental Museum Proposed to be Established at the India House" (Jan. 1799), in ibid., pp. 16–18.

[125] Hastings to Charles Wilkins [1799], in ibid., pp. 19–20; Hastings to Chairman of the Court of Directors, 15 Nov. 1799, in ibid., p. 23.

of this sounded rather like the system of conciliation that Hastings had developed as governor-general. It was only fitting, therefore, that the directors prominently displayed a portrait of him in the museum upon its completion in 1801.[126]

In the meantime, there were signs that the efforts of Hastings and the directors were finding an audience among Britain's political classes. This audience included Henry Dundas, the head of the Board of Control, a government body formed by Pitt's India Act to supervise the Company. A patron of letters himself, Dundas seems to have admired the scholarship of Jones and other Company officials. Certainly, notwithstanding his biographers' claims to the contrary, he appreciated its political value.[127] Early in discussions on the renewal of the Company's charter, he engaged John Bruce, an Edinburgh professor, to research and write a history of the Company state.[128] As Bruce put it, in telling language, the work was "a means of conciliating the opinions of the parties interested in the subsequent renewal."[129] It would do this not only by defending the Company's hybrid constitution but also by serving as an example of its leaders' promotion of knowledge. For his labors, Bruce was appointed by the directors as the Company's assistant historiographer. He also continued to do Dundas' bidding. It was under this dual aegis that he undertook his next project, "a general History of Indian Affairs."[130] Like his earlier work, the history was intended first and foremost to legitimize

---

[126] "Some Account of a Hindu Temple, and a Bust, of which Elegant Engravings are Placed in the Oriental Library of the Hon. East India Company, Leadenhall Street," *European Magazine* 42 (Dec. 1802), pp. 448–9.

[127] For these claims, see Holden Furber, *Henry Dundas, First Viscount Melville, 1742–1811: Political Manager of Scotland, Statesman, Administrator of British India* (Oxford, 1931), p. 296; Michael Fry, *The Dundas Despotism* (Edinburgh, 1992), p. 184.

[128] [John Bruce], *Historical View of Plans, for the Government of British India, and Regulation of Trade to the East Indies* (London, 1793).

[129] Bruce to Directors, draft [1818], BL, IOR H/456e, p. 233G.

[130] Bruce to Alexander Adamson, 16 May 1793, ibid., p. 2. The work Bruce eventually published was narrower in scope: John Bruce, *Annals of the Honorable East-India Company, from Their Establishment by the Charter of Queen Elizabeth, 1600, to the Union of the London and English East-India Companies, 1707–8*, 3 vols. (London, 1810).

the Company state. It would "be divided into the Political, and Commercial Branches" but show that these were "interwoven."[131] It would also incorporate, and draw attention to, the research of scholar-officials across the Company's territories. Bruce solicited contributions from Jones and other members of the Asiatic Society as well as from authorities in Benares, Bombay, Madras, and elsewhere. His project thus marked an attempt to credit Dundas and the directors in London for scholarship carried out in India.

Dundas' engagement of Bruce was but one among many signs of Hastings' and the directors' public success. The earlier Indian "floodtide of panegyric" on Hastings' scholarly patronage was now being matched in Britain.[132] Following his acquittal, Hastings appeared in print as "the distinguished patron of ... literature"; "the enlightened politician, the comprehensive genius, and polite scholar."[133] One pamphleteer credited him with inspiring Lord Macartney's mission to China, which, like those he had sent to Tibet, combined "attention to ... commerce" with "service to ... science."[134] At the same time, the directors were increasingly coming in for praise on the same account. The writer and antiquarian Thomas Maurice adduced their patronage as proof that these "enlightened ... merchants" were free from "the meanness of avarice." He described their blending of "Trade and Science" as conducive to a world in which the two "travelled, side by side."[135] Such accolades demonstrated both what the directors wanted to hear and the willingness of their clients to oblige.

---

[131] Bruce to Alexander Adamson, 1794, BL, IOR H/456e, p. 75. See also Olivera Jokic, "Commanding Correspondence: Letters and the 'Evidence of Experience' in the Letterbook of John Bruce, the East India Company Historiographer," *Eighteenth Century* 52 (2011), p. 113.

[132] For the phrase, see Burke, Speech (21 Apr. 1789), in E. A. Bond, ed., *Speeches of the Managers and Counsel in the Trial of Warren Hastings*, 3 vols. (London, 1860), vol. II, p. 5.

[133] Eliza Hamilton, *Translation of the Letters of a Hindoo Rajah*, 2 vols. (London, 1796), vol. I, dedication; [Hastings, ed.], *Debates*, p. 504.

[134] *The Merits of Mr. Pitt and Mr. Hastings, as Ministers in War and in Peace, Impartially Stated* (London, 1794), pp. 49–52.

[135] Thomas Maurice, *Indian Antiquities*, 7 vols. (London [1793]–1800), vol. I, pp. xv, lxvi n.

There were many further examples. John Gilchrist, writing from Bengal, rejoiced at the cherishing of letters "by a sovereign Company of British Merchants."[136] Patrick Russell proclaimed that this was "a splendid era" for the Company, owing to its happy union of "commercial concerns" and "Science."[137] Joseph Hager pronounced that Britain was indebted to the directors as much for their devotion to scholars as for their "Commercial enterprise."[138] David Macpherson held that their "encouragement of literature and science have raised the mercantile character to the highest degree of exaltation."[139] And yet, this last encomium was different. There was something defensive about it, coming as it did in 1805. By this time, the Company state was threatened from within by a governor-general with altogether different ideas about knowledge.

CONCLUSION

In the last decade and a half of the eighteenth century, Hastings' idea of conciliation – of legitimizing the Company state through scholarly patronage – was promulgated, tarnished, expanded, contracted, and ultimately widely embraced. Ironies and paradoxes abounded. A critic of the Company state, Hastings was thrust into the role of its defender. A likely source for Hastings' idea of conciliation, Burke emerged as its greatest skeptic. An intimate of Macpherson, Jones partnered with his enemy Cornwallis. And the more the Company changed, the more its ideas about knowledge stayed the same.

The idea of conciliation withstood the reforms of Pitt, Dundas, and Cornwallis largely because these fundamentally preserved the Company state. In the 1780s, Dundas had considered ending the Company's political role, but Cornwallis, and later experience,

---

[136] Gilchrist, *Dictionary*, vol. I, p. i.

[137] Patrick Russell, *An Account of Indian Serpents, Collected on the Coast of Coromandel* (London, 1796), p. viii.

[138] Joseph Hager, *A Dissertation on the Newly Discovered Babylonian Inscriptions* (London, 1801), p. xi.

[139] David Macpherson, *Annals of Commerce, Manufactures, Fisheries, and Navigation*, 4 vols. (London, 1805), vol. I, dedication.

convinced him against this.[140] As he told the Commons in 1793, no political economist "has as yet supposed that an extensive empire can be administered by a commercial association"; yet he found the Company "to be an organ of government, and of trade, which has experimentally proved itself."[141] The resulting Charter Act renewed the Company's privileges for twenty years and thus ensured that the raison d'être for conciliation remained. It also provided evidence that Hastings' system of conciliation had been effective. Certainly, signs to the contrary could be found. Some scholar-officials complained that the directors had done "nothing" for them.[142] Tafazzul's failure in Awadh revealed the limits of the strategy of employing learned elites as political agents. Still, on the cusp of the nineteenth century, the Company's constitution appeared secure and conciliation entrenched in its ideology. As Richard Wellesley, Earl of Mornington sailed for India in late 1797, perhaps only he foresaw the challenges to both that his governor-generalship would bring.

[140] Furber, *Henry Dundas*, pp. 130–31; C. H. Philips, *The East India Company, 1784–1834*, 2nd edn (Manchester, 1961), pp. 71–2.

[141] Henry Dundas, Speech in House of Commons Debate (23 Apr. 1793), in *Parliamentary History*, vol. XXX, cols. 651–3.

[142] Jonathan Scott, preface to [Inayat-Allah Kamboh] Einaiut Oolah, *Bahar-Danush; or, Garden of Knowledge. An Oriental Romance*, trans. Scott, 3 vols. (Shrewsbury, 1799), vol. I, pp. xiv–xv. For another complaint, about a lack of support from the Bombay administration, see Charles Reynolds to Alexander Adamson, 18 Mar. 1795, BL, IOR H/456e, p. 187.

3   The Politics of the College of Fort William

"The College must stand or the Empire must fall."[1] So declared Lord Wellesley in reference to the College of Fort William.[2] The year was 1802, his pet project was threatened with abolition, and the threat came from the Company's Court of Directors. Since being appointed governor-general of Bengal four years earlier, Wellesley had quarreled with his nominal masters. The topics of controversy ranged from his fiscal and administrative policies to his personal conduct to his wars and diplomacy. Yet it was that Calcutta seminary for Company servants to which Wellesley vowed to devote the rest of his political life, over which he threatened to resign the governor-generalship, and upon which he later would look back as his proudest achievement.[3] Why was the college so important to Wellesley? Why did it so antagonize the directors? How did it respond to, and affect, the Company's thinking about knowledge, which had come to revolve around the idea of conciliation?

Modern studies offer limited help in answering these questions. The ideas that shaped Wellesley, his college, and the directors' enmity toward it have been little understood. To start with, the ambitions of the man have been underestimated. Wellesley, the elder brother of the Duke of Wellington, has been seen by historians as "viceregal,"

---

[1] Marquess Wellesley to David Scott, 12 Aug. 1802, in Robert Rouiere Pearce, *Memoirs and Correspondence of the Most Noble Richard Marquess Wellesley*, 3 vols. (London, 1846–7), vol. II, p. 212.

[2] The Earl of Mornington, as he was styled when he took up the governor-generalship, was created Marquess Wellesley in 1799.

[3] Wellesley to Earl of Dartmouth, 5 Aug. 1802, in ibid., vol. II, pp. 214, 217; Wellesley to Charles Metcalfe, Aug. 1839, in *The Wellesley Papers* [ed. L. S. Benjamin], 2 vols. (London, 1914), vol. II, p. 350; Wellesley to W. B. Bayley, 21 Mar. 1841, in John William Kaye, *Lives of Indian Officers*, 2 vols. (London, 1867), vol. I, p. 488.

an avatar of Lord Curzon a century later.[4] But this is putting things mildly. As one contemporary recalled, Wellesley was "regal" in everything he did and "unbounded in the authority of a name which filled all India."[5] According to no less than Curzon, Wellesley exercised "a single and self-centred rule" – an "autocracy" – that would have been "impossible" in his own day.[6] To brand Wellesley a proconsul, an instrument of the British state, or an architect of the Raj is to ignore his intention to rule as a king. Jeremy Bentham was right, albeit late, in characterizing the regime forged by Wellesley as a "sort of local Monarchy."[7] The forging of this regime, in turn, explains the college controversy. For all of the personal, financial, and – it has been alleged – cultural issues that divided Wellesley and the directors, what mattered by far the most was his hostility to the Company state.[8] Wellesley argued that the Company's constitution jumbled together "the conflicting characters of merchant and sovereign," and that the directors were incapable of putting their sovereign duties before their "mercantile interests, prejudices, and profits."[9]

[4] Iris Butler, *The Eldest Brother: The Marquess Wellesley, the Duke of Wellington's Eldest Brother* (London, 1973), pp. 23–4; C. A. Bayly, *Imperial Meridian: The British Empire and the World, 1780–1830* (London, 1989), pp. 111, 209.

[5] [Charles Marsh], "Society in India," *New Monthly Magazine* 22 (1828), p. 234. Wellesley thus argued against any "interference of the Crown" in the government of British India, which ought to be left to the governor-general. Wellesley to Henry Dundas, 27 Jan. 1800, in Dundas and Wellesley, *Two Views of British India: The Private Correspondence of Mr. Dundas and Lord Wellesley, 1798–1801*, ed. Edward Ingram (Bath, 1969), p. 223.

[6] George Nathaniel Curzon, *British Government in India: The Story of the Viceroys and Government Houses*, 2 vols. (London, 1925), vol. II, pp. 9, 108, 115.

[7] Jeremy Bentham, *Plan of Parliamentary Reform* (London, 1817), p. xciv. For more contemporary allusions to Wellesley's kingly style of rule, see Sir James Mackintosh to Richard Sharp, 14 Aug. 1804, in Mackintosh, *Memoirs of the Life of the Right Honourable Sir James Mackintosh*, ed. Robert James Mackintosh, 2nd edn, 2 vols. (London, 1836), vol. I, p. 212; Viscount Valentia, *Voyages and Travels to India, Ceylon, the Red Sea, Abyssinia, and Egypt*, 3 vols. (London, 1809), vol. I, pp. 235–6.

[8] For discussions of these issues, see C. H. Philips, *The East India Company, 1784–1834*, 2nd edn (Manchester, 1961), pp. 125–30; Ainslie Thomas Embree, *Charles Grant and British Rule in India* (London, 1962), pp. 187–94; David Kopf, *British Orientalism and the Bengal Renaissance: The Dynamics of Indian Modernization, 1773–1835* (Berkeley, 1969), pp. 133–5.

[9] Wellesley to Viscount Castlereagh, 25 Jul. 1803, in *DMW*, vol. III, p. 202.

The directors, for their part, understood that Wellesley sought "to establish a new species of Government," to subvert their authority, and to assume "all the political powers of British India."[10] Both parties saw the college as central to this attempt.

A close examination of the college controversy shows that it turned on the danger the institution posed to the Company state. The college served to aggrandize Wellesley at the directors' expense and to establish his legitimacy with multiple audiences. It would do this not through conciliation but through the projection of an image of grandeur consonant with a kingly territorial sovereignty. In a sign of the reach and impact of Wellesley's ideas, the directors continued to fear them for years after his departure.

THE COLLEGE CONTROVERSY

Wellesley made it clear that his founding of the college was part of an assault on the foundations of the Company state. And yet the directors at first did not appreciate the danger they faced. Only upon further examination – and provocation – did the directors attempt to abolish the institution. They were blocked, however, by the Board of Control, whose constitutional role now entered into the controversy. Unable to close the college, the directors decided to establish one of their own in Hertfordshire. Haileybury College would absorb some of the functions and, they hoped, the prestige of the College of Fort William. Nonetheless, it evinced no new ideas about knowledge. The directors remained wedded, at least for the time being, to the idea of conciliation.

Wellesley opened the controversy on 10 July 1800, with a dispatch entitled "The Governor-General's Notes with Respect to the Foundation of a College at Fort William." The political nature of the institution was implied in the first sentence: "The British possessions

---

[10] Copy of a Proposed Dispatch to the Bengal Government, Approved by Twenty-Three of the Twenty-Four Directors of the Hon. East-India Company, Dated April 3, 1805 (London, 1806), p. 17; Directors to Board of Control, 6 Nov. 1805, in P. J. Marshall, Problems of Empire: Britain and India 1757–1813 (London, 1968), p. 143.

in India now constitute one of the most extensive and populous empires in the world." To the officials who administered this empire, Wellesley continued, "commercial or mercantile knowledge" was entirely inapplicable. The "commercial education" they typically received in Britain was not merely unnecessary; it was positively inimical. In the following pages, Wellesley broached several issues connected with the institution he had already founded in consequence, such as the age at which "writers" should enroll, where they should reside, and which subjects they should study. Undergirding all of his plans, however, was a claim that the Company's territory had outgrown its mode of government, and that ultimate power must be vested in the office of the governor-general. His most concrete proposal in this regard was to wrest away from the directors' control of civil service appointments. With the founding of the college, he held, the governor-general was best placed to determine writers' starting ranks and destinations. In symbolic ways too, the college was intended to strengthen Wellesley's authority. Not only would he serve as its visitor, a role often played by the Crown at Oxford and Cambridge colleges, but he dated its founding to the first anniversary of the conquest of Mysore. The choice was revealing. Wellesley had invaded Mysore against the directors' wishes, and in furtherance of a large-scale territorial vision of British India. He now said in public what he had long said in private: Such an empire must be ruled not by "a commercial concern" but by "a powerful sovereign."[11]

The directors were slow to grasp this challenge to their authority, or, at least, its full magnitude. Upon the arrival of Wellesley's dispatch in spring 1801, they reacted with ambivalence.[12] The influential Charles Grant pronounced the college "highly commendable," and noted only three partial objections from his fellow directors:

[11] Marquess Wellesley, "The Governor-General's Notes with Respect to the Foundation of a College at Fort William" (10 Jul. 1800), in DMW, vol. II, pp. 325–9, 351, 355, 358.
[12] See John Bowen, "The East India Company's Education of Its Own Servants," JRAS (1955), p. 108; Philips, East India Company, pp. 125–6.

(1) That it is far too expensive for the Company's finances;
(2) That it ought not to comprehend the young men of other
Presidencies; (3) That it should be confined chiefly to learning
properly Oriental, and not to include a revising course of
European Literature, which would be better and more cheaply
provided at home.

Grant thought "these objections have weight, particularly the
last."[13] But he agreed on the need for a better educated civil service.
Furthermore, he cheered the appointments of his fellow Evangelicals
David Brown and Claudius Buchanan as provost and vice-provost.
Neither Grant nor the other directors initially saw the institution
as especially dangerous. Perhaps they were inclined to dismiss
Wellesley's rhetoric as harmless bluster. Some may have been pla-
cated by a revision drawn up by Grant at the urging of Wellesley's
ally among the directors, David Scott.[14] Others may not have read
the dispatch's eighty-nine paragraphs very closely. In any case, Scott
expressed a cautious optimism that "we must all approve such an
institution," and that "time for reflection and reasoning" would convince enough of the skeptics.[15] On the contrary, by the end of the
year, the directors as a body were set against the college, for they had
grown to understand the intentions of its founder.

The first alarm was sounded by none other than the former
governor-general Warren Hastings. Scott had sent him Wellesley's
dispatch in June 1801 in the hope of enlisting his support.[16] In letters
of July and October, Hastings commended the institution in general. But he criticized certain features that he argued undermined
the directors' authority. He objected, in particular, to Wellesley's

---

[13] Grant to David Brown, 19 Jun. 1801, in Henry Morris, *The Life of Charles Grant:
Sometime Member of Parliament for Inverness-Shire and Director of the East India
Company* (London, 1904), pp. 241–2.

[14] See Embree, *Charles Grant*, pp. 192–3.

[15] Scott to Wellesley, 9 Jan. 1801, in Scott, *The Correspondence of David Scott*, ed. C. H.
Philips, 2 vols. (London, 1951), vol. II, p. 297; Scott to Lord Teignmouth, 9 May 1801,
in ibid., vol. II, p. 306.

[16] Scott to Hastings, 11 Jun. 1801, in ibid., vol. II, pp. 309–10.

proposal to assume the "extraordinary privilege" of deciding the destinations of writers.[17] This would have a result "to be avoided in every delegation of a remote authority, that of transferring the sense of ... fidelity, from the Company to the person of the Governor General." Hastings also apparently suspected that Wellesley would try in other ways to make the college a vehicle for his own aggrandizement. He enjoined the directors to frame new rules for the college that would set "clearly defined bounds" to the "discretion" of the visitor. If Hastings saw the irony of giving this advice when he had once sought greater independence from the directors, then he did not show it. He did display an awareness that the college was likely to be "unpopular" with that body.[18]

Two further developments underscored the subversive potential of the college and hardened the directors against it. Reports reached London, first, of Wellesley's extravagant spending and, second, of his renewed encouragement of private trade.[19] In both cases, Wellesley had disregarded the directors' instructions as well as the Company's commercial interests. The unsanctioned and expensive college thus came to seem part of a pattern of defiant assault on the foundations of the Company state. As the directors wrote in January 1802, its establishment without their permission was

> a departure from our established system; the tendency of all such deviations is to weaken the authority which is constitutionally placed in this country; for, when measures are once adopted, which either pledge the faith of government, or incur great expense, the exercise of control, in such cases, is in effect frustrated.[20]

By now, additional issues had crept into discussions of the college in metropolitan political circles. Some commentators feared it would

---

[17] Warren Hastings, "A Letter of Warren Hastings on the Civil Service of the East India Company" (19 Jul. 1801), ed. W. H. Hutton, *English Historical Review* 44 (1929), p. 638.

[18] Hastings to Directors, 18 to 19 Oct. 1801, BL, IOR H/487, pp. 224, 226, 228.

[19] Philips, *East India Company*, p. 126.

[20] Public Despatch to Bengal (27 Jan. 1802), in *Letters of the Marquis Wellesley Respecting the College of Fort William* (London, 1812), p. 59.

become a sink of Jacobinism or lead to disruptive "colonization" (British settlement) in India. By contrast, some Evangelicals envisioned the college as an instrument for spreading the word of God. But the directors, after faulting Wellesley for disobedience, ordered its abolition on the simple ground of expense.

It was at this point that the Board of Control entered the controversy and raised it to a new pitch. Lord Dartmouth, the president of the board, favored Wellesley and the college and edited the directors' order to make it seem merely provisional.[21] Under better financial conditions, in the new wording of the dispatch, the college would merit "the most serious consideration."[22] Accordingly, Wellesley waited for conditions to improve and then, in August 1802, wrote the directors that he had stayed the college's abolition.[23] When the letter reached London, Dartmouth's successor, Lord Castlereagh, pushed the directors to endorse a dispatch he had penned in support of Wellesley's decision.[24] But the directors now stated that their financial justification had been a pretext and that larger questions were at issue.[25] In a draft dispatch of July 1803, they objected not only that the college had been "formed without our sanction" but also that its "plan and scope" endangered the Company's constitution. This constitution, they held, was "of a mixed nature, being partly Commercial and partly Political," and Wellesley threatened to degrade "the Commercial part." This was the tendency, allegedly, of his aspersions on mercantile knowledge and of his "high assumptions of title" and "splendour." For that matter, his grab for control of writers' appointments seemed to have more to do with his own

---

[21] Dartmouth to Wellesley, 2 Feb. 1802, Staffordshire County Record Office, D(W)1778/I/ii/1589.

[22] Public Despatch to Bengal [showing alterations by Board of Control] (27 Jan. 1802), BL, IOR E/4/652, p. 86.

[23] For this strategy, see Merrick Shawe to Henry Wellesley, 20 Jun. 1802, BL, Mss Eur E176, pp. 547–8.

[24] Prakash Chandra, "The Establishment of the Fort William College," *Calcutta Review* 51 (1934), p. 166; Philips, *East India Company*, pp. 127–8.

[25] Directors to Board of Control, 1 and 19 Jul. 1803, BL, IOR H/487, pp. 399, 445.

"power" than, as he claimed, "the good of the service."[26] No wonder then that Castlereagh's intervention "produced a hurricane at the
India House."[27] In the directors' estimation the survival of the college might mean the demise of the Company state.

The controversy had grown to involve, in Castlereagh's words,
"the general System of India Government."[28] At issue now was the
constitutional relationship of the directors not only to the governor-
general but also to the Board of Control. When Henry Dundas and
William Pitt had drawn up plans for the board two decades earlier,
they had left the extent of its powers somewhat uncertain. After
all, it must be able to exert control when necessary without appearing to infringe the chartered rights of the Company. Along with the
draft dispatch of July 1803, however, the directors sent a letter stat-
ing that "they consider the Authority of the Board to be confined to
an absolute or partial negative."[29] According to them, the board had
overstepped its bounds in changing the meaning of one dispatch and
in seeking to originate another. Of course, things looked otherwise
to Castlereagh. In his view, the directors themselves were "aiming
at the extension of their authority" far beyond what Dundas and
Pitt had envisioned. If allowed to stand, their construction would
not only exclude "the Board of Controul (that is, the State) from all
effectual direction" but would lead to further "attempts at undue
authority."[30] After Castlereagh rejected the directors' draft, along
with their argument, both sides took legal counsel. The directors
seemed to have the stronger case, but the board was prepared to bring
its case before parliament.[31] Finally, in order to prevent an open

---

[26] Draft Public Despatch to Bengal (19 Jul. 1803), ibid., pp. 456, 459, 461, 469, 471–2,
506–9.
[27] Castlereagh to Viscount Melville, 1 Aug. 1803, Public Record Office of Northern
Ireland, D3030/L/8.
[28] Ibid.
[29] Directors to Board of Control, 19 Jul. 1803, p. 451.
[30] Castlereagh to Viscount Melville, 4 Aug. 1803, Public Record Office of Northern
Ireland, D3030/L/9.
[31] P. E. Roberts, *India Under Wellesley* (London, 1929), pp. 160–62; Chandra,
"Establishment," pp. 168–70.

confrontation, the two parties agreed on a compromise. The ambiguity of their respective powers would be allowed to continue – as would Wellesley's college.

Already, the directors had been developing a response to the college that went beyond simple abolition. As early as the start of the controversy, they had recognized a political as well as a practical need to offer something in its stead. Their draft dispatch of January 1802 put forward a dual remedy. First, a seminary giving basic linguistic instruction might replace the College of Fort William. Second, "regulations" might be adopted for the prior and fuller education of writers in England. Dartmouth undercut both proposals. He made the one seem largely a means to save costs and expunged the other entirely.[32] Far from rebutting Wellesley's charges, therefore, his modified dispatch reinforced them.[33] No wonder that amid the climactic volley of correspondence with the board, the directors felt the need to disclaim being led "by the narrow views of commercial habits." They protested that this was "a stale and unjust imputation." Had they not encouraged "the literary talents of Individuals" and "the literary spirit in general"?[34] In the negotiations with the board, the directors won a concession: limiting admission to the college to writers assigned to Bengal. In addition, they ordered Wellesley to specify which expenses were "requisite for ... the study of the Native Languages" and which, by implication, could be cut.[35] So began in earnest a scheme not to abolish the college but, instead, to diminish it. Further reductions would play a part in this scheme. So too would the establishment of Haileybury College.

Having failed to destroy Wellesley's college, the directors set about building a college of their own to overshadow it. The East India College, or Haileybury, took shape in a report of 1804 and was formally established in Hertfordshire the following year. Grant, the

---

[32] Public Despatch to Bengal [showing alterations] (27 Jan. 1802), pp. 67–71.

[33] See Charles Grant, Speech in East India House Debate (5 Mar. 1817), *AJ* 4 (1817), p. 273.

[34] Directors to Board of Control, 1 Jul. 1803, pp. 405–6.

[35] Public Despatch to Bengal (2 Sept. 1803), BL, IOR E/4/654, pp. 653–4.

prime mover of the enterprise, insisted that it was no reaction to
Wellesley, for its origins dated back to 1796.[36] But while the directors
had discussed a "plan" or "regulations" for educating writers – "most
probably" at Oxford or Cambridge – the idea of a new institution
seems to have arisen only once it became clear that Wellesley's college would persist.[37] Indeed, the primary purpose of Haileybury was
to counter the menace of Wellesley. Its course of instruction would
precede and largely replace that of his college and would uphold the
hybrid constitution of the Company. On the one hand, according to
the 1804 report, it should include "Mercantile Accounts" and prepare
writers for "Commercial Operations." On the other hand, it should
also comprehend every other subject connected with the "Affairs of
our Empire."[38] As a later plan concurred, writers must be trained to
serve not only as "Factors and Merchants" but also as "Magistrates,
Ambassadors, and Provincial Governors." The Company's "extension of dominion" increased its responsibilities; Haileybury's curriculum ensured that it could meet them.[39] And yet, for all of the
directors' seriousness of purpose, encapsulated by the forbidding edifice they commissioned, Haileybury smacked of reaction instead of
initiative. It bespoke no new ideas about knowledge. According to a
notice in the press, the college would stand as "a lasting memorial"
of the Company's patronage "of literature and science."[40] This statement, authored by the directors or on their behalf, did no more than
invoke the idea of conciliation.

[36] "Report of the Committee Appointed to Enquire into the Plan for Forming an
Establishment at Home for the Education of Young Men Intended for the Company's
Civil Service in India, 26 October 1804," in Anthony Farrington, ed., *The Records
of the East India College Haileybury and Other Institutions* (London, 1976), p. 14;
Grant to Sir James Mackintosh, 17 Sept. 1805, in Morris, *Life*, p. 245.

[37] Grant to Sir James Mackintosh [c. 1801–2], in Morris, *Life*, p. 244; Public Despatch to
Bengal [showing alterations] (27 Jan. 1802), p. 67; "Report of the Committee," p. 14.

[38] "Report of the Committee," pp. 16–17.

[39] *A Preliminary View of the Establishment of the Honourable East-India Company in
Hertfordshire for the Education of Young Persons Appointed to the Civil Service in
India* ([Hertfordshire,] 1806), pp. 3–4.

[40] "Varieties, Literary and Philosophical," *Monthly Magazine* 29 (London, Mar. 1810),
p. 164.

MIGHT AND SPLENDOR

Wellesley had other ideas. Apart from subverting the directors, the College of Fort William was meant to secure his legitimacy. Wellesley sought to do this, not through conciliation, but through the projection of might and splendor instead. The collection, display, and transmission of knowledge at the institution were designed to uphold his kingly territorial sovereignty. They served, at an ideological level, to ennoble him and to enlarge the sphere of his authority. Wellesley marshalled the resources of the college, notably at its annual disputations, to cultivate audiences in Britain, British India, Europe, and Asia. What was studied and taught at the college mattered less, ultimately, than the grand impression it made.

It was telling of Wellesley's ambitions that he eschewed the idea of conciliation, which had figured in the Company's ideology for the past three decades. Since this idea blurred the distinction between sovereign and merchant – both could conciliate – it must be repudiated. The flexibility that sullied the idea for Wellesley did allow others to attach it to his College of Fort William. Warren Hastings, for one, expressed hope that the "political uses" of the college would include "ingratiating our countrymen with the ... people of India."[41] Others deployed the idea explicitly. One student, in a printed essay, held that by patronizing "natives of learning," the college would help "greatly to conciliate ... India."[42] At least one professor likewise invoked the idea by name in a request for patronage addressed to the college council.[43] Wellesley, by contrast, seldom wrote of "conciliation" as governor-general and never, it seems, in connection with scholarly patronage. Later, as lord lieutenant of

---

[41] Hastings, "Letter," p. 635.

[42] W. P. Elliott, "Of the Advantages to Be Derived from an Academical Institution in India; Considered in a Moral, Literary, and Political Point of View," in *Primitiae Orientalis*, 3 vols. [vol. 1 titled *Essays by the Students of the College of Fort William*] (Calcutta, 1802–4), vol. I, p. 32.

[43] Gilchrist to College Council, 19 Aug. 1803, PCFW, vol. 559, p. 272.

Ireland, he would advocate "conciliating" Catholics.[44] But here he sought neither to unmake the rule of a company nor to make himself into a king. In the Indian context, conciliation was linked to three things Wellesley hated: councils, compromise, and commercial sovereignty. Instead of a system of conciliation, he devised a campaign to raise his standing in the eyes of multiple constituencies.

One political frontier of the college lay in Britain, where the enmity of the directors compelled Wellesley to find other sources of support. He sent his dispatches on the college to notables like the king and prime minister, and enlarged on them in letters to allies like David Scott.[45] His campaign seems to have widened after the directors ordered the institution abolished in 1801. A composition saved in his brother Henry's papers and apparently intended for publication stressed the "Political Magnitude" of the college and asked how "any men" could judge it "on considerations purely Mercantile."[46] Wellesley's efforts went further. He also sought to staff the college with men of influence residing at the metropole. In an early letter to Henry Dundas, he proposed to appoint as professors James Mackintosh, James Rennell, Thomas Maurice, and Charles Grant (the director's son).[47] Mackintosh was a famous lawyer, writer, and philosopher; Rennell and Maurice were likewise well regarded and connected scholars; and although Grant was merely a student, his father would play a large role in determining the fate of the college. Ultimately, reductions imposed by the directors would force Wellesley to recruit from a less distinguished expatriate pool. Still, the Company's territories in India were home to at least a few scholars of metropolitan renown. One such was James Dinwiddie, who had served as the astronomer on Lord Macartney's

[44] In this context too, "conciliation" had a flexible meaning. As one pamphlet put it, this "comely word" took on "a thousand different shapes." [John Swift Emerson], One Year of the Administration of His Excellency the Marquess of Wellesley in Ireland (London, 1823), pp. 22–3.
[45] Pearce, Memoirs and Correspondence, vol. II, pp. 200–201, 217.
[46] "Copy of a Letter from a Gentleman in Calcutta to His Friend in England, Dated July 14th 1802," BL, Mss Eur E176, p. 196.
[47] Wellesley to Dundas, 18 Aug. 1800, in Dundas and Wellesley, Two Views, p. 283.

mission to China and who now maintained a wide scientific correspondence from Calcutta.[48] No doubt Dinwiddie's reputation and connections informed the decision of Wellesley, as early as August 1800,
to find a place for him at the college.[49]

Among metropolitan Britons, Evangelicals became the most fer-
vent champions of the College of Fort William. This was a constituency that Wellesley assiduously cultivated. At first, he sought Grant's
support in particular – hence the appointments of Grant's friends
David Brown and Claudius Buchanan, and the plan to appoint his son.
But as Grant emerged as the leading voice of opposition to the college –
or at least as the principal author of the directors' letters on the subject – Wellesley increasingly appealed to other Evangelicals instead.
He was helped in this task by Brown and Buchanan, as well as by the
Baptist missionaries who resided at the nearby Danish settlement of
Serampore. Wellesley attached the missionaries to the college by hiring
their press to do its printing and by hiring their chief, William Carey,
as professor of Bengali. These employments kept the mission solvent
and gave it respectability at a time when the Company still prohibited
proselytization in its territories.[50] What most endeared Wellesley to
Evangelicals, however, was his creation of a department dedicated to
translating scripture into Asian languages. As one Serampore pamphlet
put it, "Our hope of success in this great undertaking depends chiefly
on the patronage of the College of Fort William."[51] Such endorse-
ments, along with the lobbying of Brown and Buchanan, garnered the
support of religious leaders for Wellesley and his institution.[52] As late
as the debates over the renewal of the Company's charter in 1813, the

---

[48] William Jardine Proudfoot, *Biographical Memoir of James Dinwiddie, LL.D.*
(Liverpool, 1868), pp. 26, 102.

[49] James Dinwiddie, Journal (25 Aug. 1800), Dalhousie University Archives, Dinwiddie
Fonds B60.

[50] William Carey to William Cuninghame, 7 Aug. 1805, NLS, Acc.4505, pp. 31–2; Kopf,
British Orientalism, pp. 75–7.

[51] W. Carey et al., *Proposals for a Subscription for Translating the Holy Scriptures*
(Serampore, 1806), p. 7.

[52] Wilberforce to Archdeacon Wrangham, 23 Nov. 1807, in Robert Isaac Wilberforce and
Samuel Wilberforce, *The Life of William Wilberforce*, 5 vols. (London, 1838), vol. III,

fortunes of the college and of Christianity in the East could be seen as intertwined. On this occasion, Wellesley himself proposed "combining religion with learning" by connecting the college to the local ecclesiastical establishment.[53] By his own admission, Wellesley's contribution to the Evangelical cause had been cautious and limited.[54] It was enough to put pressure on Grant, however, and may have helped to save the college from total destruction.

Another political frontier of the college lay in British India, where the institution was meant to elevate Wellesley in the eyes of his "subjects."[55] Soon after his arrival, Wellesley complained that the unassuming style of Sir John Shore had lowered "the person, dignity and authority of the Governor-General."[56] Not only had the subordinate presidencies of Bombay and Madras become insubordinate but even his council now refused to pay the "respect due" to him. This lent the government he had inherited the character less "of a monarchy" than of a "republic" – or, he might have written, of a trading company.[57] Defiance had also trickled down the ranks. Soon, Wellesley augured, "the Europeans settled at Calcutta will control the government, if they do not overturn it." What was needed was "a thorough reform in private manners," and the College of Fort William would be the vehicle for effecting it.[58] Wellesley emphasized protocol and discipline, formed a loyal coterie of students, and promoted them to the top ranks of the civil service. And yet none of this forestalled the emergence of disorders at the institution itself, which in turn came to preoccupy him. After eight students were expelled for misbehavior, Wellesley was observed passing by the college buildings in his carriage,

pp. 352–3; Watson to Duke of Grafton, 10 Dec. 1807, in Richard Watson, *Anecdotes of the Life of Richard Watson* (London, 1817), p. 373.

[53] Wellesley, Speech in HL Deb (9 Apr. 1813), vol. XXV, col. 697.

[54] Penelope Carson, *The East India Company and Religion, 1698–1858* (Woodbridge, UK, 2012), pp. 133–4.

[55] On Wellesley's telling use of this term, see Curzon, *British Government*, vol. II, p. 174.

[56] Wellesley to Lord Grenville, 18 Nov. 1798, in *Report on the Manuscripts of J. B. Fortescue, Esq., Preserved at Dropmore*, 9 vols. (London, 1892–1915), vol. IV, p. 383.

[57] Wellesley to Dundas, 25 Jan. 1800, in Dundas and Wellesley, *Two Views*, p. 216.

[58] Wellesley to Grenville, 18 Nov. 1798, p. 384.

looking "hard in at the Windows."[59] He must have been even more dis-turbed by reports that older civil servants were slandering the college with the encouragement of the directors.[60] One student described an atmosphere of growing paranoia: Opinions were closely guarded; infor-mants had an ear out for expressions of disaffection.[61] For Wellesley, the problems of establishing authority in Britain and British India were connected: These were two fronts in the same campaign.

This campaign was not aimed at Europeans alone: Wellesley also sought to earn "the obedience and respect of the [Indian] people."[62] And he likewise sought to do this in ways that depended upon the College of Fort William. His "Notes" on the college echoed the rationale Hastings had given twenty years earlier for establishing the Calcutta Madrasa. With the decline of the Mughals, Wellesley wrote, "all the public institu-tions calculated to promote education and good morals were neglected." He suggested that by employing Indian teachers and scholars the college would help them reclaim their honor and livelihood. He also proposed to make the Madrasa, along with its Hindu counterpart in Benares, "the means of aiding the study of the laws and languages in the College." He concluded, "These arrangements respecting the native Colleges, while they contribute to the happiness of our native subjects, will qualify them to form a more just estimate of the mild and benevolent spirit of the British Government."[63] For all of its intended embodiment of mild-ness and benevolence, however, the college was also meant to inspire awe and obedience. Before the directors' cuts forced him to use exist-ing buildings for the college, Wellesley had planned to build a walled compound with a great hall, a chapel, and an observatory.[64] It was dif-ficult to find a large enough site in the desired vicinity of Garden Reach,

[59] Richard Blechynden, Diary (5 May 1801), BL, Add. MS 45617, f. 79v.
[60] David Brown to Charles Grant, 15 Jan. 1805, in Kaye, Lives, vol. I, p. 481.
[61] William Fraser to father, 21 Aug. 1804, Reelig House, bundle 76.
[62] Wellesley to Dundas, 25 Jan. 1800, p. 216.
[63] Wellesley, "Governor-General's Notes," pp. 351–2.
[64] Claudius Buchanan to Charles Grant, 23 Aug. 1800, in Hugh Pearson, Memoirs of the Life and Writings of the Rev. Claudius Buchanan, 2 vols. (Oxford, 1817), vol. I, p. 205; James Dinwiddie, Journal (23 and 29 Sept. 1800), Dalhousie University Archives, Dinwiddie Fonds B61; S. Davis, Minute (8 Aug. 1814), BL, IOR H/488, p. 610.

so several plots were acquired and joined together.[65] Displaced Indian residents of the area were compensated but not always satisfactorily.[66] Several residents threw themselves before Wellesley's carriage, whereupon "he ordered them ... sent to the police who ... confined them to hard labour for one month." Dinwiddie, who recorded this incident, thought the punishment harsh: Lord Cornwallis had once been halted thusly and had taken no such action.[67] For Wellesley, however, the dignity of the institution was paramount. He was even said to have ordered a nearby brickworks dismantled, lest it spoil the view.[68]

Another blot on the horizon was not so easily expunged: the Egyptian expedition of Napoleon. News of this venture "to answer at once the purposes of science and conquest" greeted Wellesley upon his arrival in Calcutta in 1798.[69] Soon, he was using the fears it stoked of a French invasion of India to justify expansionist designs to authorities in Britain.[70] Yet Egypt and India were linked not only in military strategy but also in the classical imaginary. In recent years, Sir William Jones had spawned a raft of philological and mythological links between the two ancient civilizations. If Jones' Asiatic Society had drawn European attention to British discoveries in India, then Napoleon's *Commission des Sciences et des Arts* threatened to refocus it on French ones in Egypt. The exploits of this corps of some one hundred and fifty savants, ranging from the antiquarian to the zoological, would have been familiar to Wellesley. The commission was famous enough in Britain to inspire no fewer than three

[65] Wellesley, "Notes," p. 350; Dinwiddie, Journal (29 Sept. 1800); William Hickey, *Memoirs of William Hickey*, ed. Alfred Spencer, 5th edn, 4 vols. (London, 1950), vol. IV, pp. 237–8.

[66] Some petitioned the government for additional relief. West Bengal State Archives, Bengal Revenue Proceedings (1 Dec. 1801), nos. 13–14.

[67] James Dinwiddie, Journal (5 Feb. 1801), Dalhousie University Archives, Dinwiddie Fonds B63.

[68] James Dinwiddie, Journal (19 Nov. 1800), ibid., Dinwiddie Fonds B62.

[69] *Selections from the Calcutta Gazettes*, 5 vols. (Calcutta, 1864–8), vol. III, p. 202.

[70] G. S. Misra, "Napoleon's Egyptian Expedition and Its Repercussions on Wellesley's Policy," *Journal of the Uttar Pradesh Historical Society* new ser. 3 (1955); Edward Ingram, "The Geopolitics of the First British Expedition to Egypt – III: The Red Sea Campaign, 1800–1801," *Middle Eastern Studies* 31 (1995).

James Gillray cartoons.[71] Apart from the scale of its operations – the first edition of the resulting *Description de l'Égypte* (1809–18) filled twenty-three volumes – what was novel about the commission was its close identification with the French state. To quote one historian, "The British had done nothing of the sort in India."[72] Napoleon had thus thrown down a gauntlet, and with the College of Fort William Wellesley took it up. An early memorandum on the college expected that it would impress "the learned world in Europe."[73] In the coming years, its continental reputation would inspire a strain of gasconade.[74] The Egyptian expedition may have marked a high point in the Anglo-French national rivalry over art and science, but the college marked Wellesley's entry into this arena as a sovereign in his own right.[75]

The college was also intended to boost Wellesley's standing among the sovereigns of Asia, most directly by training a diplomatic corps. It offered some subjects, like Marathi, with an eye to their utility in negotiations.[76] But for Wellesley, the practical was often subordinate to the ornamental. As he advised the leader of an embassy to the Arabian states, "the greatest attention is requisite to points of ceremony and appearance. Any concessions in points of that nature on the part of an Ambassador to an Eastern court, tend to degrade his consequence and to impede the progress of his negotiation."[77] In diplomatic settings, Wellesley suggested, knowledge itself was an

---

[71] Andrew Bednarski, *Holding Egypt: Tracing the Reception of the* Description de l'Égypte *in Nineteenth-Century Britain* (London, 2005), pp. 16–20.

[72] Charles Coulston Gillispie, *Science and Polity in France: The Revolutionary and Napoleonic Years* (Princeton, 2004), p. 599.

[73] "On the Comparative Advantages of a College in Calcutta & in Its Vicinity" [c. 1801], BL, Add. MS 13862, f. 45r.

[74] Abraham Lockett to College Council, 29 Sept. 1810, PCFW, vol. 561, p. 335; Thomas Roebuck, *Annals of the College of Fort William* (Calcutta, 1819), p. vii.

[75] On this rivalry, see Maya Jasanoff, *Edge of Empire: Lives, Culture, and Conquest in the East, 1750–1850* (New York, 2005); Holger Hoock, *Empires of the Imagination: Politics, War and the Arts in the British World, 1750–1850* (London, 2010).

[76] See J. Webbe to N. B. Edmonstone, 19 Jun. 1802, in *DMW*, vol. V, pp. 193–4.

[77] Wellesley to Home Popham, 16 Oct. 1801, in *DMW*, vol. V, p. 155.

ornament that imparted prestige to the wearer. Among senior diplomats, he favored Neil Benjamin Edmonstone, not only for his Eastern learning but also for his gentlemanly display of it.[78] Wellesley's ambitions for kingship and extended territory demanded an increased supply of residents, agents, and other "political" personnel. He told Edmonstone in early 1800 that too few Company servants possessed the knowledge and "dignity" needed to represent him.[79] But a solution was near at hand. In March, Wellesley informed Dundas that he planned to establish an institution where writers might acquire both qualifications.[80] Within a few months, Edmonstone was busy finding and training able diplomats in his new role as professor of Persian at the College of Fort William.

Not only the college's diplomatic training but also its literary apparatus was calculated to enhance Wellesley's regional standing. The development of its library into one of the finest in India was as much a political as a scholarly enterprise. The library's greatest treasures were plundered from the palace of Tipu Sultan after the conquest of Mysore in 1799. Wellesley wanted Tipu's fate to dissuade other would-be challengers.[81] But he wanted the fate of his library to convey an additional message. The collection had been a regal appurtenance, after all, and still carried associations with sovereignty.[82] By preserving it and penetrating its secrets, Wellesley offered the "native princes" a demonstration of his fitness to be king. He continued to bolster this claim. His survey of Mysore in 1800 yielded various "ancient inscriptions and valuable manuscripts."[83]

---

[78] See [Robert] Montgomery Martin, preface to *DMW*, vol. III, p. xii n; Marla Karen Chancey, "In the Company's Secret Service: Neil Benjamin Edmonstone and the First Indian Imperialists, 1780–1820" (PhD dissertation, Florida State University, 2003), chs. 7–10 *passim*.

[79] Edmonstone to Archibald Edmonstone, 6 Mar. 1800, Cambridge University Library, Add. 7616/2/21.

[80] Wellesley to Robert Dundas, 5 Mar. 1800, in *DMW*, vol. II, p. 232.

[81] Wellesley to Directors, 11 May 1799, in *DMW*, vol. I, p. 578.

[82] Joshua Ehrlich, "Plunder and Prestige: Tipu Sultan's Library and the Making of British India," *South Asia: Journal of South Asian Studies* 43 (2020).

[83] *Asiatic Annual Register* 8 (London, 1809), "Chronicle," p. 29.

His embassies to Persia and Arabia in the following years spared "neither trouble nor expense to procure whatever was rare or valuable" for the repository.[84] From 1804, the college council sponsored manuscript expeditions to Mysore, Travancore, Ceylon, and elsewhere.[85] And within a decade-and-a-half, the library could boast over eight thousand print holdings in addition to some three thousand manuscript ones.[86]

Besides preserving works, the college was publishing them, on the order of one hundred original volumes in its first four years.[87] The vice-provost Buchanan, presumably at Wellesley's urging, sought "to swell the annual Catalogue" and was "very little solicitous about the expence."[88] The publications included grammars, dictionaries, letters, dialogues, fables, prayer-books, and ethical treatises in Persian, Arabic, Sanskrit, Bengali, Hindustani, and Marathi.[89] Many copies would have been destined for the libraries of rulers and elites across India. Wellesley suggested this when he announced that "the operation of these useful labours, will not be confined to the limits ... of this Empire."[90] The college munshi (teacher) Mir Sher Ali Afsus could boast of one of his productions that "five hundred copies were struck off, and reached distant places."[91] Wellesley no doubt shared the belief of Professor John Gilchrist that "the Nations of India" would praise him as the "Reviver and Patron of Oriental Literature."[92]

---

[84] Charles Stewart, *A Descriptive Catalogue of the Oriental Library of the Late Tippoo Sultan of Mysore* (Cambridge, 1809), p. 190.

[85] Claudius Buchanan, *Christian Researches in Asia: With Notices of the Translation of the Scriptures into the Oriental Languages* (Cambridge, 1811), p. 91; Kopf, *British Orientalism*, pp. 67, 188.

[86] Sisir Kumar Das, *Sahibs and Munshis: An Account of the College of Fort William*, repr. edn (Calcutta, 2001), pp. 103–5.

[87] [Claudius Buchanan, ed.], *The College of Fort William in Bengal* (London, 1805), p. 156.

[88] Matthew Lumsden to College Council, 2 May 1810, PCFW, vol. 561, p. 239.

[89] See Roebuck, *Annals*, appendix, pp. 21–45.

[90] Wellesley, Speech (30 Mar. 1803), in Roebuck, *Annals*, p. 41.

[91] [Mir Sher Ali Afsus], *The Araish-i-Mahfil; or, Ornament of the Assembly* [1805], trans. Major Henry Court (Allahabad, 1871), p. 3.

[92] John Gilchrist, dedication and introduction to [Mir Sher Ali Afsus] Meer Sher Ulee Ufsos, trans., *The Rose Garden of Hindoostan* (Calcutta, 1802), pp. [iii], vii.

Gilchrist also alluded to the fact that scholars had come from far and wide to teach the students, manage the library, and compose and translate texts.[93] These scholars soon numbered over one hundred and hailed, in Buchanan's words, "from every quarter of India, and from the parts beyond, from Persia and Arabia."[94] In 1805, the "learned Malay" Tuanko Attil was recruited from Natal, on the coast of Sumatra.[95] In that year too, Buchanan sought to hire a Sinophone Armenian from Macao, though this plan was scotched by the directors.[96] Many of the scholars were recruited through Company or kinship networks; others had seen an advertisement issued by Wellesley for "men of learning and knowledge."[97] It was one measure of the sundry origins of the college pandits that "there are few (not being of the same district) who will give the same account of their faith, or refer to the same sacred books."[98] Such a group, according to Buchanan, could only have been assembled "by the influence of the supreme government, as exerted by the Marquis Wellesley."[99]

This was a circumstance that Wellesley emphasized in his 1802 letter staying the directors' order to abolish the college. "Many learned natives," he warned, "are now attached to the institution who have been invited ... by my especial authority, from distant parts of Asia." To suddenly rescind their employment – "to violate our faith" – surely would "be an act of the most flagrant impolicy."

---

[93] Ibid., pp. vii–viii.
[94] Claudius Buchanan, *Memoir of the Expediency of an Ecclesiastical Establishment for British India* (London, 1805), p. 81.
[95] NAI, Bengal Public Consultations (21 Aug. 1806), no. 21; Buchanan, *Christian Researches*, p. 80.
[96] Elmer H. Cutts, "Early Nineteenth Century Chinese Studies in Bengal," *Indian Historical Quarterly* 20 (1944), pp. 117–18.
[97] For the first group, see Maulavi Ikram 'Ali, *Ikhwanu-S-Safa; or, Brothers of Purity* [1810], trans. John Platts (London, 1869), pp. ix–x; Ruth Gabriel, "Learned Communities and British Educational Experiments in North India: 1780–1830" (PhD dissertation, University of Virginia, 1979), pp. 177–81. For the second group, see Pearson, *Memoirs*, vol. I, p. 212; Mir Amman, *Bāgh o Bahār; or Tales of the Four Darweshes* [1804], trans. Duncan Forbes (London, 1857), p. [1].
[98] Buchanan, *Memoir*, p. 26.
[99] Buchanan, *Christian Researches*, p. 3.

Ought these "learned natives" to "be driven forth to the extremities of Asia, to report ... that the British Government was unable to support ... learning"?[100] Wellesley was arguing that these informants and advisers of far-flung sovereigns were arbiters of his and his government's reputation. Their recruitment enlarged the sphere of his influence and thus served as a complement to more forceful strategies of expansion.[101] As if to endorse this notion, the college pandits credited Wellesley with securing power not only through arms but also through "science, and the ... regard of the learned."[102] They obviously knew how to flatter their patron: Wellesley would keep this address and later make it available to the editor of his papers.

The various audiences and messages of the College of Fort William mingled in the grandiose spectacle of its "Public Disputations in the Oriental Languages." This annual event at Government House was designed to attract "all Calcutta" – Europeans and "natives of rank and learning" – and indeed it did.[103] According to one attendee, "all the college and private moonshis were present, with all the native and foreign eastern merchants who pretend to any learning, and crowds of Europeans."[104] In 1804, an envoy from the pasha of Baghdad joined in the pageantry, as part of a mission to shore up the alliance recently forged against Napoleon. For that matter, the audience was not limited to physical spectators. Reports were printed in octavo volumes, in the official gazette, and in local and metropolitan journals. As the missionary professor Carey put it, "thousands of the learned in distant nations will exult in this triumph of Literature."[105] At the center of the proceedings sat the governor-general himself.

---

[100] Wellesley to Directors, 5 Aug. 1802, in *DMW*, vol. II, p. 663.

[101] For Wellesley's fostering of ties with intermediaries as a strategy of expansion, see Paul K. Macdonald, *Networks of Domination: The Social Foundations of Peripheral Conquest in International Politics* (Oxford, 2014), ch. 3.

[102] "Address from the Pundits of the College" (31 Jul. 1805), in *DMW*, vol. IV, p. 628.

[103] Buchanan to W. P. Elliott, 17 Nov. 1800, in Pearson, *Memoirs*, vol. I, p. 209. The first disputations of 1802 were held in the Writers' Buildings, as Government House had not yet been completed.

[104] Maria Graham, *Journal of a Residence in India* (Edinburgh, 1812), p. 138.

[105] William Carey, Speech (20 Sept. 1804), in *Primitiae Orientalis*, vol. III, p. 115.

The following account dates from 1819, but most of what it describes originated with Wellesley:

> In a state chair, covered with crimson velvet and richly gilt, with a group of aid-de-camps and secretaries standing behind him, sat the Marquis of Hastings [the governor-general]. Two servants with state punka[h]s of crimson silk were fanning him, and behind them again were several native servants bearing silver staffs. Next him, on either side, were seated the examiners, and below them again, the most distinguished ladies of the presidency. Next, in an open space, were two small rostrums for the disputants, and chairs for the professors; the room behind these, and fronting the marquis, was quite filled with company, and in the rear of all, the body guard was drawn up in full uniforms of scarlet with naked sabres.[106]

After presiding over the disputations, Wellesley presented the top students with gold medals engraved with the motto, *Redit a nobis Aurora diemque reducit*.[107] He then delivered a speech extolling the college's ideals and achievements – or, as one student put it, "a piece of bombast ... intended to exalt himself."[108] A grand dinner was held in the evening.

Whether judged by Indian or British, Asian or European standards, there was an unmistakable kingliness to all of this. One Malay scribe, visiting Bengal in 1810, construed the disputations as part of the ritual life of a raja's palace. Unable to comprehend the languages

---

[106] [Moyle Sherer], *Sketches of India: Written by an Officer for Fire-Side Travellers at-Home* (London, 1821), pp. 119–20. For comparison, see "A Colored Plan of a Hall for Public Exercises for the College of Fort William," BL, Add. MS 13901C; William Fraser to father, 30 Mar. 1803, Reelig House, bundle 75, f. 24v; Notes, Mount Stuart, HA/21/19.

[107] "The Dawn returns down there/Bringing them back the light of our previous day." Virgil, *The Georgics of Virgil: A Translation*, trans. David Ferry (New York, 2005), p. 20. For the medals, see Robert P. Puddester, *Medals of British India with Rarity and Valuations: Volume One: Commemorative and Historical Medals from 1750 to 1947* (London, 2002), pp. 16–18.

[108] William Fraser to father, 1 Aug. 1803, Reelig House, vol. 28, p. 195.

being spoken, the scribe, Ibrahim, relied on his eyes to interpret "the manners and customs of the great Rajah of the English." He remarked on the plenitude of the "palace," "the splendour of the throne," the hierarchy of the "court," and the beauty of the raja's "wives" (ladies in attendance).[109] No doubt the envoy from Baghdad better grasped the proceedings, yet he too hailed the governor-general as a sovereign: "Kings approach his threshold with offerings of respect."[110] Meanwhile, the trappings of sovereignty at the disputations were equally intelligible according to European models. Buchanan analogized the governor-general's speech at the college to "the King's speech in Parliament."[111] A student participant described Wellesley as a "King ... seated in all his Glory."[112] Clearly, rather than impart a single image of authority, the disputations were designed to accommodate multiple interpretations and attachments.

What was meant to bind spectators' impressions into a coherent language of rule was a collective sense of awe at the majesty of the ruler. Ibrahim described his arrival on the scene as an ascent into "heaven": "I was no longer in the world I had left," and it was "fortunate ... that I lived to see the wonders that were within."[113] Others responded in a similar fashion. For one British visitor, the sight of Government House was too dazzling to "be conveyed by words": The hall where the disputations were held was a "magic ground" that "brought to my mind some of the enchanted castles described in the Arabian tales."[114] The directors, for their part, were said to be astonished at reports of the disputations.[115] Most, no doubt, concluded with one official that they were "a very vain miserable piece

---

[109] Ibrahim, "An Account of Bengal, and of a Visit to the Government House, by Ibrahim, the Son of Candu the Merchant," trans. John Leyden, in Graham, *Journal*, pp. 201–7.

[110] Suleiman Aga, Address (20 Oct. 1804), Cambridge University Library, Oriental MSS Add. 286.

[111] Buchanan to Wellesley, 6 Mar. 1806, BL, Add. MS 37284, f. 35v.

[112] William Fraser to father, 30 Mar. 1803, f. 25r.

[113] Ibrahim, "Account of Bengal," p. 202.

[114] J. Johnson, *The Oriental Voyager; or, Descriptive Sketches and Cursory Remarks, on a Voyage to India and China* (London, 1807), p. 100.

[115] Buchanan to Wellesley, 6 Mar. 1806, f. 38v.

of Business."[116] It was Wellesley's ally David Scott who best appreciated his counterargument. By confirming his ascendance "in the eyes of other men," Scott conceived, the college might sustain "the charm by which that immense eastern empire could alone be held."[117] "Charm" was an apt word, for there was something talismanic about Wellesley's scaffolding of sovereignty, as if the constituent elements mattered less than the magnificence of their arrangement.[118] Knowledge held pride of place among these elements; to debate whether Wellesley was an Anglicist or an Orientalist is to miss the fact that its provenance was beside the point.

REVERBERATIONS

In the summer of 1805, Wellesley vacated his gilt chair and departed for England. His warring with the Marathas had finally upset his pact with the Board of Control and led to his effective recall. But this would not be the end of his impact. For one thing, the College of Fort William still rankled with the directors. Even after they scaled back the college, its association with its founder meant that it continued to loom as a threat. Residual aggravations included a natural history establishment, which Wellesley had envisioned as an outgrowth of the college, and the library of Tipu Sultan, which he had claimed for the college's repository. So sweeping were the directors' apprehensions that they extended to scholar-officials formerly employed at the institution. Wellesley had left the scene, but his ideas about knowledge lingered.

By the time of Wellesley's departure, the directors had cast aside any reservations they had had about openly disavowing him or his college. In a draft dispatch, they beheld such

[116] Edward Strachey, Minute (Jul. 1814), BL, IOR H/488, p. 600.
[117] Scott to Wellesley, 8 Sept. 1803, in Scott, *Correspondence*, vol II, p. 431.
[118] For the "scaffolding" of sovereignty as the "aesthetic, artistic, theatrical, and symbolic structures" that establish and maintain it, see Zvi Ben-Dor Benite, Stefanos Geroulanos, and Nicole Jerr, introduction to Benite, Geroulanos, and Jerr, eds., *The Scaffolding of Sovereignty: Global and Aesthetic Perspectives on the History of a Concept* (New York, 2017), p. 3.

assumpointns of new authority by the Governor General himself, that the character of our Indian Government has in his hands undergone an essential change. It has in fact been turned into a pure and simple despotism; the powers of the Supreme Council have been completely absorbed; the Subordinate Governments have been reduced nearly to the condition of Provinces of the Bengal Presidency; the authority of the Court of Directors has, in many instances, been disregarded ....[119]

Wellesley, as the directors repeated to the board, had "invaded" the Company's constitution and infringed its "rights and privileges."[120] Their reappointment of the trusty, if elderly, Lord Cornwallis as governor-general was an effort to repair some of the damage. Cornwallis died less than three months into his second stint in office. He spent much of that time trying to undo Wellesley's legacy, including by cutting down the college.[121] His acting replacement George Barlow, though better disposed toward both Wellesley and the college, took the same course out of deference to the directors. He meekly followed orders to retrench, which the directors took the occasion of Lord Castlereagh's resignation from the board to transmit.[122] In a matter of months, the college's staff and prizes were reduced, and its curriculum restricted to the study of a few languages.

And yet, even these measures failed to propitiate the directors. One lingering irritant was the Institution for Promoting the Natural History of India. Having founded the institution in 1800 as an annex to the college, Wellesley separated it in 1804 in an attempt to evade the coming retrenchments. At the same time, he appointed Francis Buchanan to head the institution and to enlarge it from a menagerie

---

[119] Draft Public Despatch to Bengal (26 Mar. 1805), BL, IOR H/486, pp. 7–8.

[120] Directors to Board of Control, 6 Nov. 1805, p. 143.

[121] "Narrative of Marquis Cornwallis's Proceedings in India" (Sept. 1805), TNA, PRO 30/11/210, ff. 15v–16v.

[122] Barlow to Charles Grant, 22 Mar. and 30 Nov. 1806, BL, Mss Eur F176/29, pp. 55–7, 100–4; Public Despatch to Bengal (21 May 1806), BL, IOR E/4/659, pp. 1019–30; Public Despatch to Bengal (23 Jul. 1806), BL, IOR E/4/660, pp. 151–5.

into a research center. Whereas it was soon receiving specimens from across the region, the directors' India Museum was languishing for want of contributions.[123] The directors' displeasure must have been compounded by Wellesley's suggestion that the extension of "the boundaries of ... science" went hand in hand with the extension of territory.[124] From 1804, he seems to have conceived of the institution as a means to sustain a greater vision of the college despite the directors' reductions. Accordingly, he also proposed to build an experimental farm, which, along with the institution, would form a scientific cluster around his country seat.[125] He left before this design could be implemented. The institution itself lasted some months more before succumbing to cuts imposed by the directors.[126]

If the directors were annoyed at the college's extension in the form of the natural history institution, then they were incensed at its retention of the library of Tipu Sultan. Upon founding the college, Wellesley had canceled an order of the army's prize committee allotting most of the collection to the directors' Oriental Library.[127] "It is obvious," he declared, "that these manuscripts may be rendered highly useful to the purposes of the new institution, and that much more public advantage can be derived from them" there than in London.[128] Unappeased by Wellesley's offer to transmit those works "merely valuable as curiosities," the directors grumbled at their library being "superceded by the interception of contributions

---

[123] Mildred Archer, "India and Natural History: The Rôle of the East India Company, 1785–1858," *History Today* 9 (1959), p. 738; Ray Desmond, *The India Museum, 1801–1879* (London, 1982), p. 19.

[124] Marquess Wellesley, "Minute of the Governor-General on the Natural History of India" (26 Jul. 1804), in *DMW*, vol. IV, p. 675.

[125] Marquess Wellesley, "Minute of the Governor-General on the Improvement of Indian Agriculture" (1 Jun. 1805), in *DMW*, vol. IV, p. 676.

[126] Extract Public Despatch to Bengal (28 Feb. 1806), BL, IOR F/4/199/4471, pp. 17–20; Extract Bengal Public Consultations (30 Apr. 1807), ibid., pp. 59–62. For the site's survival as a public garden, see Eugenia W. Herbert, *Flora's Empire: British Gardens in India* (Philadelphia, 2011), pp. 83–96.

[127] For the order, see "Extract from the Proceedings of the Committee of Prize" (May to Jun. 1799), BL, Eur Mss E196, f. 51r.

[128] Wellesley, "Governor-General's Notes," p. 353.

intended for it."[129] After Wellesley's departure in 1805, they recurred to the subject of Tipu's collection, "which we have always intended should be preserved in the Company's Library."[130] Of the twelve trunks of books and manuscripts sent by the college in response, however, only one was designated for that repository. The rest were addressed to a relation of the vice-provost Buchanan "for the purpose of being presented, in the name of the College" to universities and collections in Britain. At this the directors exploded, declaring

> our decided disapprobation of this act of our College, & our displeasure at the unprecedented & disrespectful form & manner in which it has been executed.
>
> Hitherto no Department subordinate to our authority had ever presumed to dispose of the Company's Property without our consent, much less make Presents ... in its own name, as if it were an Establishment independent of our Control.[131]

Two members of the college council offered to resign, although the fault apparently lay with Buchanan.[132] The new governor-general, Lord Minto, ordered the council to send the directors everything originally allotted to them.[133] This resolved the immediate issue but could not remove its underlying causes. The directors' aversion to Wellesley cast a long shadow over their relations with the College of Fort William.

The suspicions of the directors even extended to scholar-officials whom Wellesley had patronized in India. These included onetime personnel of the College of Fort William upon their return to Britain. Charles Stewart found a position at Haileybury; no doubt it helped that he brought a catalogue of Tipu's books with him. Other

---

[129] Ibid.; Draft Public Despatch to Bengal (19 Jul. 1803), p. 526.

[130] Public Despatch to Bengal (15 Jun. 1805), BL, IOR E/4/658, p. 32.

[131] Public Despatch to Bengal (28 Feb. 1806), BL, IOR E/4/659, pp. 569–71.

[132] G. S. A. Ranking, "History of the College of Fort William from Its First Foundation," *Bengal Past and Present* 21 (1920), pp. 182–3; Rosane Rocher and Ludo Rocher, *The Making of Western Indology: Henry Thomas Colebrooke and the East India Company* (Abingdon, UK, 2012), pp. 66–7.

[133] Governor-General to College Council, 27 Nov. 1806, BL, Mss Eur E196, ff. 82v–83r.

candidates for such employment were decidedly less fortunate. John Gilchrist found that his association with Wellesley was positively "productive of harm": The directors, believing him a partisan of the College of Fort William, were reluctant to hire him or to grant him a pension.[134] Similar treatment awaited Francis Buchanan, who had headed the natural history establishment. Buchanan's ties to Wellesley and his voyage home with him "prejudiced them [the directors] so much against me that there is no saying the lengths they may go."[135] Wellesley's college and the ideas it embodied still troubled the directors. At one time, they had seen scholar-officials as assets; now, they were as likely to see them as liabilities.

CONCLUSION

In only a few years, Wellesley had upended the politics of the Company. Central to his rebellion was the College of Fort William. When he declared that "the College must stand or the Empire must fall," the empire he meant was very different from the one he had been sent to administer. It was not just that Wellesley conquered and annexed on a larger scale than his predecessors, and adopted greater pomp and ceremony. He was the first governor-general who sought to undo the Company state and the ideas about knowledge that legitimized it.

The future prospects for Wellesley's own ideas were mixed. On the one hand, his kingly pretensions were unlikely to be imitated. Wellesley could make such pretensions only because the directors feared provoking the ministry, and he paid for them back at home when they sponsored an inquiry against him.[136] On the other hand, Wellesley's embrace of large-scale territorial sovereignty would be difficult, if not impossible, to reverse. The Company now ruled

[134] J[ohn] B[orthwick] G[ilchrist], *Dr. Gilchrist's Statement of His Case and Conduct,* bound with Jonathan Scott and John Borthwick Gilchrist, *Introductory Address to the Honorable Court of Proprietors of the East India Company* [Hertford, 1806], UCL Library Special Collections, Hume Tracts, vol. 119, pp. 30, 53.
[135] Buchanan to John Hamilton, 17 Jul. 1806, National Records of Scotland, GD161/18/8.
[136] Philips, *East India Company,* pp. 144–50.

vast tracts in the south, north, west, and east of India, which its representatives would feel obligated to preserve. Wellesley's ideas about knowledge were another matter. Would the college remain a magic "charm," to quote David Scott, in the absence of its founder? Even setting aside the impact of the directors' cuts, it was doubtful whether Wellesley's successors would share his devotion to the institution. The former governor-general Lord Teignmouth (Sir John Shore) had doubts on this score, as did the director Charles Grant, long before the outcome of the controversy was assured.[137] For their part, presumably, the directors would stop any governor-general from restoring the college, lest he try to realize its subversive potential.

At the same time, the depth of the directors' own commitment to knowledge had become newly uncertain. Would they continue to dedicate resources to Haileybury? Was there something incongruous in modeling their college on one they had sought to abolish? For that matter, was there something incongruous in filling their museum with the spoils of conquests of which they had disapproved? Finally, and most importantly, did the idea of conciliation still have currency in the wake of Wellesley's rebellion? It had become more difficult to make the case not only for commercial sovereignty but also for scholarly patronage as its complement. The College of Fort William had sponsored more publications in five years than the Company had in its entire previous history. Perhaps it was this awkward fact that led the directors, in 1806, to claim that the college had rendered no "advantages ... to Literature." They dismissed its publications as "a few elementary School Books" that might have appeared under their patronage "though the College had never existed."[138] These statements demonstrated new concerns about the loyalty of the Company's scholar-officials. Wellesley's "reign" had ended, but its reverberations were only just beginning to be felt.

---

[137] Lord Teignmouth to Grant, 30 Mar. 1801, cited in Lord Teignmouth, *Memoir of the Life and Correspondence of John Lord Teignmouth*, 2 vols. (London, 1843), vol. II, pp. 31–2; Grant to Brown, 19 Jun. 1801, p. 242.

[138] Public Despatch to Bengal (28 Feb. 1806), pp. 574–7.

4   Scholar-Officials and the Later Company State

Upon landing at Madras in 1803, the young surgeon John Leyden took stock of his surroundings. Fellow servants of the Company, he quickly perceived,

> fell naturally into two divisions. The mercantile party, consisting chiefly of men of old standing, versed in trade, and inspired with a spirit in no respect superior to that of the most pitiful pettifogging pedlar, nor in their views a whit more enlarged; in short, men whose sole consideration is to make money .... [T]his is the party that stands highest in credit with the East India Company. There is another party for whom I am more at a loss to find an epithet .... [T]hey have discovered that we are not merely merchants in India, but legislators and governors; and they assert that our conduct there ought to be calculated for stability and security ....

Leyden considered his options. On the one hand, he might adopt the outlook of the "mercantile party," and "by strict economy, endeavour to amass a few thousand pounds in the course of twenty years." On the other hand, he might adopt the outlook of that second division of his colleagues. He might acquire a "knowledge of India, its laws, relations, politics and languages," and fill a "more respectable" role helping to consolidate an empire. Leyden settled on the latter option. By 1805, he was well on his way to realizing his decided ambition: "to become a furious Orientalist."[1]

The twinning of intellectual ambition and a sense of the imperatives of sovereignty defined Leyden's generation of Company

---

[1] Leyden to [James] Ballantyne, 24 Oct. 1805, in Leyden, *The Poetical Works of Dr. John Leyden* (London, 1875), pp. lxxviii–lxxix.

scholar-officials. More than the movements of Romanticism, Evangelicalism, or Utilitarianism, it was the Company's recent evolution that impressed itself on their minds.[2] The Mysore war of 1798–9 and the Maratha war of 1803–5 dramatically enlarged the Company's dominions. These conflicts also destroyed and weakened, respectively, its two major rivals, lending its conquests for the first time the appearance of permanence.[3] For that matter, the Battle of Delhi during the latter conflict rendered the once mighty Mughal Empire a vassal state of the Company. "What a revolution," as one student at the College of Fort William put it: "The Emperor of Hindoostan glad ... to receive the protection of a mercantile association."[4] But could a mercantile association secure "a greater empire than any Emperor of Delhi reigned over," to quote one professor at the college?[5] Along with a belief that the Company's situation had changed came a regret, on the part of critics, that its constitution had not changed accordingly. The opposition to the Company state stirred up by Lord Wellesley and his college would not simply disappear in the years following his departure. On the contrary, attempts to alter the balance between the Company's mercantile and sovereign characters would only intensify.

Ideas about knowledge would continue to feature in these attempts. The Charter Act of 1813 tied the Company's patronage of scholars to its collection of land revenue. European scholar-officials and their Indian collaborators, meanwhile, increasingly tailored their intellectual projects to the aim of territorial expansion. Overall, such expansion was encouraging engagement with Indian society

---

[2] On these influences, see respectively Michael J. Franklin, ed., *Romantic Representations of British India* (London, 2006); Penelope Carson, *The East India Company and Religion, 1698–1858* (Woodbridge, UK, 2012); Eric Stokes, *The English Utilitarians and India* (Oxford, 1959).

[3] See Governor-General in Council to Secret Committee of Directors, 13 Jul. 1804, in *DMW*, vol. IV, pp. 144, 176. Cf. Francis G. Hutchins, *The Illusion of Permanence: British Imperialism in India* (Princeton, 1967), p. 5.

[4] William Fraser to Edward Fraser, 3 Apr. 1804, Reelig House, bundle 76, f. 4r.

[5] Henry Thomas Colebrooke to George Colebrooke, 9 Aug. 1802, in Sir T. E. Colebrooke, *The Life of H. T. Colebrooke* (London, 1873), p. 211.

and raising the prospect of greater involvement in Indian education. The Court of Directors was slow to embrace this prospect. But by the 1820s, the need for new ideas about knowledge could not be ignored any longer.

FROM PATRONAGE CLAUSE TO EDUCATION CLAUSE

Few laws pertaining to the Company have been as much discussed, by contemporaries and by historians, as section forty-three of the Charter Act of 1813:

> [I]t shall be lawful for the Governor-General in Council to direct, that, out of any surplus which may remain of the rents, revenues, and profits arising from … territorial acquisitions … a sum of not less than one lack of rupees in each year, shall be set apart and applied to the revival and improvement of literature and the encouragement of the learned natives of India, and for the introduction and promotion of a knowledge of the sciences among the inhabitants of the British territories in India.[6]

Since Victorian times, histories of Indian education have often begun with the enactment by parliament of this "education clause." Despite its later appellation, however, the section was meant less to institute a new system for spreading learning than to invigorate an old one for supporting the learned. What was initially significant about the clause was that it linked the Company's patronage of scholars to its collection of land revenue. Its meaning shifted to center on Indian education only in the course of a years-long debate on the character and responsibilities of the Company.

To trace the original meaning of section forty-three requires briefly reconstructing the life and mind of its author. The life is more easily reconstructed, for the author was the prominent yet reticent Robert Percy "Bobus" Smith. Smith distinguished himself as a Latinist at Eton and Cambridge and, before entering parliament,

---

[6] 53 Geo. III, c. 155, s. 43.

served as the Company's advocate-general of Bengal. In that role, he would have interacted with maulvis and pandits. He is also known to have befriended several fellow British scholar-officials. John Leyden came out on the same ship in 1803 and would recall enjoying "the society of the excellent R. Smith, whose profound comprehensive & versatile mind with equal ease fathomed the Abysses, unravelled the subtilties & amused itself with the playthings of literature & science."[7] Sir James Mackintosh, after taking up a legal appointment in Bombay, told a common friend that "I have heard a great deal of Bobus. His fame is greater than that of any pundit since the time of M[a]nu."[8] Smith was a consummate literary socialite. He wrote for the *Microcosm* at Eton, founded the King of Clubs in London, and frequented the Asiatic Society in Calcutta. After returning to Europe in 1811, he consorted with Madame de Staël, who remarked that "due to his personality he comes in contact with everyone."[9] In limited circles, Smith was celebrated as "a well of old poetry and ingenious philosophy."[10] A young Thomas Babington Macaulay, meeting Smith in 1833, pronounced him "a great authority on Indian matters."[11] And yet Smith seems to have confined his written scholarship to legal reports. He left little correspondence. Nor, despite early political ambitions, did he cut much of a figure in parliament.[12] His surviving letters reveal an enthusiasm for Wellesley's imperial vision, tempered slightly by a classicist's

---

[7] Leyden to William Erskine, 15 Sept. 1804, NLS, MS 3383, 147r.

[8] Mackintosh to Richard Sharp, 29 Jun. 1804, cited in Mackintosh, *Memoirs of the Life of the Right Honourable Sir James Mackintosh*, ed. Robert James Mackintosh, 2 vols. (London, 1835), vol. I, p. 208.

[9] Germaine de Staël to Lord and Lady Lansdowne, 24 Jan. 1816, in de Staël, *Correspondance Générale*, 9 vols. (Paris, 1960–2017), vol. IX, p. 390.

[10] Baron Holland to Thomas Grenville, 6 Sept. 1832, Centre for Buckinghamshire Studies, D 56/7/25.

[11] Macaulay to Hannah Macaulay, 21 Dec. 1833, in Macaulay, *The Letters of Thomas Babington Macaulay*, ed. Thomas Pinney, 6 vols. (Cambridge, 1974–81), vol. II, p. 365.

[12] Thomas de Quincey, "Dr. Parr and His Contemporaries" (1831), in de Quincey, *The Works of Thomas de Quincey*, ed. Frederick Burnwick, 21 vols. (London, 2000), vol. VIII, pp. 7–9; M. H. Port and R. G. Thorne, "Smith, Robert Percy (1770–1845)," in Thorne, ed., *The House of Commons 1790–1820*, 5 vols. (London, 1986), vol. V, pp. 201–3.

wariness of luxury and overextension.[13] He praised Lord Minto, who
arrived in 1807, as "a good quiet sensible Governor G[enera]l."[14] The
two were evidently friends.[15]

Smith's friendship with Minto underpins one plausible theory
of the origins and meaning of section forty-three. In a minute of 1811,
Minto proposed to form a few Hindu and Islamic seminaries, and
to reform the Benares Sanskrit College and the Calcutta Madrasa.
What was most striking about the minute was its claim that, since
a widespread "want of ... education" hindered efforts toward "better
government," the Company should promote "the more general diffusion of knowledge among the great body of the people."[16] These
lines held out the prospect of a new policy of mass education, as
distinct from scholarly patronage. And yet, the rest of the minute
did not match up to this radical prospect. As a later educationalist
would complain, "nothing whatsoever ... is proposed, or even alluded
to, as regards 'the great body of the people' .... [N]o classes whatever of the community are provided for, but the learned and more
respectable classes."[17] A colleague would agree: Minto intended to
encourage those "natives of India ... who are already learned."[18] Both
readers viewed the minute through the prism of later debates, yet it is
hard to disagree with their conclusion. There was nothing very new
about the measures Minto advocated: Previous governors-general
had formed and reformed colleges. They too had mused about influ-
encing Indian society at large but had focused on conciliating elites.

---

[13] Smith to James Mackintosh, 2 Aug. 1804, BL, Add. MS 78764, ff. 1v–2r; Smith to
Baron Holland, 18 Aug. 1805 and 22 Sept. 1807, BL, Add. MS 51801, ff. 50r–v, 55r. For
this wariness, see also Robert Percy Smith, *Early Writings of Robert Percy Smith*, ed.
R. V. S. (Chiswick, 1850), pp. 48–52.

[14] Smith to James Mackintosh, 14 Feb. 1808, BL, Add. MS 78764, f. 8v.

[15] Earl of Minto to family, Apr. 1808, in Minto, *Lord Minto in India: Life and Letters of
Gilbert Elliot, First Earl of Minto, from 1807 to 1814*, ed. Countess of Minto (London,
1880), p. 88.

[16] Governor-General in Council, Minute (6 Mar. 1811), in PP (1831–2), vol. 735-I, p. 484.

[17] [Alexander Duff], "The Early or Exclusively Oriental Period of Government Education
in Bengal," *Calcutta Review* 3 (1845), p. 260 [emphasis removed].

[18] William Adam, *Adam's Reports on Vernacular Education in Bengal and Behar,
Submitted to Government in 1835, 1836 and 1838*, ed. J. Long (Calcutta, 1868), p. 310.

If indeed Minto's minute provided the basis for section forty-three, then that basis consisted of little more than a reframing of the Company's existing policy.

Section forty-three may have had other origins. According to the chairman of the directors, Robert Thornton, parliament, presumably including Smith, was unaware of Minto's minute.[19] The timing makes it possible that Thornton was mistaken.[20] Another possibility, however, is that section forty-three resembles Minto's minute because both derived from a memorandum of 1806. Penned by the scholar-official Henry Thomas Colebrooke and addressed to the previous governor-general, Sir George Barlow, this memorandum at some point ended up in Minto's papers. Its call for "publick instruction" was akin to Minto's call for the "general diffusion of knowledge." And it envisioned the formation or reformation of institutions in the same places. Still, these institutions – at Barelli, Jaunpur, Nadia, and Tirhut – would not be colleges but merely libraries, and would be meant for the use of the same discrete constituencies. Colebrooke's plan of 1806, therefore, had even less to do with popular education than Minto's plan of 1811. It is hard to determine the exact relationship among the three documents. Colebrooke was appointed to Minto's council and signed the minute, so it is likely that he had a hand in its composition. He was on friendly terms with Smith, so it is also likely that he exchanged ideas with him throughout the period when both were in Calcutta. In at least one way, however, the memorandum seems directly connected to section forty-three: Colebrooke cited as the cost of his plan the identical sum of one lakh of rupees. For that matter, he presented the support of knowledge as a duty imposed by the "domination" of territory.[21]

---

[19] Robert Thornton to Marquess of Hastings, 5 Sept. 1813, Mount Stuart, HA/9/28.

[20] See Michael Hancher, "Reading and Writing the Law: Macaulay in India," in Michael Freeman and Fiona Smith, eds., *Law and Language: Current Legal Issues* (Oxford, 2013), pp. 195–6.

[21] [Henry Thomas Colebrooke], "Remarks Delivered to Sir G. Barlow in 1806," NLS, MS 11726, ff. 1r–7v. Colebrooke's authorship of the memorandum can be gleaned from a reference to "the encouragement lately given by myself to a Sanscrit Printing Press."

This was something that Wellesley – but not Minto – had done, and that Smith would do in his remarks proposing section forty-three.

Smith's remarks before parliament yoked the Company's old idea of conciliation to its increasingly conspicuous territorial sovereignty. Still, their ambiguity, which endured in the language of the Charter Act, allowed for multiple readings. Several reports of the session of the Commons on 2 July 1813 noticed the speech. One summarized it thus: "Mr. R. Smith read certain clauses, the effect of which was to apply part of any surplus to the establishment of colleges, schools, and lectures, in India, to promote the sciences, and revival of oriental literature, and also to afford marks of honour and distinction on the natives."[22] A second report differed slightly. In this version, Smith proposed "to lay aside a modicum for founding schools for the literature of the natives, wherein they should be themselves the teachers; and for communicating the sciences to them through the medium of Europeans."[23] A third report included further details, one of which was especially significant: The outlay "would be but just," it quoted Smith as saying, "as we extracted from this people 17 millions yearly."[24] None of the reports suggested that Smith had meant to advance a new policy of education. Absent was any reference even to "public instruction" or the "diffusion of knowledge." They suggested instead that he sought to patronize Indian learned elites and European scholar-officials. These, after all, were the likeliest beneficiaries of the "modicum" to be spent and of the "marks of honour" to be conferred. The reports revealed something else: that Smith had emphasized that the sum should be drawn from the Company's land revenue and that he saw the measure as fulfilling a duty imposed by its extraction of such

Colebrooke helped set up such a press in Calcutta in 1806. Ibid., f. 3v. For details on the press, see Colebrooke to father, 9 Jun. 1806, in Colebrooke, *Life*, p. 227; David Kopf, *British Orientalism and the Bengal Renaissance: The Dynamics of Indian Modernization, 1773–1835* (Berkeley, 1969), p. 118.

[22] Smith, Speech in HC Deb (2 Jul. 1813), *Morning Post* (3 Jul. 1813), p. [3].

[23] Smith, Speech in HC Deb (2 Jul. 1813), vol. XXVI, cols. 1098–9 [emphasis removed].

[24] Smith, Speech in HC Deb (2 Jul. 1813), *Morning Chronicle* (3 Jul. 1813), p. [2].

revenue in the first place. His clarity on this point contrasted with the ambiguity of many of his comments and of the resulting statutory language. The Charter Act was passed on 21 July. Thorny decisions remained about how to spend the annual lakh of rupees.

For help with these decisions, the Board of Control turned to the librarian and resident orientalist of East India House, Charles Wilkins. Wilkins returned a detailed memorandum many of whose suggestions were novel but whose spirit was in keeping with the idea of conciliation. His main suggestion was to conduct a survey of all of the "Pandits, or learned men ... who, of course, are mostly Brahmans," and to note which of them "appear to be the most distinguished, and to have the greatest influence over the rest." By discovering which individuals were "of the highest Cast and literary rank," the Company would discover too which "ought, in good policy, to be the chief objects of encouragement." Wilkins' remarks were premised on the notion that "the Hindu Hierarchy" safeguarded India's political stability. Thus, he warned that "the clause in question [section forty-three] cannot be acted upon with too much circumspection." In seeking to effect the "improvement" and "introduction" of knowledge, the Company must take care to conciliate, and not to demean, the leading pandits. Rather than subject them to the "subordination and discipline" of colleges, the Company should place them in charge of existing seats of learning. It should also bring them into its scientific establishments and encourage scholar-officials to cooperate with them. There was no necessary contradiction between the "ancient" knowledge of Indians and the "modern" knowledge of Europeans. "A reciprocal communication of knowledge" was possible and productive of political benefits. For Wilkins, however, it could be so only if the Company upheld the Indian social order. To "interfere with the education of the natives" and risk disturbing that order was "politically" dangerous.[25]

So afraid was Wilkins of this prospect that in the first draft of his memorandum he had expressed a wish that "'the clause in the act

---

[25] Wilkins to [John Sullivan], 25 Aug. 1813, BL, Add. MS 29234, ff. 204r–211v, 243r–v.

had not been moved.'"[26] As it happened, this was exactly the view of his old friend and patron Warren Hastings. That the board next consulted the former governor-general reflected both his scholarly reputation and his political rehabilitation. It also reflected the impression he had made recently in parliament and the press with his testimony during the charter negotiations. For one old schoolmate, it was as if "the world has just found out that Mr. Hastings, now 84, is a great man."[27] His testimony had led backward in time, opposing the expansionism of Wellesley along with the inroads of Evangelicals and free merchants.[28] Once a critic of the Company state, Hastings, in retirement, had become one of its defenders (and pensioners). On questions of knowledge, therefore, he enjoined the board and directors to follow the example of his administration. He reminded them that in the city of Benares, whose pandits were especially renowned, they possessed a "powerful instrument of conciliation." Yet ultimately, Hastings' concern not to disrupt India's social order ran even deeper than that of his friend. Regarding section forty-three he was forced to conclude that "no specific plan can be devised for its operation." He continued, "If the Braminical establishment has any wants, let the professors of it represent them. Let them be even invited to represent them."[29] This argument did not preclude engaging with pandits; it did insist that such engagement occur on their terms. Hastings made it clear that he opposed any unsolicited interference in Indian education.

The directors' dispatch on the subject of section forty-three, after being lightly revised by the board, was communicated in June 1814.[30] It did little more than weave together the judgments of

---

[26] John Sullivan to Warren Hastings, 10 Oct. 1813, BL, Add. MS 29188, f. 276v.

[27] William Vincent to William Francklin, 10 Jul. 1813, National Library of India, R 19/14.

[28] See Hastings, Speech in HC Deb (30 Mar. 1813), vol. XXV, cols. 415–29; Hastings, Speech in HL Deb (5 Apr. 1813), vol. XXV, cols. 553–63.

[29] Warren Hastings, "My Observations on Mr. Wilkins' Plan" (7 Oct. 1813), BL, Add. MS 29234, ff. 212r–215v.

[30] For the original draft and modifications, see Draft Paragraphs to Bengal (1 Jun. 1814), BL, IOR F/3/31, pp. 25–43.

Wilkins and Hastings. Some of its advice was positive. It repeated their call to award "natives of caste and of reputation" with honors and "pecuniary assistance." It pointed out that attentions to the pandits of Benares might prove a "powerful instrument of ... conciliation." It endorsed the forging of "links of communication" between Indian learned elites and European scholar-officials. Nevertheless, its overall tendency was negative. It concurred that the objects of section forty-three could not "be attained through the medium of public colleges." And it echoed Hastings' refusal "to devise any specific plan" for the clause's implementation. Finally, in a sign of the directors' wariness toward scholar-officials (discussed later in this chapter), it ordered the new governor-general, Lord Moira, not to "adopt any arrangement" without authorization. With its limp proposal to give "effect in the course of time to the liberal intentions of the Legislature," the directors' dispatch fell dead from the East Indiaman that carried it.[31] Smith had linked the idea of conciliation to large-scale territorial sovereignty. But the directors, like their two informants, resisted this new affiliation.

The dispatch came closest to reckoning with the Company's altered situation in a few paragraphs on the subject of "village teachers." Paraphrasing Wilkins and Hastings, it described these teachers as "public servants" the support of whom had long been a "distinguished feature of internal polity." It instructed Moira to investigate their present state and wants and to guarantee "their just rights and immunities."[32] Doing so was in keeping with the policy of conciliating elites, but it also presented a chance to reach beyond this constituency. In the understanding of the directors, informed by Wilkins and Hastings, village teachers were elites who mixed with commoners and commanded their respect. Integrating them into the Company's machinery might extend its grasp downwards from the upper classes and inwards from the coastal presidencies. And this

---

[31] Extract Public Despatch to Bengal (3 Jun. 1814), in *GIED*, pp. 94–6.
[32] Ibid, pp. 95–6.

might be just the beginning. Hastings wrote that his comments on village teachers "may be repeated of the village Bramins officiating in ... religious worship."[33] Wilkins offered that "Though I would not interfere with the religion of the natives, I see no objection why Government should not ... exercise a controul over its ministers." What both men imagined was an alliance between the Company and India's "national clergy" analogous to that which had shaped the development of European states.[34] This line of thought was pregnant with radical implications, including not just curbing the spread of Christianity but also enshrining Hinduism as the official faith. Neither Hastings nor Wilkins pursued these implications. Despite pushing at the boundaries of conciliation, they advanced no new idea to replace it. Meanwhile, the directors seem not to have recurred to the subject of village teachers; Moira proposed merely to offer them little moral manuals.[35]

Moira's response to section forty-three was shaped by a number of sources in addition to the directors' dispatch. He received advice on the subject from at least a half-dozen Europeans based in Calcutta alone. Some of these individuals, mainly officials, reprised the plans of Colebrooke and Minto to establish a few elite institutions; others, mainly missionaries and their supporters, called for a larger number of popular schools.[36] Noncommittal as to these various schemes, Moira had greater reason to listen to the powerful director Charles Grant. In correspondence, Grant urged him to establish schools and to distribute tracts that would improve "the moral & intellectual condition of our Indian Subjects."[37] Grant's rationale was partly religious.

---

[33] Hastings, "My Observations," f. 212v.

[34] Wilkins to [Sullivan], 25 Aug. 1813, f. 243r.

[35] Lord Moira, Minute (2 Oct. 1815), in H. Sharp, ed., *Selections from Educational Records*, Part I: *1781–1839* (Calcutta, 1920), pp. 24–5.

[36] J. Sargent, *The Life of the Rev. T. T. Thomason* (London, 1833), pp. 222–5; Kopf, *British Orientalism*, pp. 148–51; M. A. Laird, *Missionaries and Education in Bengal 1793–1837* (Oxford, 1972), pp. 68–9.

[37] Grant to Marquess of Hastings, 11 Sept. 1819, Mount Stuart, HA/9/47. Moira was created Marquess of Hastings in 1816 but will be referred to as Moira throughout this discussion to avoid confusion with Warren Hastings (no relation).

He had added similar language to the Charter Act as part of a clause allowing proselytization in the Company's territories.[38] His recently reprinted *Observations on the State of Society* (1792) depicted education as the surest route to Christianization in India.[39] Nonetheless, Grant was a complex figure. Religious considerations mingled with other kinds in the thought of the Company man. And while he disapproved of further conquests, he insisted that those that had already been made imparted certain responsibilities.[40] In one letter to Moira, he described the Company's "acquisition of territorial dominion" as a watershed that created imperatives "of preservation & of progressive refinement." It was in keeping with these imperatives that he urged Moira to establish schools and distribute moral treatises, for "as the Minds of that people [Indians] are enlarg'd by greater knowledge in things compatible with their superstition, they may be expected to become more readily susceptible of encreas'd influence from our superior lights & principles."[41] This was an Evangelical and providential outlook, but it was also a political one. The "preservation" to which Grant alluded was that of the Company state.

Preservation was likewise a recurrent theme in the letters addressed to Moira by Hastings. Even the ostensibly subtle innovations proposed by Grant, however, alarmed the former governor-general. Upon Moira's appointment in 1812, he contacted Hastings, and promptly received congratulations and a dinner invitation.[42] At the start of the ensuing correspondence, Hastings expressed an uneasiness about the changes that had occurred since his own administration: "in the system of government ... in its foreign policy and relations, its vast extension of territory, its regulations of law, finance, and even rights of property .... I fear I shall have to add commercial

---

[38] Carson, *The East India Company and Religion*, pp. 37, 147.

[39] Charles Grant, *Observations on the State of Society among the Asiatic Subjects of Great-Britain* ["written chiefly in the year 1792"] (London, 1797).

[40] Ainslie Thomas Embree, *Charles Grant and British Rule in India* (London, 1962).

[41] Grant to Marquess of Hastings, Apr. 1817, Mount Stuart, HA/9/35.

[42] Moira to Hastings, 11 Nov. 1812, BL, Add. MS 39871, ff. 118r–122r; Hastings to Charles Hastings, 13 Nov. 1812, Huntington Library, HA 6194.

competitions."[43] As his contemporary poems attest, Hastings saw the age as one of imperial decline rather than triumph.[44] He enjoined Moira to revert to the time-honored usages, policies, and institutions of the Company state. He counseled him to seek the good opinion of the directors and of the British public. He urged him to communicate with Indians and to observe "their relative ranks in society." Finally, mirroring his and Wilkins' remarks to the board, he exhorted Moira not to disturb the social order by propagating Christianity.[45] Cultivating British and Indian political classes and negotiating with them – these were the hallmarks of Hastings' system of conciliation. Having once devised this system out of necessity, he now embraced it. As ever, it centered on scholarly patronage.

Hastings recommended to Moira several scholarly ventures. One was an intellectual commerce with Bhutan and Tibet. Though the Qing had barred Europeans from these places, Hastings believed that high-caste, well-connected Gosains might retrace the steps of his envoys. Any diplomatic gains would be modest. Yet, Hastings reasoned, "It opens a new, and almost untried field of knowledge ... and who can set bounds to its discoveries?"[46] Citing similar reasons, he encouraged Moira to commission a history of the neighboring kingdom of Nepal. Such a work, Hastings claimed, would appeal to the British "public: a powerful body ... and no inefficient dispensers of fame." It ought to focus on commerce, which according to him was "the most useful of all subjects" and yet one lately neglected by scholar-officials.[47] If Hastings thus adhered to his idea of conciliation, then he nonetheless made several concessions to the times. In the belief that Muslim elites "have now scarcely any existence," he focused on Hindu ones and stressed the need to insulate

---

[43] Hastings to Moira, 12 Nov. 1812, Mount Stuart, HA/10.
[44] Stuart Gillespie, "Warren Hastings as a Translator of Latin Poetry," *Translation and Literature* 26 (2017), pp. 200–202.
[45] Hastings to Moira, 2 Dec. 1812, Mount Stuart, HA/12/19.
[46] Hastings to Moira, 24 Dec. 1812, ibid.
[47] Hastings to Marquess of Hastings, 3 Jan. 1817, Mount Stuart, HA/9/35.

and accommodate them.[48] He reiterated his verdict on Wilkins' plan: The Company should "abstain from all interference ... but such as they [pandits] themselves shall solicit."[49] His concern was that the Company had strayed too far from its old constitution. Restoring his system of conciliation would help to bring it back within bounds.

Hastings and Grant espoused two different ideas about knowledge, between which Moira at first vacillated. The choice was between conciliating political classes through scholarly patronage and shaping Indian society through education. In an early response to Hastings, Moira wrote that many of the Company's problems stemmed "from the discarding that tone of conciliation ... with which you tempered ... your measures."[50] He delayed responding to the directors' dispatch until after an extensive tour of northern India in 1814–15. Among the stops on Moira's itinerary was Benares, the focus of so much interest among the various commentators on section forty-three. Expectations duly heightened, he was "particularly curious to assure myself of the state of learning" at the Company's Sanskrit college.[51] In the event he was disappointed. He came away convinced by what he had seen and heard that "the instruction communicated at this college was wretchedly superficial." Still, in a line that would have pleased Hastings, Moira hoped that with the "co-operation of some of the principal natives," he could render the college "effective for its professed ends."[52]

This thinking would change dramatically. In a dispatch of the following year, Moira described "the existing native colleges" as lacking "any embers capable of being fanned into life." Thus, he argued, the funds authorized by parliament should be spent instead on founding and maintaining experimental schools. Underpinning this turn from patronizing scholars to providing education was a sense that the

---

[48] Hastings, Speech in HL Deb (5 Apr. 1813), col. 560.

[49] Hastings to Moira, 14 Sept. 1814, Mount Stuart, HA/9/28.

[50] Moira to Hastings, 3 Feb. 1814, BL, Add. MS 29189, f. 127v.

[51] Moira, Minute (2 Oct. 1815), p. 27.

[52] Marquess of Hastings, *The Private Journal of the Marquess of Hastings*, ed. Marchioness of Hastings, 2 vols. (London, 1858), vol. I, p. 128.

Company had reached a climacteric. Its "extensions of territory" and success in "securing the new possessions" now warranted a bolder mission: to "cultivate" the "intellect" of an "immense population." There were limits to Moira's proposed "revolution." He reasoned that it was "most likely to succeed" with the cooperation of "natives of birth and education." And he left as a matter for future deliberation "the nature as well as the extent" of the Company's "interference" in Indian society. Nonetheless, he proposed that the Company might diffuse knowledge "to places and persons now out of its reach."[53] Endorsing conciliation and education, but with the latter ultimately in view, Moira supplied a coda to the first career of section forty-three and a preview of the second.

Moira did little in the following years to effect his "revolution," leaving the founding of schools to individuals and associations. Not only was he distracted by wars with the Gurkhas, Pindaris, and Marathas, but he was delayed by the failure of the requisite revenue surplus to materialize.[54] One association that sprang up in the meantime was the Calcutta School Book Society (CSBS), which counted officials, missionaries, and Indian scholars as its members. The CSBS engaged Moira as its sponsor and, in its first proceedings, asked him and other leaders to forgo the "patronage of learning" for "the general march of Mind."[55] Moira accepted this proposition. Already, he had announced that any funds granted under section forty-three must be spent not on "literary" works but on Indian education.[56] Besides the CSBS, he contributed to a school founded by his wife in Barrackpore and to similar ventures in Bengal and Rajputana. These actions, though small and unofficial, drew forth from the governor-general grand musings on the basis of Company rule in India. "How is it,"

---

[53] Moira, Minute (2 Oct. 1815), pp. 25–9.

[54] On the indebtedness of the Company's territorial account to its commercial one throughout this period, see C. H. Philips, *The East India Company, 1784–1834*, 2nd edn (Manchester, 1961), p. 303.

[55] "Proceedings Prior to the Final Establishment of the Society, &c." (1817), in *The Second Report of the Calcutta School Book Society's Proceedings* (Calcutta, 1819), p. 68.

[56] Extract Bombay Public Consultations, 8 May 1816, BL, IOR F/4/523/12491, p. 19.

Moira queried, "that we maintain sovereignty over this immense mass?" His answer was "equity." But equity first required education. Through education, he averred, the lower classes would learn to appreciate their rights, and the upper classes would give up some of their privileges.[57] These changes might be in the ultimate interests of Christianity; they were certainly in the immediate interests of the government. In 1817, Moira described the "expansion of intellect" as good for the state and urged young officials to promote "the education of a rising generation."[58] Moira himself, however, was to play even less of a role in this project in the following years. The second half of his decade in office was marred by illness, debts, and quarrels with the home authorities.[59] Moira was the first British statesman to call for "public education" in India.[60] But he conceded that his efforts had been "nothing" next to those of others.[61]

SCHOLAR-OFFICIALS AND SCHOLARLY INSTITUTIONS IN INDIA

The story of the changing meaning of section forty-three captures something of the Company's changing ideas about knowledge in the early nineteenth century. And yet education was not the only politico-intellectual avenue opened by the growth of the Company's dominions. In another ramification, scholar-officials in India now turned their efforts to extending and securing the control of the state. This trend was visible across a growing range of scholarly institutions, and in projects to digest reams of information on the Company's territories. The designs of scholar-officials, however, had little impact on the higher reaches of discourse or policy. Unwilling to

[57] Marquess of Hastings, *Private Journal*, vol. II, pp. 149–50, 156–9, 346–7.
[58] Marquess of Hastings, Speech (30 Jun. 1817), in Thomas Roebuck, *Annals of the College of Fort William* (Calcutta, 1819), pp. 542–3.
[59] Richard John Bingle, "The Decline of the Marquess of Hastings," in Donovan Williams and E. Daniel Potts, eds., *Essays in Indian History in Honour of Cuthbert Collin Davies* (New York, 1973).
[60] Moira, Minute (2 Oct. 1815), p. 24.
[61] Marquess of Hastings, *Summary of the Administration of the Indian Government, from October 1813, to January 1823* (London, 1824), p. 33.

embrace these officials' expansionist views, the directors withheld their patronage and approbation.

The foremost site in India for the fusion of intellectual and territorial ambitions remained the College of Fort William. Its reduction notwithstanding, the college, and, in particular, its disputations, continued to evoke something of the vision of its founder, Wellesley. For that matter, it still employed European professors in addition to scores of Indian munshis and pandits. It maintained a sizeable library with books in many languages and a printing press with founts of English and various "Oriental" types. Most importantly, the college continued to dispense considerable literary patronage. In an artful bit of bookkeeping meant to evade the directors' cuts, Wellesley had set up a separate fund for this purpose in 1805.[62] In the next decade and a half, the college council subsidized more than one hundred publications.[63] It thus helped to sustain the Serampore Mission Press and the Asiatic Society. From 1812, the College of Fort St. George performed a similar range of functions in Madras. Apart from training civil servants, it too employed European and Indian scholars, published and patronized works, and sponsored private initiatives.[64] The effect of both colleges was centripetal as well as centrifugal: attracting scholars and deploying them to conduct research. One official spoke for many in describing the college as bound up with the "interests ... of the government of this extensive and populous territory."[65]

Other institutions fostered the same perspective. The Calcutta Botanic Garden, according to its manager, Nathaniel Wallich, had a "sphere of ... operations" to match that of the Company's government. Its specimens, he wrote in 1819, "have derived from every variety of soil and climate ... within our Indian possessions," and had been cultivated and disseminated to "a corresponding

[62] Rosane Rocher and Ludo Rocher, *The Making of Western Indology: Henry Thomas Colebrooke and the East India Company* (Abingdon, UK, 2012), pp. 65–6.
[63] Roebuck, *Annals*, appendix, pp. 21–45.
[64] Thomas R. Trautmann, *Languages and Nations: The Dravidian Proof in Colonial Madras* (Berkeley, 2006), ch. 4.
[65] George Hewett, Speech (7 Aug. 1811), in Roebuck, *Annals*, p. 275.

degree."[66] As microcosms of the territorial state, the Company's botanic gardens – in Bangalore and Saharanpur as well as Calcutta – brought its concerns within the scope of individual intellectual exertion. The same was true of the museum founded in 1802 by the governor of Madras, Lord Clive, and entrusted to the superintendence of the botanist and naturalist Benjamin Heyne. Clive, a disciple of Wellesley, not only approved Heyne's plan to exhibit "the natural Productions and Curiosities of this Country." He also ordered him to investigate thirty-six subjects, ranging from its climate to the customs of its inhabitants.[67] Heyne's commission, evidently, was to help to secure the Company's control of the vast tracts captured from the late Tipu Sultan. Versions of this rationale attached to additional scientific institutions. The astronomical observatories of Bombay and Madras came to be justified as emblems of territorial power.[68] After all, apart from defining local time and place and aiding navigation, they now facilitated ambitious terrestrial surveys.

For many scholar-officials, an appointment to one of the new surveys offered the best chance to further the twin causes of science and the state. The Mysore survey begun in 1799, in particular, was a wide-ranging enterprise, intellectually as well as geographically. The survey's initial sponsor, Wellesley, decreed that it "should not be confined to mere military or Geographical information." Instead, it should comprehend every kind of knowledge useful for "establishing and conducting our government."[69] The breadth of this enterprise explains why Heyne, John Leyden, and Colin Mackenzie – men of differing talents – all saw in it tantalizing possibilities. In 1815, Mackenzie was appointed the first "Surveyor-General of India." By this time, the Company's surveys had crisscrossed the peninsula and

---

[66] NAI, Bengal Public Proceedings (7 Jan. 1820), no. 55.

[67] Extract Madras Public Consultations (2 Apr. and 18 Jun. 1802), BL, IOR F/4/152/2601, pp. 3–9, 11–22.

[68] See Simon Schaffer, "The Bombay Case: Astronomers, Instrument Makers and the East India Company," *Journal for the History of Astronomy* 43 (2012), p. 158.

[69] Marquess Wellesley, Minute (4 Sept. 1799), cited in R. H. Phillimore, *Historical Records of the Survey of India*, 5 vols. (Dehra Dun, 1945–68), vol. II, p. 91.

reached as far north as the Himalayas and the Sutlej. In 1818, the same year that the Company became "paramount" in India, Moira acknowledged that they had gone hand in hand with "the consolidation of our Empire."[70] For that matter, dedicated surveys did not offer the only opportunities for surveying. The Company's military and diplomatic missions did so as well. The embassies of John Malcolm to Persia and of Mountstuart Elphinstone to Peshawar furnished, in equal measure, arguments for the integration of British India and materials for the exploration of neighboring lands.[71]

Scholar-officials used not only institutions but also grand projects to forward their politico-intellectual agenda. Most ambitiously, they sought to digest a vast array of information on the Company's lands and subjects. In 1805, James Mackintosh informed Wellesley of plans for a work entitled "The History and Present State of the British Dominions in India." Not only would this work justify "our national policy in the East," but it would yield "new conclusions of political science" and "rules for the conduct of statesmen." It was to be based on information gleaned from Company officials and their networks throughout India. Thus, Mackintosh asked Wellesley to order "all the civil and military servants, to transmit answers ... to such ... queries as I should send." "By this means," he explained, "I might hope to accumulate valuable materials of various sorts, especially statistical, which ... would furnish the means of applying principles of political economy to the condition of this country."[72] Mackintosh's letter from Bombay reached Wellesley only after he had resigned, but he recommended the scheme to his successor, Lord Cornwallis, and

---

[70] Marquess of Hastings, Minute (6 Jan. 1818), cited in ibid., vol. III, p. 302.

[71] Ibid., vol. II, pp. 65–7, 173–6; Jack Harrington, *Sir John Malcolm and the Creation of British India* (Basingstoke, 2010), pp. 83–94; Shah Mahmoud Hanifi, ed., *Mountstuart Elphinstone in South Asia: Pioneer of British Colonial Rule* (London, 2019), chs. 1–5 passim.

[72] Mackintosh to Wellesley, 16 Jul. 1805, in Robert Rouiere Pearce, *Memoirs and Correspondence of the Most Noble Richard Marquess Wellesley*, 3 vols. (London, 1846–7), vol. II, pp. 380–83.

promised to take it up with the directors.[73] The latter approach bore fruit in a dispatch of 1806 instructing officials to cooperate fully with Mackintosh's requests.[74] In the meantime, "desirous to make a trial" of his method, Mackintosh had drawn up a narrower *Plan of a Comparative Vocabulary of Indian Languages* (1806).[75]

It was at this point that Mackintosh's exertions began to attract the interest of other scholar-officials. After Minto referred the narrower plan to the council of the College of Fort William, one member, Henry Thomas Colebrooke, offered to enlarge it into "a very grand undertaking."[76] Whereas Mackintosh had proposed to collect specimens of Indian languages, Colebrooke proposed to compile entire vocabularies.[77] Meanwhile, Leyden had proposed something even grander: a comparative analysis of a plethora of Eastern languages.[78] Although the council chose Colebrooke's plan over Mackintosh's, this put an end neither to Leyden's plan nor to others that emerged in the following years. Not all of the scholar-officials who framed these projects were directly inspired by Mackintosh, but all shared similar political and intellectual aims. In Serampore and Calcutta, William Carey was starting work on "A Universal Dictionary of the Oriental Languages Derived from Sanskrit."[79] In the same environs, Francis Irvine was drawing up "a physical survey and philosophical statement of the characters of the tribes of this vast country."[80] In Bombay and Madras, respectively, William Erskine and Francis Whyte Ellis

---

[73] Wellesley to Mackintosh, 20 Nov. 1805, BL, Add. MS 78765, ff. 52r–53v.

[74] Extract Public Despatch to Bengal (9 Apr. 1806), NLS, MS 11726, ff. 30r-v.

[75] Mackintosh to Lord Minto, 31 Jul. 1807, ibid., f. 11v.

[76] Colebrooke to father, 14 Sept. 1807, in Colebrooke, *Life*, pp. 228–9.

[77] Colebrooke, Minute (15 Aug. 1807), NLS, MS 11726, ff. 32v–34v.

[78] Leyden to Barlow, 2 Jan. 1807, BL, Add. MS 26566, ff. 3r–4v.

[79] George Smith, *The Life of William Carey, D.D.*, 2nd edn (London, 1887), p. 221; M. Siddiq Khan, "William Carey and the Serampore Books (1800–1834)," *Libri* 11 (1961), pp. 235–6. Carey was more interested in religion than empire but saw the spread of the latter as conducive to that of the former.

[80] Mackintosh to John Whishaw, 13 Aug. 1811, in Whishaw, *The "Pope" of Holland House: Selections from the Correspondence of John Whishaw and His Friends, 1813–1840*, ed. Lady Seymour (London, 1906), p. 287.

were embarking on great studies of Indian languages and history.[81] And, following his Mysore survey, Mackenzie was arranging sundry collections for his intended magnum opus: "a Statistical & Historical View" of the "Geography of India."[82] These scholar-officials all hitched their fortunes to "the acquisition of British India," as Leyden described it, and to "the necessity of regulating accurately its interior and exterior relations."[83] Their argument was the one gaining ground at the Company's scholarly institutions: Assimilating new territories politically required assimilating them intellectually.

As sound as this argument may have been, it did not appeal to the directors, who sought to curtail the new or new-modeled institutions and projects. This policy was in evidence at the College of Fort William, whose functions and budget they continued to trim. By 1820, a professoriate once numbering over one dozen had been whittled down to just three.[84] Some professors were dismissed; others left in frustration, including in short succession two lecturers of natural philosophy.[85] Even those who stayed, meanwhile, frequently had reason to feel unappreciated. In 1811, the directors again condemned the college's publications as expensive, ill-executed, and unworthy of patronage.[86] Matthew Lumsden, the author of one of the offending works, protested at these remarks: "The utility of the College has never yet been fully acknowledged by the authorities at home .... [I]t can flourish only by means of their decided

[81] P. Hardy, introduction to William Erskine, *A History of India under the Two First Sovereigns of the House of Taimur, Baber and Humayun* (1854), repr. edn, 2 vols. (Karachi, 1974); Jane Rendall, "Scottish Orientalism: From Robertson to James Mill," *Historical Journal* 25 (1982), p. 62; Trautmann, *Languages and Nations*, pp. 83–4, 108–15.

[82] Mackenzie to C. M. Ricketts, 15 Jun. 1815, Mount Stuart, HA/9/32.

[83] John Leyden, "Plan for Investigating the Languages, Literature, Antiquities, & History of the Dekkan," BL, Add. MS 26600, f. 109v.

[84] Public Despatch to Bengal (28 Jun. 1820), BL, IOR E/4/699, pp. 814–16.

[85] David Hare to James Dinwiddie, 16 Jan. 1810, Dalhousie University Archives, Dinwiddie Fonds A51; William Jardine Proudfoot, *Biographical Memoir of James Dinwiddie, LL.D.* (Liverpool, 1868), pp. 119–21.

[86] Extract Public Despatch to Bengal (10 Jul. 1811), BL, IOR F/4/503/12029, pp. 1–2.

approbation and support."[87] A resulting letter from the college council to the directors, seeking their "assurance" on this point, proved unavailing.[88] In 1815, they ordered that the college's literary fund be reduced and its patronage confined to "works of real utility."[89] "Without exception," according to a later memorandum, the publications of the college had put their authors in debt.[90] Finances at the College of Fort St. George were even more constrained.[91]

The directors were no better disposed toward the Company's scientific establishments. The Calcutta Botanic Garden they merely tolerated. They repeatedly sought to limit its activities to ones with commercial value; its manager Wallich endured because he "knew how to appeal to the Company's material interests."[92] In 1808, the governor of Madras, Sir George Barlow, abolished Heyne's office as botanist and naturalist. In response to Heyne's plea that the political "usefulness of natural History is generally admitted," Barlow replied that he was "not at Liberty ... to continue the Appointment."[93] Not only was the presidency's natural history museum closed but its botanical gardens were permitted to languish. By the 1810s, those built up over many years by Heyne and the physician-general James Anderson now lay "totally neglected and barren," "in a sad state of ruin."[94] Astronomy, meanwhile, suffered from lackluster support at all three

---

[87] Lumsden to College Council, 11 Nov. 1812, PCFW, vol. 562, pp. 268–9.

[88] College Council to Directors, 29 Dec. 1812, ibid., p. 299.

[89] Extract Public Despatch to Bengal (6 Mar. and 19 May 1815), BL, IOR F/4/587/14202, pp. 3–4, 5–6. For figures, see Kopf, British Orientalism, p. 220.

[90] College Council to Governor-General in Council, 22 Dec. 1823, PCFW, vol. 567, p. 354.

[91] Here the directors' retrenchments culminated in an 1823 order confining literary patronage to "essential" works. Peter L. Schmitthenner, Telugu Resurgence: C. P. Brown and Cultural Consolidation in Nineteenth-Century South India (New Delhi, 2001), p. 107.

[92] David Arnold, "Plant Capitalism and Company Science: The Indian Career of Nathaniel Wallich," MAS 42 (2008), p. 911; Mark Harrison, "The Calcutta Botanic Garden and the Wider World, 1817–46," in Uma Das Gupta, ed., Science and Modern India: An Institutional History, c.1784–1947 (Delhi, 2011), p. 237.

[93] Tamil Nadu Archives, Madras Public Consultations (3 Jun. 1808), pp. 3837, 3856.

[94] Maria Graham, Journal of a Residence in India (Edinburgh, 1812), p. 125; Benjamin Heyne, Tracts, Historical and Statistical, on India (London, 1814), p. 411.

presidencies. Plans for new observatories were put off or rejected; the one at Madras was cut back and threatened with closure.[95] In the last instance, scholar-officials remonstrated with Governor Barlow and Governor-General Minto alike.[96] But there was little that either man could do given the determination of the directors.

And so it went with the Company's surveys. In the absence of steady sponsorship, these assumed "a chaotic, if not anarchic, character."[97] At one point, William Lambton complained that "neither the extent nor principle of my plan have been in the least understood by the Court of Directors."[98] While Lambton's trigonometrical survey fared better than Mackenzie's Mysore one, this was largely because it posed less of a threat to that body. Lambton presented himself as a disinterested man of science and distinguished the work of surveying from that of building a territorial empire. Thus, as one of his allies put it,

> when the fame of Conquest & extensive Dominion has passed
> away, a page may remain on the records of science, to shew
> that under the fostering & liberal protection of the East India
> Company, a survey has been carried on ... not inferior ... to the
> brilliant labors of the English & French astronomers.[99]

Mackenzie, meanwhile, struggled to make such a case for his survey. Appeals to the interests of commerce and the idea of conciliation could not disguise its Wellesleyan mandate.[100] Nor, in private

---

[95] Joydeep Sen, *Astronomy in India, 1784–1876* (London, 2014), ch. 2.

[96] William Petrie, Memorandum (4 Sept. 1808), NLS, MS 11726, ff. 36r–42r; Andrew Scott to Petrie, 9 Sept. 1808, ibid., ff. 44r–47r.

[97] Matthew H. Edney, *Mapping an Empire: The Geographical Construction of British India, 1765–1843* (Chicago, 1997), p. 162.

[98] Lambton to Samuel Peach, 28 Jun. 1802, Cleveland Public Library, 091.92 L179L.

[99] Petrie, Memorandum (4 Sept. 1808), f. 41v.

[100] For such appeals, see Peter Robb, "Completing 'Our Stock of Geography', or an Object 'Still More Sublime': Colin Mackenzie's Survey of Mysore, 1799–1810," *JRAS* 3rd ser. 8 (1998), p. 201. For Mackenzie's belief that the Company must become a "Paramount Power" in order to ensure "the tranquillity of all India," see Mackenzie to [Thomas Middleton], 11 Feb 1819, BL, Add. MS 9871, f. 56v.

correspondence, did he even attempt to disguise his antipathy toward the directors. He told Leyden, "I feel very little obliged by them, & if they & their System go to pot, I am not bound to bewail either their Justice or their Indulgence."[101] Mackenzie's sense of grievance endured long after the termination of the Mysore survey. His appointment as surveyor-general of India was less a reward than a cost-cutting measure. Now burdened with administrative duties, Mackenzie was forced to give up his plans for a great "Statistical & Historical" work. Though he still hoped to organize and catalogue his materials, in the end, he would fail to accomplish even this.[102]

Mackenzie was hardly alone in being disappointed: Few of his contemporaries realized their great projects either. The main reason for this, dwarfing even the decline of scholarly institutions, was the drying up of scholarly patronage.[103] Leading officials sometimes commanded the resources to undertake ambitious works independently. As the resident at Mysore, Mark Wilks could draw on staff, state papers, and local learned men to write a history of the province.[104] Matters were different for their subordinates, who now found opportunities for scholarship limited. This, in 1815, was the complaint of the army officer and political assistant John Briggs. From bases in the Deccan, Briggs had long been working on a comprehensive "History of the Mohamedan Conquests" and had collected some eleven volumes of notes and translations.

---

[101] Mackenzie to Leyden, 13 Nov. 1809, NLS, MS 3380, f. 117r.

[102] Mackenzie to Alexander Johnston, 1 Feb. 1817, in Johnston, "Biographical Sketch of the Literary Career of the Late Colonel Colin Mackenzie," *JRAS* 1 (1834), p. 343; Mackenzie to [Thomas Middleton], 4 Jun. 1818, BL, Add. MS 9871, ff. 26r–27r.

[103] There were other reasons too: Mackintosh and Colebrooke found few contributors; Erskine was charged with defalcation and sent off in disgrace; Carey's work was destroyed in a fire; and further accidents befell Ellis and his papers. Khan, "William Carey," p. 236; Jane Rendall, "The Political Ideas and Activities of Sir James Mackintosh (1765–1832): A Study in Whiggism Between 1789 and 1832" (PhD dissertation, University of London, 1972), pp. 203–5; Trautmann, *Languages and Nations*, pp. 84–6, 107, 113; Rocher and Rocher, *Making of Western Indology*, p. 72.

[104] Mark Wilks, *Historical Sketches of the South of India, in an Attempt to Trace the History of Mysoor*, 3 vols. (London, 1810–17), vol. I, p. x; Su Fang Ng, "Indian Interpreters in the Making of Colonial Historiography: New Light on Mark Wilks' *Historical Sketches of the South of India* (1810–1817)," *English Historical Review* 84 (2019).

With the departure of his patrons Wilks and Malcolm, however, Briggs "was deprived of almost all the literary patronage I could have once secured in India." For one thing, a remote posting prevented his "acquiring either interest or acquaintance among the people in power in Madras." For another, he had already written to the College of Fort William two years earlier and never received so much as a response.[105] In 1817, Briggs finally abandoned the project after the contents of his library were variously destroyed or scattered.[106] The mishap resulted from the Maratha peshwa's [prime minister's] sacking of the Poona residency, yet the larger issue remained a lack of patronage. Some of Briggs' "valuable Oriental MSS" might have been replaced, and assistants hired to track down or reconstruct his other papers. Despite pleas on his behalf, however, "no adequate compensation" was granted by the Company.[107]

Governors and governors-general of the era were not uniformly inattentive to scholar-officials. Minto was sometimes willing to assist fellow Scots in particular. The surveyor Francis Buchanan, who had feared that he would never be able to return to India, was brought out again by Minto in 1806.[108] Soon, a colleague and rival could remark that "his views have met the aid and encouragement of Government" and that his research was benefitting from this "powerful assistance."[109] Another of Minto's protégés was Leyden, who hailed from near his ancestral seat and had been recommended by no less a literary light than Walter Scott. Minto favored the orientalist with appointments to Calcutta's Court of Requests, college,

[105] Briggs to Colin Mackenzie, 17 Sept. 1815, BL, Mss Eur F303/442.

[106] John Briggs, preface to Firishta, *Tarikh-i Firishta*, trans. Briggs, as *History of the Rise of the Mahomedan Power in India, till the Year A.D. 1612*, 4 vols. (London, 1829), vol. I, p. viii.

[107] John Briggs, cited in Evans Bell, *Memoir of General John Briggs* (London, 1885), p. 101.

[108] Buchanan to John Hamilton, 17 Jul. 1806, National Records of Scotland, GD161/18/8. For details, see Mark F. Watson and Henry J. Noltie, "Career, Collections, Reports and Publications of Dr Francis Buchanan (Later Hamilton), 1762–1829: Natural History Studies in Nepal, Burma (Myanmar), Bangladesh and India (Part 2)," *Annals of Science* (in press).

[109] Thomas Hardwicke to James Edward Smith, 4 Nov. 1807, Linnean Society of London, GB-110/JES/COR/22/82.

and mint, and, upon his expedition to Java in 1811, to the post of chief translator. Leyden's ties to the governor-general put him in demand as an intermediary and must also have made him an object of envy.[110] One apparent rival was Irvine, who complained to his father in 1810 that "Lord Minto's distribution of patronage is ... self-willed & unfair."[111] Two years later, however, Minto granted Irvine a monthly salary to complete a work of "Political, Moral, and Statistical economy."[112] Irvine, along with Buchanan and Leyden, now belonged to the small set of scholar-officials who enjoyed the governor-general's patronage.

And yet none of these three enjoyed a happy fate in the Company's service. Despairing of his future in India, Buchanan returned to Scotland in 1815.[113] Leyden complained of being tasked with the work of four or even ten officials; overextension contributed to the illness that killed him in 1811.[114] Unlike Buchanan and Leyden, Irvine could pursue his scholarship uninterrupted by other responsibilities. Nonetheless, he claimed that having to constantly justify his salary resulted in delays.[115] In 1813, he was told that, having paid him through a use "of the publick funds not ... strictly warranted," Minto was "anxious to take with him to England some report of the progress of that work."[116] Apart from the fact that Irvine had little to show for his efforts thus far, his unsanctioned salary clearly put Minto in an awkward position with the directors.[117] When Irvine's contract ended the following year, he was informed that "Government cannot on any account grant you

---

[110] See I. M. Brown, "John Leyden (1775–1811): His Life and Works" (PhD dissertation, University of Edinburgh, 1955), pp. 468, 483, 510–11, 518–20.

[111] Irvine to father, 5 Aug. 1810, NLS, Acc.13147.

[112] Governor-General in Council to Irvine, 25 Sept. 1812, BL, F/4/427/10436, p. 170.

[113] Marika Vicziany, "Imperialism, Botany and Statistics in Early Nineteenth-Century India: The Surveys of Francis Buchanan (1762–1829)," MAS 20 (1986), p. 654.

[114] Leyden to Oliva Raffles, 10 May 1808, NLS, MS 971, f. 53v; Brown, "John Leyden," p. 555; John Bastin, Sir Stamford Raffles and Some of His Friends and Contemporaries: A Memoir of the Founder of Singapore (Singapore, 2019), pp. 66, 71.

[115] Irvine to Minto, 28 Jan. 1812, NLS, MS 11727, f. 2v.

[116] N. B. Edmonstone to Irvine, 18 Nov. 1813, ibid., f. 90r.

[117] See Irvine to Minto, 6 Dec. 1813 and 7 May 1814, ibid., ff. 94r–96r.

any further pecuniary assistance."[118] In 1815, the directors denounced not only his salary but also his apparent attempt to force upon them new "duties in the administration of India."[119] For some time, Irvine still hoped to complete his great work but was impeded by debts, "bad health & worse spirits."[120] Finally, in 1820, he relocated with his wife and children to Australia and thence, in 1824, back to Scotland.[121] Like Buchanan's disillusionment and Leyden's death, Irvine's failure to complete his treatise undoubtedly owed to multiple causes. The common factor, however, was the directors' reluctance to support their endeavors on account of their political implications.

SCHOLAR-OFFICIALS AND SCHOLARLY INSTITUTIONS IN BRITAIN

The directors' break with scholar-officials was clearest in Britain at the institutions they superintended directly. Haileybury College and the India Museum, which they had founded as centers of learning, now languished as a result of their distrust and disesteem. At the same time, these institutions became sites of conflict over the character of the Company. The directors were forced, if not to develop new ideas about knowledge, then at least to confront the diminishing relevance of conciliation. Company scholarship was becoming so bound up with territorial expansion that eventually the directors lost interest in it. By the 1820s, they had reached the conclusion that they had little to gain politically from scholarly patronage.

Scarcely had the imposing edifice of Haileybury College gone up than it began to seem inapposite. Once envisioned as a counterweight to the College of Fort William, Haileybury now lacked an ideological purpose. Even if the directors still felt that their college must overshadow its Calcutta counterpart, it was less economical to feed the one than to

---

[118] Governor-General in Council to Irvine, 7 Apr. 1814, ibid., f. 97r.

[119] Extract Public Despatch to Bengal (6 Mar. 1815), BL, IOR F/4/489/11870, pp. 1–2.

[120] Irvine to father, 4 Oct. 1815, 8 Feb. 1816, and 16 Mar. 1820, NLS, Acc.13147.

[121] Dennis Wright, "Descendants of Capt Francis Irvine, 1786–1855" (self-published booklet, 2014), pp. 4–6.

starve the other. Their aversion to scholar-officials, meanwhile, manifested itself in a reluctance to employ that cadre or to train students to enter it. As Jonathan Scott apprised the directors, they had access to scores of returned officials like himself who had already added much to the "stock of Oriental information."[122] But they mostly kept these men at a distance from the college, dealing brusquely with Scott and spurning overtures from John Gilchrist and Thomas Roebuck.[123] Equally telling were conditions at the college library. "The neglect of the Directors is scandalous," wrote one student in 1806, upon finding its shelves empty.[124] A year later, Charles Stewart marveled that "many of the writers attached to this College ... have never yet seen an Arabic or Persian Manuscript."[125] Part of the problem was that some books could only be obtained from India, but even these seem not to have been well treated or, when necessary, replaced. As late as 1828, a professor could grumble at "the miserable state of our supply of Hindustani books."[126] Such issues notwithstanding, many staff and students seem to have found Haileybury unobjectionable. The political economist Thomas Robert Malthus spent a long career at the institution and defended it in print.[127] In light of the "merely rudimental learning" offered there, however, it was the instilment of *esprit de corps* that advocates cited in its favor.[128] This was a markedly humbler mission for a university than that announced by Wellesley or, at one time, by the directors.

---

[122] Jonathan Scott, *Observations on the Oriental Department of the Hon. Company's East India College, at Hertford* (Hertford [1806]), BL, IOR H/488, pp. 678–9, 719–21.

[123] Scott to Charles Grant, Jun. 1805, BL, Add. MS 29190, f. 29v; Scott to Directors, 3 Dec. 1805, ibid., ff. 30r–v; Directors to Roebuck, 8 Oct. 1807, in [John Gilchrist], *The British Indian Monitor*, 2 vols. (Edinburgh, 1806–8), vol. II, p. xv; John Borthwick Gilchrist to College Committee, 1 and 2 Jun. 1818, BL, IOR, J/1/33/221–2. The directors' aversion to Gilchrist seems to have long outlasted their suspicion that he was an agent of Wellesley.

[124] Alexander Fraser to father, 6 Aug. 1806, Reelig House, vol. 32, p. 224.

[125] Stewart to Charles Wilkins, 30 Sept. 1807, BL, IOR J/1/23/410.

[126] James Michael to College Committee, 12 Dec. 1828, BL, IOR J/2/7/276.

[127] See Timothy L. Alborn, "Boys to Men: Moral Restraint at Haileybury College," in Brian Dolan, ed., *Malthus, Medicine, and Morality: "Malthusianism" after 1798* (Amsterdam, 2000).

[128] Scott, *Observations*, p. 687; Bernard S. Cohn, "Recruitment and Training of British Civil Servants in India, 1600–1800," in Cohn, *An Anthropologist among the Historians and Other Essays* (Delhi, 1987), pp. 537–45.

Controversies over Haileybury did, at least, force the directors to revisit the Company's relations with knowledge. In debates at East India House, proprietors (shareholders) defined these relations in ways that clashed with the idea of conciliation.[129] According to one view, the Company should interest itself only in knowledge that was practically relevant to its trade. Thus, for Randle Jackson, the founding of Haileybury was a sign that Wellesley's "mania had reached the directors in England":

It was too much to expect, that young gentlemen would descend from the rostrum, – where they had been displaying their acquirements in ... high branches of human knowledge – to count bales and to measure muslins.... Surely, if they [the directors] wished to form a good and active merchant, they would not commence by making him a Doctor of Laws or an expounder of philosophy.... Instead of sending out writers qualified for the purposes of commerce, they prepared to pervade India with an army of young Grotiuses and Puffendorfs – whose qualifications were too high for the situations they were intended to fill – whose minds could not descend to the drudgery of the counting-house ....

Jackson's comments reportedly drew a mixture of laughter and cheers from the audience of directors and proprietors.[130] Charles Grant, in a later speech, and Malthus, in a pamphlet, noted that fewer than one-sixth of the Company's civil servants were now involved in trade.[131] Nonetheless, these comments highlighted a tendency, prevalent among the directors, to think of the Company as still fundamentally a trading outfit. It was left to other proprietors, like the

---

[129] On these debates, which comprehended much else besides, see Callie Wilkinson, "The East India College Debate and the Fashioning of Imperial Officials, 1806–1858," *Historical Journal* 60 (2017).

[130] Randle Jackson, Speech in East India House Debate (18 Dec. 1816), *AJ* 3 (1817), p. 156 [emphasis removed].

[131] Charles Grant, Speech in East India House Debate (6 Feb. 1817), *AJ* 3 (1817), p. 373; T. R. Malthus, *Statements Respecting the East-India College* (London, 1817), p. 92.

member of parliament Douglas Kinnaird, to articulate the opposing view. According to Kinnaird,

> It were to be wished, indeed, that in transferring the name and some of the forms of lord Wellesley's college at Calcutta, some attention had been paid to the objects which the noble lord had in view .... His objects were not confined merely to the education of the Company's civil servants, as was the case here ... but his aim was to found at the same time a seat of learning, the civilizing effects and advantages of which were to be diffused throughout the whole empire .... He wisely thought that the most effectual mode of governing sixty millions of people, was to scatter the seeds of learning and of science amongst them .... Lord Wellesley's object was to establish a source from whence the fountain of science might diffuse its waters over the whole territory of India.

Kinnaird envisioned "securing" the Company's territories through "an enlightened system of government."[132] The directors, in 1817, were unable to unite around such an idea. If, to quote Malthus, "In the establishment of the East-India college, the feelings of the sovereign conspicuously predominated," then, in its subsequent management, these feelings evidently took a backseat.[133]

The India Museum and Oriental Library was the focus of a parallel set of conflicts, which likewise arose from its failure to meet expectations. These expectations had been set as early as 1799, when Charles Wilkins, applying to serve as the museum's curator, had pledged to advance the cause of "Eastern learning" and of "science in general." To this end, he had drawn up a prospectus for a counterpart to the Asiatic Society. "Under the patronage of the Court of Directors," this body was to hold meetings, conduct research, and publish a journal on the premises. He anticipated little difficulty in

---

[132] Douglas Kinnaird, Speech in East India House Debate (20 Feb. 1817), *AJ* 4 (1817), pp. 47–8.
[133] Malthus, *Statements*, p. 487.

finding suitable members: Many scholar-officials had retired in the vicinity of London.[134] Wilkins' plan may explain why some current or former officials, like Warren Hastings, offered up their collections despite the directors' paying little if anything for them.[135] But the directors never adopted the plan. Nor, after the first few years, did they take more than a sporadic interest in the repository's holdings. They did make some effort, apparently, to acquire items that had monetary value or commercial applications. But "a place to store and deploy capital," as one historian has called the museum and library, was a far cry from Wilkins' vision.[136]

Conditions at the place, meanwhile, were notorious. As late as the 1830s, the library had no catalogue and the museum's comprised "some tattered loose leaves, in manuscript." According to one critic, the reading room was poorly staffed and organized, not to mention frequently disturbed by casual visitors. More than one critic accused the directors of allowing the library's valuable manuscripts to deteriorate through wanton neglect. Some collections, reportedly, were succumbing to dirt, damp, or termites.[137] Others, years after arrival, lay "packed in the cases in which they had been sent."[138] Thus, one commentator reasoned that the Company must "not wish for visitors" to its museum and library; another that "the public benefited as little by them almost as if they had no existence."[139]

The directors were not only negligent of their repository but also antagonistic toward the scholar-officials who contributed to it.

[134] Charles Wilkins, "Sketch of a Plan for an Oriental Museum Proposed to be Established at the India House" (Jan. 1799), in A. J. Arberry, *The Library of the India Office: A Historical Sketch* (London, 1938), p. 18.

[135] See [Peter Gordon], "The Oriental Repository at the India House," *Alexander's East India and Colonial Magazine* 10–11 (1835–6), vol. X, pp. 131–4.

[136] Jessica Ratcliff, "Hand-in-Hand with the Survey: Surveying and the Accumulation of Knowledge Capital at India House during the Napoleonic Wars," *Notes and Records: The Royal Society Journal of the History of Science* 73 (2019), p. 160.

[137] [Gordon], "Oriental Repository," vol. X, pp. 140, 427, vol. XI, pp. 126–7.

[138] William Gowan, Speech in East India House Debate (19 Mar. 1834), *AJ* 13 (1834), p. 295.

[139] Ibid.; "Her Majesty's East India House," *East India Magazine* (Mar. 1841), p. 221.

One such official was Colin Mackenzie, who was willing to offer the directors his collection, notwithstanding his grievances against them.[140] "I sincerely hope you will be able to dispose of your valuable collection to advantage, to the East India Company," warned William Francklin in 1818; "I am sorry to say that they have discarded me & mine long since, & never sent me even thanks for the offer."[141] Four years later, the Bengal government bought Mackenzie's trove from his widow for a sum the directors decried as exorbitant.[142] This was an outcome of which other scholar-officials, like Francklin, or indeed Francis Buchanan, could only have dreamed. When Buchanan donated his manuscripts and specimens to the directors' museum in 1815, they gave him a "very cold" reception.[143] They accepted "my collection with such contempt and arrogance," he fumed, "that I would neither ask nor receive any favour from so scoundrely a body."[144] Buchanan saw the directors' lack of "approval of my conduct or of thankfulness for my present" as a result of their still-commercial priorities.[145] His surveys of India – its "appearance," "productions," "antiquities," "inhabitants," and "history" – could "in no manner interest" them, except insofar as they might "obtain credit."[146] According to Buchanan, the directors valued his work not as an asset to their government but instead only as an accessory to their trade. Ascribing to these "Cheese monger Emperors" an unstatesmanlike "jealousy," Buchanan echoed his old patron Wellesley.[147]

---

[140] Mackenzie to Ricketts, 15 Jun. 1815.

[141] Francklin to Mackenzie, 22 Oct. 1818, BL, Mss Eur F303/442.

[142] David M. Blake, "Colin Mackenzie: Collector Extraordinary," *British Library Journal* 17 (1991), p. 141.

[143] A. Allan to [Benjamin Sydenham], 14 Feb. 1816, National Records of Scotland, GD161/19/2/21.

[144] Buchanan to Nathaniel Wallich, 4 Feb. 1817, Natural History Museum, MSS BUC, p. 149. For details, see Watson and Noltie, "Career."

[145] Buchanan to Nathaniel Wallich, 17 Jul. 1816, Natural History Museum, MSS BUC, pp. 147–8.

[146] Buchanan to Benjamin Sydenham, 4 Mar. 1816, National Records of Scotland, GD161/19/2/17–18.

[147] Ibid.; Buchanan to Wallich, 4 Feb. 1817, p. 149.

The India Museum, like Haileybury, emerged as a site of conflict over the Company's relations with knowledge. Having been founded to advertise the fruits of the Company's trade, it was filling up instead with the spoils of the Company's conquests. The books and other belongings of Tipu Sultan, in particular, sat incongruously at East India House.[148] In adorning their headquarters with the trappings of a territorial empire, the directors risked undercutting their commercial sovereignty.[149] A delicate balancing act thus could be observed in the receptions they hosted for visiting dignitaries. The Mamluk chief Muhammad Bey al-Alfi and the Persian ambassador Mirza Abu'l Hasan were conducted on tours that illustrated the Company's hybrid character. Both were shown the museum and library. Abu'l Hasan admired the "high-ceilinged room" with shelves of "neatly ranged books in Arabic and Persian."[150] Al-Alfi, at least according to the *Times*, assumed "a solemnity of demeanor suited to the idea he must entertain of the first Corporate Body in the world."[151] Exhibiting curiosities, however, was not quite the same thing as encouraging scholarship. If the directors saw political value in the one, then it was far from clear that they still saw it in the other. The writer Peter Gordon, who criticized the Company in the 1830s, was being hyperbolic when he held that it "excels every other Government in its hatred of knowledge."[152] That he could point to the state of its museum as evidence, however, did provide a measure of the directors' waning interest in scholarship.

So too did the abolition, in 1817, of the office of historiographer, which had existed for half of a century. After pensioning off the

[148] For remarks by contemporaries to the effect that East India House was fit for merchants but not sovereigns, see John McAleer, "Exhibiting the 'Strangest of All Empires': The East India Company, East India House, and Britain's Asian Empire," in Stephanie Barczewski and Martin Farr, eds., *The Mackenzie Moment and Imperial History: Essays in Honour of John M. Mackenzie* (Basingstoke, 2019), pp. 30–32.

[149] Joshua Ehrlich, "Plunder and Prestige: Tipu Sultan's Library and the Making of British India," *South Asia: Journal of South Asian Studies* 43 (2020), pp. 488–90.

[150] Mirza Abul Hassan Khan, *A Persian at the Court of King George 1809–10: The Journal of Mirza Abul Hassan Khan*, ed. and trans. Margaret Morris Cloake (London, 1988), p. 74.

[151] "Elfi Bey," *Times* (9 Dec. 1803).

[152] [Gordon], "Oriental Repository," vol. X, p. 547.

longtime occupant, John Bruce, the directors entrusted the writing of the Company's annals to a "literary hack." According to Bruce, the directors' only concern in the matter was "to save my Salary."[153] In addition, however, they seem to have lost faith in the conciliatory value of his labors. If they had hired him in 1793 because he had helped to renew the Company's charter on favorable terms, then they must have been disappointed when he failed to replicate the feat in 1813.[154] Besides, the directors now seemed to be making a habit of squandering literary talent. Having long employed Charles Lamb as an accountant, in 1819 they hired James Mill and Thomas Love Peacock as preparers of correspondence. Mill's *History of British India* (1818), which was dismissive of Company scholarship, neither attracted nor repelled them on political grounds.[155] In their new way of thinking, it simply established his qualifications as a clerk.[156]

It was no wonder that the Company's scholarly institutions were beginning to be eclipsed by other ones at the metropole. One sign of this trend was that scholar-officials were donating their collections to universities, museums, and especially the Royal Asiatic Society. With the society's founding in 1823, Wilkins' plan was finally realized – albeit under the aegis of the Crown instead of the Company. The society kept a museum and library, held meetings, published a journal, and patronized scholars – everything Wilkins had sought in vain from the directors. Its prospectus may have alluded to this fact with its expression of "surprise" that such a body had not

---

[153] Bruce to Hugh Inglis, 30 Jun. 1817, BL, IOR H/456e, pp. 362–3.

[154] For Bruce's efforts on the later occasion, see John Bruce, *Annals of the Honorable East-India Company, from Their Establishment by the Charter of Queen Elizabeth, 1600, to the Union of the London and English East-India Companies, 1707–8*, 3 vols. (London, 1810), vol. I, p. vii; John Bruce, *Report on the Negociation, Between the Honorable East-India Company and the Public, Respecting the Renewal of the Company's Exclusive Privileges of Trade, for Twenty Years from March, 1794* (London, 1811), p. iii; William Foster, *John Company* (London, 1926), pp. 241–2.

[155] On this dismissiveness, see Javed Majeed, *Ungoverned Imaginings: James Mill's The History of British India and Orientalism* (Oxford, 1992).

[156] See William Foster, *The East India House: Its History and Associations* (London, 1924), pp. 195–7.

been established sooner. The document slighted the directors in other ways, omitting to mention them and announcing as founding members several of their adversaries.[157] Henry Thomas Colebrooke, the society's driving force, did ask for the directors' "countenance and support," but only as an afterthought; and it took four years and a pointed reminder to obtain from them a modest annual grant.[158] Thus, despite being comprised largely of retired Company officials, like Colebrooke, the society charted an independent course. It was to focus on the parts of Asia "under British dominion" and serve as "the main link" that secured them "in the bonds of literature, science, and art."[159] The directors and their commercial ideas, such language implied, were no longer integral to British orientalism. Nor, by this time, did the directors bother to contest the point.

INDIAN COLLABORATORS AND THE TURN TO EDUCATION

The Royal Asiatic Society's prospectus did suggest a domain of knowledge in which the directors and the Company might yet play a leading role: The society, it held, would not "interfere with the views and proceedings of ... associations for promoting Education in the East."[160] In India, such associations were being led not only by missionaries and their allies but also by a new range of Indian scholar-collaborators. Indeed, the territorial expansion that so profoundly influenced scholar-officials encouraged, too, a broadening and deepening of their Indian connections. The flourishing of education associations was but one result of this. Another was the framing of great projects by Indians hopeful of the Company's patronage. And yet, while the same Indian scholar-collaborators were often involved

---

[157] "Asiatic Society of London: Prospectus" (16 Jan. 1823), *AJ* 15 (1823), pp. 264–5.

[158] Minute of Council (15 Mar. 1823), cited in C. F. Beckingham, "A History of the Royal Asiatic Society, 1823–1973," in Stuart Simmonds and Simon Digby, eds., *The Royal Asiatic Society: Its History and Treasures* (Leiden, 1979), p. 27; Rocher and Rocher, *Making of Western Indology*, p. 166.

[159] "Asiatic Society of London: Prospectus," p. 265; "Twelfth Annual Report of the Council," *JRAS* 2 (1835), p. xxvi.

[160] "Asiatic Society of London: Prospectus," p. 264.

in both kinds of endeavor, they found much greater support for the first kind than for the second.

Expansion altered the pattern of collaboration between European scholar-officials and Indians in several ways. First, it opened to the former wider horizons, the exploration of which required greater manpower and expertise. If scholar-officials once had tended to employ a single maulvi or pandit – the forming of groups to compile and translate laws being an exception – then the institutions and projects to which they now turned called for teams of Indian scholars as a matter of necessity.[161] Francis Buchanan surveyed Bengal with a complement of several dozen, including clerks, collectors, and draughtsmen – not to mention a military escort.[162] Colin Mackenzie employed an even larger "native establishment," at times numbering over one hundred, on his survey of Mysore.[163] Horace Hayman Wilson assembled his mammoth Sanskrit dictionary from texts prepared by numerous "native assistants."[164] And even some less well-placed officials, like Francis Irvine, built extensive Indian networks to gather and process material for their vast schemes.[165] In some respects, therefore, such projects were at least as much Indian as European.[166] The political ideas that set and kept them in motion, however, were those of the scholar-officials who sought to extend and consolidate the Company's dominions.

[161] See Ruth Gabriel, "Learned Communities and British Educational Experiments in North India: 1780–1830" (PhD dissertation, University of Virginia, 1979), ch. 5; Thomas R. Trautmann, introduction to Trautmann, ed., *The Madras School of Orientalism: Producing Knowledge in Colonial South India* (New Delhi, 2009), p. 11.

[162] Ray Desmond, *The European Discovery of the Indian Flora* (Oxford: Oxford University Press, 1992), p. 78.

[163] Tobias Wolffhardt, *Unearthing the Past to Forge the Future: Colin Mackenzie, the Early Colonial State and the Comprehensive Survey of India*, trans. Jane Rafferty (New York, 2018), p. 121.

[164] Horace Hayman Wilson, *A Dictionary, Sanscrit and English: Translated, Amended and Enlarged, from an Original Compilation Prepared by Learned Natives for the College of Fort William* (Calcutta, 1819), p. iii.

[165] Extract Bengal Public Consultations (7 Apr. 1814), BL, IOR F/4/489/11870, pp. 7–10.

[166] See Kapil Raj, *Relocating Modern Science: Circulation and the Construction of Knowledge in South Asia and Europe, 1650–1900* (Basingstoke, 2007); Rama Sundari Mantena, *The Origins of Modern Historiography in India: Antiquarianism and Philology, 1780–1880* (Basingstoke, 2012).

A second effect of expansion was thus to deter many Indian rulers and learned elites from collaborating with scholar-officials. The rise in this period of complaints of Brahman obfuscation can be explained only partly by Evangelical and anti-Maratha prejudices.[167] The duping of Francis Wilford by his chief pandit in Benares may not have been a political act: Likely the pandit was trying to please his patron.[168] Different, however, was the case of pandits obstructing scholar-officials in Poona, the seat of the Maratha peshwa. In 1806, the residency officer and aspiring orientalist E. S. Frissell described the situation to James Mackintosh:

> I have not been inattentive to your wishes respecting a Catalogue Raison[n]é of the Peshwa[']s Shanscrit MSS, but I am very sorry to tell you that I have reason to fear the accomplishment of them will be impracticable. When one asks a native of rank for any information respecting any thing belonging to him, his family, his occupations, his connections, his possessions of whatever kind they may be, he invariably thinks that there is something sinister in your motive, and takes alarm. No persons are allowed to look at the Peshwa[']s books, but two or three of his favorite Pundits.[169]

Suspicions of this kind may explain why Claudius Buchanan had to overcome opposition from court Brahmans to obtain a catalogue of manuscripts in Travancore, or why the College of Fort William struggled to procure manuscripts through the Company's residents in Basra, Delhi, Lucknow, and Hyderabad.[170] Benjamin Heyne, for

---

[167] On these, see Susan Bayly, *Caste, Society and Politics in India from the Eighteenth Century to the Modern Age* (Cambridge, 1999), pp. 88–93, 110–11.

[168] C. A. Bayly, "Orientalists, Informants and Critics in Benares, 1790–1860," in Jamal Malik, ed., *Perspectives of Mutual Encounters in South Asian History, 1760–1860* (Leiden, 2000), pp. 103–11; Nigel Leask, "Francis Wilford and the Colonial Construction of Hindu Geography, 1799–1822," in Amanda Gilroy, ed., *Romantic Geographies: Discourses of Travel 1775–1844* (Manchester, 2000), pp. 214–19.

[169] Frissell to Mackintosh, 13 Jun. 1806, BL, Add. MS 78765, f. 73r. On Frissell, see "Deaths Abroad," *Monthly Magazine* 25 (May 1808), p. 378.

[170] Matthew Lumsden to College Council, 18 Sept. 1810, PCFW, vol. 561, p. 325; Claudius Buchanan, *Christian Researches in Asia: With Notices of the Translation of the Scriptures into the Oriental Languages* (Cambridge, 1811), p. 93.

that matter, ascribed his difficulties in investigating the minerals of the Carnatic to the nawab's distrust of Europeans.[171] These places all fell without the sphere of the Company's formal control but, it might be surmised, within that of its ambition. By contrast, learned elites in longer-established dominions like Bengal may have been becoming more, not less, willing to collaborate. And rulers of dependent states like Mysore, Tanjore, and Baroda readily furnished the Company with valuable manuscripts.[172] It was the unstable periphery of the Company's territory, however, that most interested scholar-officials. And they turned to new partners to bring it under intellectual control.

A final effect of expansion was to throw up a wider range of Indian scholar-collaborators. This was especially true in the south, where the Company's inroads deprived pandits of their royal patrons yet created openings for other men of letters.[173] In Madras, scholar-officials had long found that access to pandits and their texts was mediated by the city's powerful dubashes. When Mark Wilks attempted to learn Sanskrit, they allegedly "threatened loss of cast and absolute destruction to any Bramin" who would teach him.[174] As the Madras Presidency expanded, however, new collaborators came into the Company's orbit. Mackenzie staffed his survey with Niyogis, a class of Brahmans widely regarded as sullied by their embrace of salaried employment.[175] Other scholar-officials turned to Deshasthas, a small community of Maratha Brahmans in some

---

[171] Heyne, *Tracts*, p. 112.

[172] Anand Rao Gaekwad to East India Company [Jan. 1809], BL, IO Islamic 4253; Fateh Singh Rao Gaekwad to East India Company [Jan. 1809], BL, IO Islamic 4254; Alexander Walker to Jonathan Duncan, 11 Jan. 1809, NLS, MS 13922, ff. 1r–2v; Buchanan, *Christian Researches*, p. 53; Wilks, *Historical Sketches*, vol. I, p. x.

[173] See Velcheru Narayana Rao, "Print and Prose: Pundits, *Karanams*, and the East India Company in the Making of Modern Telugu," in Stuart Blackburn and Vasudha Dalmia, eds., *India's Literary History: Essays on the Nineteenth Century* (New Delhi, 2004), pp. 150–52.

[174] John Leyden to William Erskine, 27 Nov. 1804, BL, Add. MS 26561, f. 56v.

[175] Phillip B. Wagoner, "Precolonial Intellectuals and the Production of Colonial Knowledge," *Comparative Studies in Society and History* 45 (2003), pp. 795–6.

ways as removed from Hindu society as Europeans.[176] One of this number was Vennelakanti Subbarao, who, through literary services, rose from modest origins to become a translator at the high court.[177] For that matter, Non-Brahman men of letters too now found their talents in higher demand. Of the Tamil "pandits" at the College of Fort St. George at least two were Christians and the rest, apparently, Pandarams and Vellalars.[178] Mamadi Venkayya, a Komati, compiled Telugu and Sanskrit dictionaries for the Company despite attempts by Brahmans to stop him.[179] Thiruverkadu Muttiah, a Mudaliar, served scholar-officials in Madras before being appointed a "literary translator" in Ceylon.[180] Thus, while the Company's ascent in the south may have displaced many learned elites, it created opportunities for some of their social subordinates.

This trend was not limited to the eastern side of the peninsula. A striking instance comes from Malabar, where, as late as the 1800s, the Company was still jostling for power with local rulers. Amid the turmoil, the officer Alexander Walker investigated numerous subjects with the aid of a set of Indian Christians based in Calicut. Even after being transferred elsewhere, Walker relied on these contacts for intelligence, and for assistance with his eclectic researches: on one occasion, a delivery of pepper and cardamom plants; on another, advice from a *shastri* (Sanskrit scholar) on Hindu religious practices. In return, Walker helped the men to find work in the Company's offices, where, one reported, the "Bramins take every opportunity of shewing themselves as factotum." Letters from the group to Walker recurred

---

[176] Robert Eric Frykenberg, *Guntur District 1788–1848: A History of Local Influence and Central Authority in South India* (Oxford, 1965), p. 8.

[177] [Vennelakanti Subbarao] Vennelacunty Soob Row, *The Life of Vennelacunty Soob Row*, ed. Vennelacunty Venkata Gopal Row (Madras, 1873), pp. 14, 16.

[178] A. R. Venkatachalapathy, "'Grammar, the Frame of Language': Tamil Pandits at the College of Fort St. George," in Trautmann, ed., *Madras School*, pp. 120–24.

[179] Trautmann, *Languages and Nations*, pp. 146–50.

[180] For Mootiah's activities in Madras and Ceylon, respectively, see [Thiruverkadu Muttiah] Teroovercadoo Mootiah, "An Historical and Chronological Journal, of the Life of Teroovercadoo Mootiah," *Oriental Repository* 2 (1797), pp. 569–70; General Despatch from Ceylon, 26 Feb. 1799, in S. G. Perera, ed., *The Douglas Papers* (Colombo, 1933), pp. 160–61.

to a central topic: a Malayalam history which he had hired one of their number, Joseph Passanha, to translate.[181] Noting the existence of different versions of the text tailored to the interests of different castes and families, Walker compared his translation with another commissioned by the Governor of Bombay.[182] He may also have sought to control for discrepancies by hiring Passanha instead of a pandit, who might have been more likely to be an interested party. Walker's relations with the humble translator were sometimes strained. He later claimed to have consorted only with Indians "of rank, of Education, or of Property."[183] And he bemoaned the astonishing "power and ascendancy" obtained by "Native favourites" – "men of low origin ... without much education" though "of great shrewdness."[184] Scholar-officials were beginning to ask how such upward mobility, if widely stimulated, might impact Indian society and its relations with the Company. Walker seems to have had ambivalent feelings on the subject, but this was not the case with many of his contemporaries.

For scholar-officials, it was often a short leap from investigating Indian society to calling for its alteration. The army and political officer James Tod studied Rajputs and their history with a view to raising their present standing.[185] Mackenzie displayed more popular inclinations, researching and working with many groups, and advancing broad notions of state-led "improvement."[186] Irvine

---

[181] "Native Letters: Malabar" (1801–8), NLS, MS 13718, ff. 1r–42v.

[182] Alexander Walker, "An Account of the Kerool-ood-Patty," NLS, MS 13797, pp. 2–4. See Jonathan Duncan, "Historical Remarks on the Coast of Malabar, with some Description of the Manners of Its Inhabitants," *Asiatick Researches* 5 (Calcutta, 1798), p. 1. Walker thus anticipated the modern view of the text as "a charter of validation for status groups in society." Kesavan Veluthat, "The Kēraḷōlpatti as History," in *The Early Medieval in South India* (New Delhi, 2009), p. 142.

[183] Alexander Walker [1826], cited in Sanjay Subrahmanyam, *Europe's India: Words, People, Empires, 1500–1800* (Cambridge, MA, 2017), p. 271.

[184] Alexander Walker [c. 1820], cited in Neil Rabitoy, "System v. Expediency: The Reality of Land Revenue Administration in the Bombay Presidency, 1812–1820," *MAS* 9 (1975), p. 543.

[185] Jason Freitag, *Serving Empire, Serving Nation: James Tod and the Rajputs of Rajasthan* (Leiden, 2009), pp. 108–14.

[186] Robb, "Completing 'Our Stock of Geography,'" pp. 198–201; Wolffhardt, *Unearthing the Past*, pp. 197–202.

sought "to give a new turn to the occupations of the people" and, accordingly, to the "structure of Society."[187] John Leyden, for his part, disapproved of caste distinctions and called for demystifying Brahmanical authority.[188] Among scholar-officials, however, it was Francis Buchanan who most forcefully inveighed against India's social order. In an early essay, he contrasted this order, which he took to be dominated by Brahmans, with Buddhist egalitarianism.[189] His *A Journey from Madras* (1807), as William Erskine had it, avoided the errors orientalists had committed by "confining their enquiries to men of learning, & of the upper classes."[190] In this and other works, Buchanan devoted his attention to non-Brahmanical institutions and ideologies.[191] His program went still further. In *Genealogies of the Hindus* (1819), he claimed that caste was a late invention, and that "Brahman" had once meant "merely a civilized or intelligent person."[192] Implicit in his remarks, and in those of some of his fellow scholar-officials, was an argument for education as a vehicle of social change.[193] Yet generally quicker to articulate this argument were Indian scholar-collaborators, especially ones from groups not previously favored.

They did so in conjunction with the education associations springing up in Calcutta, Madras, and Bombay. These bodies were founded by Europeans, but, in the words of Irvine, "Not the least remarkable circumstance is the support which the Natives have given" them.[194] Indian members were often social climbers. Subbarao, for instance, played a principal role in the Madras School

---

[187] Extract Bengal Public Consultations (7 Apr. 1814), p. 24.

[188] Leyden to [Robert] Knox [1804], BL, Add. MS 26561, ff. 53r–54r.

[189] Vicziany, "Imperialism," p. 632.

[190] William Erskine, Diary (24 Feb. 1811), BL, Add. MS 39945, f. 4r.

[191] William R. Pinch, *Peasants and Monks in British India* (Berkeley, 1996), pp. 150–4.

[192] [Francis Buchanan] Francis Hamilton, *Genealogies of the Hindus, Extracted from Their Sacred Writings* (Edinburgh, 1819), p. 57.

[193] For further suggestive remarks by Buchanan on the existing state of education in India, see [Francis Buchanan], *The History, Antiquities, Topography, and Statistics of Eastern India*, ed. [Robert] Montgomery Martin, 3 vols. (London, 1838).

[194] [Vennelakanti Subbarao], *Life*, pp. 64–76.

Book Society (1820).[195] His fellow members included Ram Raz, head English master of the College of Fort St. George, who had ascended from similarly modest origins.[196] The Calcutta School Book Society (1817) and Calcutta School Society (1818) attracted maulvis and pandits but also Bhadralok (gentlemen), who had risen with the coming of Company rule.[197] The Bombay Native Education Society (1822) included Hindus, Muslims, and Parsis of various castes and classes.[198] All of these associations harbored multiple and sometimes conflicting agendas. For the new scholar-collaborators, however, mass education evidently took precedence. As Ram Raz put it, "In this country education is confined to a very small portion of ... the higher class," while "the greater part of the population, are lamentably sunk in ignorance."[199] For one who had escaped penury through his studies and who held a pluralistic view of Indian society, there was reason to cheer the prospect of mass "enlightenment."[200] Other scholar-collaborators, however, struggled to reconcile this prospect with their own endeavors.

The Bhadralok Ramkamal Sen, for example, found it difficult to square his educational and intellectual aims. This could be observed in the effort to produce a Bengali-English dictionary that preoccupied him from 1817.[201] A tension ran through the project. On the one hand, Ramkamal sought to make the dictionary comprehensive and authoritative. On the other, he envisioned it as a popular work for

---

[195] Irvine to Mountstuart Elphinstone, 19 Dec. 1818, BL, Mss Eur F88/298, f. 147v.

[196] *The Second Report of the Madras School-Book Society* (Madras, 1827), pp. i–ii.

[197] *The First Report of the Calcutta School Book Society* (Calcutta, 1818), p. 26; Jana Tschurenev, *Empire, Civil Society, and the Beginnings of Colonial Education in India* (New Delhi, 2019), pp. 206–13.

[198] Tschurenev, *Empire*, pp. 260–1.

[199] R[am] R[az], "A Short Sketch of the State of Education among the Natives at Bangalore" (1824), in *Second Report of the Madras School-Book Society*, pp. 24–5.

[200] Ram Raz to Richard Clarke, 13 Oct. 1827, in R. Rickards, *India; or Facts Submitted to Illustrate the Character and Condition of the Native Inhabitants*, 2 vols. (London, 1829–32), vol. II, pp. 402–3; [Henry Harkness], preface to Rám Ráz, *Essay on the Architecture of the Hindús* (London, 1834), pp. vi–x.

[201] For details in this paragraph, see Pradyot Kumar Ray, *Dewan Ramcomul Sen and His Times* (Calcutta, 1990), pp. 182–205.

the edification of Indian students. It was hard enough to satisfy his own standards; it was harder still to satisfy those of his patrons. Whereas the council of the College of Fort William demanded scholarly rigor, the committee of the CSBS demanded accessibility. Thus, although the two groups had members in common – and even convened on the same premises – they pulled Ramkamal in opposite directions. Although the college council had a larger budget than the committee, both together still could not fund the project in its entirety. Ramkamal hoped to make up the rest of the enormous cost of paying assistants and printing the dictionary through individual sales. Yet his compromises rendered the book unfit for scholars and students alike, and upon finally appearing in 1834 it sold poorly. Ramkamal's predicament reflected the transitional character of the age: While political attention had shifted away from scholarship, it had yet to refocus on popular education. In 1817, when Ramkamal began work on the dictionary, such education was the preserve of voluntary associations. Only in the long course of his travails would it become a direct concern of the Company.

Another scholar-collaborator who struggled in the interim was the Parsi Mulla Firuz bin Kawus. The great project that consumed years of his life was an epic poem in Persian entitled *Georgenama*. His nephew described its origins thus:

> In the year 1801, the Uncle of your Memorialist learnt from the late respected Governor [of Bombay, Jonathan] Duncan, that the Governor General the most noble the Marquis Wellesley having achieved a splendid victory over Tippoo Sooltan, was much desirous of having it commemorated in Verse in the Persian language, and no English scholar in the British settlement coming forward on the occasion, the Uncle of your Memorialist offered to compile in Persian Verse not only an account of the Victory over Tippoo Sooltan, but of the whole of the British Conquests in the East, which offer Mr. Duncan very gladly accepted, pleased very justly to encourage the Uncle of your Memorialist in the undertaking.[202]

[202] NAI, Bengal Public Consultations (23 Nov. 1836), no. 2.

As the Company's territory expanded in subsequent years, so too did Mulla Firuz's commission. Eventually, the poem ran to nearly forty thousand verses and carried up to the year 1817. It related the events by which the Company "from the condition of merchants were raised to that of governors; and ... attained to absolute dominion."[203] But flattering as this work would seem to have been to the Company, it attracted only limited support from Company leaders. At one point in the text, Mulla Firuz described feeling "heartbroken," with "no friend, nor well-wisher ... no one to listen to this tale."[204] He was sponsored by one after another governor of Bombay but failed to obtain the greater rewards he sought from Moira or the directors.[205] Finally, after the Mulla died in 1830, his nephew (and executor) recast the work as an effort in the cause of popular education. As a condition for underwriting a three-volume lithograph, the Bombay government fixed its price at the "lowest that could have been conjectured."[206] But sixty rupees was a still sizeable sum. And an epic poem in erudite Persian was ill-suited as a textbook. The Mulla's magnum opus, like Ramkamal's, was caught between the decline of one politics of knowledge and the rise of another.

CONCLUSION

From the 1820s, scholar-officials, like their Indian collaborators, would increasingly hitch their fortunes to the cause of education. And no wonder: Owing largely to the directors' lack of interest,

---

[203] Mulla Rustom, Announcement, trans., in "Curious Oriental Literature," *Literary Gazette; and Journal of Belles Lettres, Arts, and Sciences, &c.* (18 Nov. 1837), p. 738.

[204] Mullá Feruz bin Káwus, *The George-Námah*, ed. Mullá Rustam bin Kaikobád, 3 vols. (Bombay, 1837), vol. II, pp. 8–9.

[205] For the directors' refusal to award a pension to the Mulla's heirs, see Despatch to Bombay (23 Jan. 1828), BL, IOR E/4/1049, pp. 12–13. For his flattery of Moira, which seems to have fallen on deaf ears, see John Malcolm to Marquess of Hastings, 20 May 1819, Mount Stuart, HA/9/35; Edward Rehatsek, *Catalogue Raisonné of the Arabic, Hindostani, Persian, and Turkish MSS. in the Mulla Firuz Library* (Bombay, 1873), pp. 159–60.

[206] Moolla Rustom Bin Kaikobad, *Contents of the George Nameh, Composed in Verses in the Persian Language* ([Bombay], 1836), p. 5.

many scholarly projects and institutions lately had fallen short. By 1819, the decline of Company scholarship was being noticed as far away as the European continent: "Literary or scientific zeal appears to be unknown to the English in India, and the spirit once called into animation by Sir William Jones seems to have now become extinct."[207] The author of these remarks, the German oriental-ist Augustus Schlegel, was surely exaggerating. Still, one direc-tor spoke for many now when he claimed that the Company did not need scholars, for India could not be "retained by the force of erudition."[208]

By contrast, the directors showed a readiness to fund the new education associations that began to appear in India in the late 1810s.[209] Why was education starting to interest them and other prominent figures in the Company in a way that scholarship had not in recent years? The answer is that with the Company's rise to "para-mountcy" came an acknowledgment of new responsibilities. Moira had suggested already that the consolidation of British India would allow the Company to attend to the intellectual needs of its subjects. More to the point, political classes in Britain and India, including growing public, increasingly expected it to do so. In both places, the Company was coming to be seen less and less as a merchant and more and more as a territorial sovereign. Not only the rise of the Company's political power but also the decline of its commerce contributed to this change. Parliament threw open the India trade in 1813 and within a decade the Company's share had dwindled to insignificance (it retained control of the China trade.) Although the Company state endured, new ideas would be requisite to legitimize it.

---

[207] August Schlegel, "Ueber den Gegenwärtigen Zustand der Indischen Philologie" (1819), *Indische Bibliothek* 1 (1820), p. 26, cited and trans. in "Asiatic Society," *AJ* 14 (1822), p. 40.

[208] Henry St. George Tucker, "The Education of the Civil Service" (1843), in Tucker, *Memorials of Indian Government: Being a Selection from the Papers of Henry St. George Tucker*, ed. John William Kaye (London, 1853), p. 431.

[209] H. Sharp, ed., *Selections from Educational Records*, Part I: *1781–1839* (Calcutta, 1920), p. 45.

The concern that scholarly patronage was encouraging a shift toward large-scale territory receded once this shift became a fait accompli. The new concern of the directors, and of other Company leaders, was that such patronage endeared them only to a small elite. "Mass" or "popular" education promised to draw in a broader swath of Indian society as well as a liberal public in Britain.

5   Education and the Persistence of the Company State

In 1854, officials observed that in recent decades there was "no Indian question upon which more had been written" than "native education."[1] Indeed, in the 1820s to 1830s, in particular, that question generated sprawling debates involving all three Company presidencies.[2] These debates had different political roots than previous ones centered on scholarly patronage. At issue now was not whether the Company could or should secure extensive territory but instead whether, having done so, it could or should govern it. Paramountcy in India imperiled the Company's hybrid constitution anew. The best option for stakeholders in the Company seemed to be to buttress its claim to good government. Herein lay the main reason to establish a system of public education, something the state in Britain was only just beginning to contemplate.[3] But was the Company capable of educating the mass of Indian society? Or must it, even now, proceed by conciliating elites?

The politics of the Company's turn to education has yet to be properly explicated. Only recently have historians begun to correct an overemphasis on one minute penned by Thomas Babington Macaulay in 1835.[4] And to the extent that a kaleidoscopic view

---

[1] Cited in Nancy Gardner Cassels, *Social Legislation of the East India Company: Public Justice Versus Public Instruction* (New Delhi, 2010), p. 339.

[2] Singapore, which figures in this chapter, belonged to the fourth presidency of the Straits Settlements until this was downgraded to a residency of Bengal in 1830.

[3] Not until 1833 would parliament begin to provide funding for schools, and not until 1870 would it establish a system of mass education. For an overview of these developments, see Gillian Sutherland, "Education," in F. M. L. Thompson, ed., *Social Agencies and Institutions*, vol. 3 of *The Cambridge Social History of Britain, 1750–1950* (Cambridge, 1990).

[4] For example, Parimala V. Rao, *Beyond Macaulay: Education in India, 1780–1860* (New Delhi, 2019).

of education debates in British India has decentered that erstwhile focal point, it has also left in its place something of an interpretive void.[5] A few complications do need to be factored into any account of how and why the Company came to fixate on education. Notably, by the 1820s, its debates had grown to include a wider range of participants. Dispatches were framed not only by the directors and Board of Control but also in many cases by the Examiner's Office.[6] From various causes, above all the turnover of generations, governing councils were becoming prone to clashes of views.[7] Finally, pressure on the Company in Britain and India now came largely from "public opinion" as voiced in meetings, petitions, and the press.[8] For all of these reasons, the debates on education were variegated and diffuse. Even so, they coalesced around the premise that the Company's legitimacy was at stake and the question of how much it could hope to shape Indian society. The idea of conciliation regained prominence in these debates but also changed in meaning in several important ways. First, it no longer entailed patronizing scholar-officials, except as translators for education purposes. Second, it did entail patronizing Indian learned elites but increasingly only to gain access to the wider populace.

---

[5] For a recent overview, see Catriona Ellis, "History of Colonial Education: Key Reflections," in Padma M. Sarangapani and Rekha Pappu, eds., *Handbook of Education Systems in South Asia* (Singapore, 2021).

[6] Martin Moir, "The Examiner's Office: The Emergence of an Administrative Elite in East India House (1804–1858)," *India Office Library and Records Report for 1977* (1979); Martin Moir, "The Examiner's Office and the Drafting of East India Company Despatches," in Kenneth Ballhatchet and John Harrison, eds., *East India Company Studies: Papers Presented to Professor Sir Cyril Philips* (Hong Kong, 1986).

[7] On this turnover, see Katherine Prior, Lance Brennan, and Robin Haines, "Bad Language: The Role of English, Persian and other Esoteric Tongues in the Dismissal of Sir Edward Colebrooke as Resident of Delhi in 1829," *MAS* 35 (2001).

[8] See A. F. Salahuddin Ahmed, *Social Ideas and Social Change in Bengal, 1818–35*, 2nd edn (Calcutta, 1976); C. A. Bayly, *Recovering Liberties: Indian Thought in the Age of Liberalism and Empire* (Cambridge, 2012), chs. 1–3; Partha Chatterjee, *The Black Hole of Empire: History of a Global Practice of Power* (Princeton, 2012), chs. 4–5; Rohit De and Robert Travers, eds., Petitioning and Political Cultures in South Asia, special issue of *MAS* 53 (2019).

Thus, even many officials who advocated conciliation now described it as merely a temporary expedient. Mass education was held to be more in keeping with the character of a powerful state.

Throughout the period, officials debated the balance to be struck between conciliation and mass education. Only briefly was this question conflated with issues of language, leading to the so-called Anglicist-Orientalist controversy. For a moment in the 1830s, thanks largely to the official Charles Edward Trevelyan, English education appeared to have prevailed. But the more lasting impact of the controversy was the end of conciliation and the triumph of mass education in Company ideology.

CONCILIATION AND MASS EDUCATION IN THE 1820s

In the 1820s, Company officials took preliminary steps toward a system of public education in India. Not all were partisans of the Company, as opposed to say the Crown, but all were invested in maintaining its legitimacy. In Bengal, Madras, Bombay, and the new settlement of Singapore, they debated which system was most likely to secure that object. These debates were wide-ranging, but they centered on the balance to be struck between conciliation and mass education. The authorities in London too discussed this point and reached a general conclusion: While the former might be necessary at present, it was the latter upon which the Company's legitimacy would ultimately depend.

In Bengal, public education had emerged as both an object of attention and a subject of debate by the beginning of the decade. Among the indications of this development were moves to reform the Benares Sanskrit College and the Calcutta Madrasa. Whereas the government hitherto had been wary of meddling in these colleges, a minute on the former announced a momentous change:

> [W]hatever effect the establishment of the institution may have had in conciliating the attachment of the people, it has hitherto proved entirely useless as a seminary of learning and it must be

feared that the discredit attaching to such a failure has gone far to destroy the influence which the liberality of endowment would otherwise have had.[9]

The report of the college committee on which this minute was based contained little that was new. As early as 1804, the committee had described the college as an object of popular "ridicule ... a band of pensioners supported by the charity of government."[10] In finally heeding such criticism, however, Lord Moira and his council signaled that education took priority over scholarly patronage. They also suggested that the opinion of the people at large took priority over that of pandits. After years of half measures designed not to upset leading Muslims, meanwhile, the same criticism was making inroads at the Calcutta Madrasa. From 1823, the fate of both institutions would be decided by the General Committee of Public Instruction.

The committee was formed by Governor-General John Adam with a view to allocating the annual grant sanctioned by parliament a decade earlier. Of its ten original members, several were scholar-officials, and most had been involved in education associations. The committee's initial plan was drawn up by the councilor Holt Mackenzie and was strongly influenced by the idea of conciliation. "To provide for the education of the great body of the people," Mackenzie reasoned, would be "impossible, at least, in the present state of things." The Company was new to its vast responsibilities, remote from Indian society, and subject to financial constraints. Hence, Mackenzie continued, "the limited classes, who are now instructed ... in the learning of the Country, should be the first object of attention." Only by offering "encouragement" to these "educated and influential classes" could the state exercise any considerable "influence." Mackenzie proposed, however, that the committee's "ultimate" aim should be "the more general diffusion of knowledge"

---

[9] Governor-General in Council, Minute (17 Mar. 182[0]), in George Nicholls, *Sketch of the Rise and Progress of the Benares Patshalla or Sanskrit College* (Allahabad, 1907), p. 38.
[10] T. Brooke, Minute (1 Jan. 1804), in ibid., p. 9.

among "the people of India." He added that the subject of public education was "full of difficulty," and that his proposals were but "hints,
on which my own mind is quite unsettled." He enjoined the committee to "prepare some well digested scheme," some "comprehensive
plan" that might be "systematically pursued."[11] If Mackenzie hoped
to resolve the tension between conciliation and mass education, then
he was to be disappointed: This tension would continue to shape the
committee's proceedings for the next decade.

Mackenzie and his colleagues went back and forth but ultimately inclined toward conciliation. Their "indecision, uncer-
tainty and vacillation" owed, at root, to a sense of the limitations
of the Company's government.[12] On the one hand, the committee
founded two institutions for learned elites: the Delhi College and the
Calcutta Sanskrit College. The latter, it wrote, "will consist of men,
who by their Brahmanical birth, as well as by their learning, exercise
a powerful influence."[13] On the other hand, the committee framed
the Agra College along egalitarian lines: While "the existing government institutions ... are exclusive ... the Agra college shall be equally
available to all classes ... as they are all unquestionably, equally the
objects of the solicitude of the Government."[14] Significantly, Horace
Hayman Wilson, the committee's most prominent scholar, did not
endorse these remarks.[15] It was Wilson who had drawn up plans for
the Calcutta Sanskrit College, and who enjoyed the closest ties to
maulvis and pandits. And yet, a majority of the committee voted

---

[11] Holt Mackenzie, Minute (17 Jul. 1823), in *GIED*, pp. 99–100.

[12] For the quote, see D. P. Sinha, *Educational Policy of the East India Company in Bengal to 1854* (Calcutta, 1964), p. 95.

[13] GCPI to [Lord Amherst], 6 Oct. 1823, in H. Sharp, ed., *Selections from Educational Records, Part I: 1781–1839* (Calcutta, 1920), p. 87. For the committee's desire to employ "respectable scholars" at the Delhi College, and to inculcate the "scheme of castes" among students, see GCPI to Delhi Local Agency, 30 Aug. 1824, BL, F/4/909/25694, p. 559; Horace Hayman Wilson [1824], cited in C. E. Trevelyan, Minute (Jan. 1834), in C. E. Trevelyan et al., *The Application of the Roman Alphabet to All the Oriental Languages* (Serampore, 1834), p. 5.

[14] GCPI to Governor-General in Council, 24 Oct. 1823, BL, F/4/909/25694, pp. 518–19.

[15] Ibid., p. 531.

against funding schools for "the mass of the people" near Delhi, on the ground that resources should be spent first on "respectable members of Indian society."[16] The committee likewise resisted giving the Calcutta Madrasa or Benares Sanskrit College a popular character, proposing instead to reform both in cooperation with "the educated classes."[17] It insisted that only by catering to "the Maulavi and Pundit" could the Company influence Indian society.[18] Already, however, this premise was being disputed.

The general committee faced two major challenges in its early years, both of which concerned its preference for conciliation. The first came from Rammohan Roy, the Bengali reformer and intellectual, who, in a letter of 1823, took issue with the projected Calcutta Sanskrit College. In the name of "the native population," Rammohan called for instruction in the "useful sciences": Sanskrit had been but "a lamentable check on the diffusion of knowledge." In urging the committee to seek the good of "society" and not just of "Hindu pundits," Rammohan was making a case for popular education.[19] This case soon found support in paragraphs of a dispatch that have been attributed to James Mill, an assistant examiner at East India House. Mill likewise urged the committee to prioritize "useful learning" and implied that its regard for the "interests and feelings" of learned elites had been excessive.[20] In responding to these two critics, the committee acknowledged their concerns, and yet firmly rejected their conclusions. It dismissed Rammohan on the ground that, while he claimed to speak for "the natives of India," his "opinions are well known to be hostile to those entertained by almost all his countrymen."[21]

---

[16] William Fraser to W. B. Bayley, 25 Sept. 1823, in Sharp, ed., *Selections*, p. 14; GCPI to William Fraser, 29 Nov. 1823, in ibid., p. 15 n.

[17] Mackenzie to Madrasa Committee, 8 Aug. 1822, cited in Sinha, *Educational Policy*, p. 50. For these reforms, see J. Kerr, *A Review of Public Instruction in the Bengal Presidency, from 1835 to 1851*, 2 vols. (Calcutta, 1853), vol. II, pp. 66–75, 142–5.

[18] GCPI to Governor-General in Council, 18 Aug. 1824, in *GIED*, p. 121.

[19] Rammohan to Governor-General in Council, 11 Dec. 1823, in *GIED*, p. 111.

[20] Extract Revenue Despatch to Bengal (18 Feb. 1824), in *GIED*, pp. 116–17.

[21] J. Harington, Minute (14 Jan. 1824), in Rammohun Roy, *The Correspondence of Raja Rammohun Roy*, ed. Dilip Kumar Biswas, 2 vols. (Calcutta, 1992–4), vol. I, p. 200.

It rebutted Mill in similar fashion by claiming that "the literary classes" were against the introduction of foreign knowledge. It also held that since these classes controlled "public feeling," they must remain the first objects of "the beneficence of the Government."[22] As one official later recalled, the committee's aim at this time was to win "over the influential and learned classes, the Pundits and Mowluvees."[23] The committee appreciated the political value of education and yet doubted the social reach of the Company.

Things were different in Madras, where Sir Thomas Munro launched perhaps "the most comprehensive plan for government involvement in education ever proposed."[24] As devised by the governor, and implemented by his Committee of Public Instruction, the plan substantially favored popular education. It entailed creating a hierarchy of institutions: at the top, a central teachers' college; at the bottom, hundreds of local *tahsildari* (township) schools. Munro recognized that many non-elites were being taught in some districts of the presidency and sought to encourage this phenomenon. On the one hand, the committee stipulated that candidates for the teachers' college be "respectably connected" and, if Hindu, preferably Brahman.[25] Munro implied that the other institutions too would cater largely to "the middle and higher classes."[26] On the other hand, the committee, with Munro's support, aimed to "make these schools free for all classes, the master to pay no more attention to the Brahmin than to the Sudra boy."[27] Most telling of all, Munro proposed to spend on the *tahsildari* schools nearly twice as much as on the teachers' college. He reasoned thus:

---

[22] GCPI to Governor-General in Council, 18 Aug. 1824, p. 121.

[23] J. R. Colvin, Note (1839), cited in Sharp, ed., *Selections*, p. 171.

[24] Robert Eric Frykenberg, "Modern Education in South India, 1784–1854: Its Roots and Its Role as a Vehicle of Integration under Company Raj," *American Historical Review* 91 (1986), p. 47.

[25] Committee of Public Instruction to N. Webb et al., 24 Jun. 1826, in PP (1831–2), vol. 735-I, p. 462.

[26] Sir Thomas Munro, Minute (10 Mar. 1826), in ibid., p. 507.

[27] Committee of Public Instruction [1826], cited in ibid., p. 462.

Whatever expense Government may incur in the education of the people will be amply repaid by the improvement of the country; for the general diffusion of knowledge is inseparably followed by more orderly habits, by increasing industry, by a taste for the comforts of life, by exertions to acquire them, and by the growing prosperity of the people.[28]

Munro's system of education was an outgrowth of his system of land tenure, which aimed to curb hereditary privileges and forge direct relations with the ryot (peasant).[29] It also chimed with Scottish Enlightenment theories concerning the emergence and progress of civil society.[30] There was as yet no "public" in India, according to Munro, but the state would justify itself by educating one into existence. While he stressed that Indian self-rule was a distant prospect, Munro saw in its gradual realization the basis of the Company's legitimacy.

After Munro's death in 1827, his system was modified and ultimately abandoned. The preference of the Madras administration shifted toward conciliation. One cause was the merger of the Committee of Public Instruction with the Board of the College of Fort St. George, several of whose members were orientalists with ties to learned elites. The combined board, backed by successive governors, questioned the wisdom of mass education. According to one report, the government's "liberality" toward "the poorer classes" was at best "coldly acknowledged by them."[31] According to another, because Munro's schools were "open to all classes," the "higher

---

[28] Munro, Minute (10 Mar. 1826), p. 507.

[29] On this system, see Burton Stein, *Thomas Munro: The Origins of the Colonial State and His Vision of Empire* (Delhi, 1989).

[30] For this influence, see Martha McLaren, *British India and British Scotland, 1780–1830: Career Building, Empire Building, and a Scottish School of Thought on Indian Governance* (Akron, 2001). For a survey of this body of thought, see Fania Oz-Salzberger, "Civil Society in the Scottish Enlightenment," in Sudipta Kaviraj and Sunil Khilnani, eds., *Civil Society: History and Possibilities* (Cambridge, 2001).

[31] Board of Public Instruction to Governor in Council, 15 Nov. 1832, in Alexander J. Arbuthnot, *Papers Relating to Public Instruction* (Madras, 1855), Appendix, p. 1.

orders" were reluctant to send their children to them.[32] Many local officials gave favorable accounts of Munro's schools, but the board gave greater weight to those who dissented. In the 1830s, Governor Sir Frederick Adam ended support for the schools and his successor, Lord Elphinstone, charted "a new direction." Munro's system, Elphinstone alleged, had "produced nothing but disappointment": The state should focus on "influential and respectable natives."[33] As one of his allies put it, in defense of plans for an elite university, "the light must touch the mountain tops before it pierces to the depths."[34]

Another system was developed by another Elphinstone: the uncle, Mountstuart, who was appointed governor of Bombay in 1819. Having served in the newly conquered areas of Poona and the Deccan, he was well aware of the need to shore up "the slippery foundation of our Government."[35] Education might not be the first priority, wrote Elphinstone, but it was the key to all of the other ones.[36] Like his counterparts in Bengal and Madras, he faced a dilemma: to conciliate elites or to educate the masses? At first, he leant toward conciliation. He kept up the *dakshina*, a grant long given by the peshwas to learned Brahmans. He also founded the Poona Hindu College "to preserve the attachment" of this class, "whose influence has a very considerable effect over the feelings and conduct of the people at large."[37] From 1823, however, Elphinstone pursued a more ambitious object: "to diffuse knowledge among all orders of the people of this country."[38]

---

[32] Board of Public Instruction to Governor in Council, 6 Dec. 1834, in ibid., Appendix, p. lvii.

[33] Lord Elphinstone, Minute (12 Dec. 1839), in ibid., Appendix, p. cxxiii.

[34] George Norton, cited in ibid., p. 47 [emphasis removed].

[35] Mountstuart Elphinstone, Minute [13 Dec. 1823], in Elphinstone, *Selections from the Minutes and Other Official Writings of the Honourable Mountstuart Elphinstone, Governor of Bombay*, ed. George W. Forrest (London, 1884), p. 101.

[36] A. L. Covernton, "The Educational Policy of Mountstuart Elphinstone," *Journal of the Bombay Branch of the Royal Asiatic Society* new ser. 1 (1925), p. 71.

[37] William Chaplin to Governor in Council, 24 Nov. 1820, in R. V. Parulekar, ed., *Selections from the Records of the Government of Bombay: Education*, 3 vols. (Bombay, 1953-7), vol. I, p. 92.

[38] Mountstuart Elphinstone, Minute [1823], cited in Kenneth Ballhatchet, *Social Policy and Social Change in Western India 1817–1830* (Oxford, 1957), p. 251.

Elphinstone maintained that some "conciliation" of Brahmans was necessary owing to their great "numbers and influence," and that educating the very "lowest" and "most despised" castes would only ensure that "our system" and "our power" never spread beyond them.[39] At times, he made a gradualist argument similar to that of Mackenzie in Calcutta: It would become easier to educate "the lower orders ... after a spirit of inquiry and improvement shall have been introduced among their superiors."[40] He proposed measures to benefit these "lower orders" from the beginning, however, and, after the advent of Munro's system, sought to afford them "the same means of instruction ... as at Madras."[41] What Elphinstone advocated was to combine the conciliation of elites and the education of the masses – to act upon almost the whole body of society.

It was largely this new degree of state social involvement that generated resistance to Elphinstone's plans. His early efforts had occasioned sundry debate. But from 1823, he would face sustained opposition from one of his councilors. Responding to Elphinstone's minute of that year, Francis Warden objected that "education, as a Government concern" would dampen "individual exertions." He preferred to "excite the zeal of individuals," in part through a proposed English-medium college. The urban upper classes would contribute to the institution, Warden predicted, and schoolmasters would arise from the student ranks. The Bombay Native School Society would handle most of the details; donations and school fees would provide most of the necessary funding. Warden was adamant, however, that "the Government should not be too forward in taking the education of the natives on itself .... From an over anxiety to complete so good a work, we run the danger of attempting too much at once, and defeating our object."[42] Elphinstone was no less adamant that, having "assumed the Government of the Natives, it

---

[39] Elphinstone, Minute [13 Dec. 1823], pp. 96–7, 105, 109.

[40] Elphinstone to Thomas Hyde Villiers, 5 Aug. 1832, in PP (1831–2), vol. 735-I, p. 293.

[41] Mountstuart Elphinstone, Minute [1826], cited in Ballhatchet, *Social Policy*, p. 274.

[42] Francis Warden, Minute (29 Dec. 1823), in PP (1831–2), vol. 735-I, pp. 519–20.

is our duty to assist in their improvement."[43] "If we are to do anything" about education, he asseverated, "we must do it through our own Agents."[44] In 1825, Elphinstone observed that in the past year he and his council had spilt more ink on the subject "than both the other Presidencies have on all subjects."[45] And yet, despite these "almost constant discussions," they remained at an impasse.[46] After Elphinstone's departure in 1827, the debate extended to the professorships endowed by wealthy Indians in his name: It would be nearly a decade until the first "Elphinstone Professors" commenced their lectures.[47] The new governor, John Malcolm, followed Elphinstone in seeking both to "conciliate ... learned Hindoos" and to spread "knowledge among all classes."[48] In these attempts, however, he too was hindered by the intractable Warden.

Yet another system was tried in Singapore and debated along similar lines as in the other presidencies. The major difference here was that the Company's interests, in the words of Sir Thomas Stamford Raffles, still lay in "trade, and not territory." As Raffles put it, upon founding the settlement in 1819, Singapore must be conducted on "purely commercial principles."[49] He repeated this view in a pamphlet of the same year that advocated

---

[43] Mountstuart Elphinstone, Minute [1824], Maharashtra State Archives, Bombay General Volumes, vol. 8/63 (1824), p. 226.

[44] Mountstuart Elphinstone, Minute (1 Mar. 1824), ibid., p. 298.

[45] Mountstuart Elphinstone, Minute (23 Aug. 1825), Maharashtra State Archives, Bombay General Volumes, vol. 8/92 (1825), p. 625.

[46] Mountstuart Elphinstone, Minute (Sept. 1826), cited in Parulekar, ed., Selections, vol. II, p. xviii.

[47] See Kenneth Ballhatchet, "The Elphinstone Professors and Elphinstone College, 1827–1840," in C. H. Philips and Mary Doreen Wainwright, eds., Indian Society and the Beginnings of Modernisation, c. 1830–1850 (London, 1976); Naheed F. Ahmad, "The Elphinstone College, Bombay, 1827–1890: A Case Study in 19th Century English Education," in Mushirul Hasan, ed., Knowledge, Power and Politics: Educational Institutions in India (New Delhi, 1998), pp. 392–7.

[48] John Malcolm, Minute (1828), in PP (1831–2), vol. 735-I, p. 526; John Malcolm, Minute (30 Jul. 1828), ibid., p. 472.

[49] Sir Thomas Stamford Raffles, "On the Administration of the Eastern Islands in 1819," in Sophia Raffles, Memoir of the Life and Public Services of Sir Thomas Stamford Raffles (London, 1830), Appendix, pp. 12–13.

the establishment of a college on the island. In continental India, he observed, the Company had disseminated knowledge as a means of augmenting "the power ... of the state." Around the Strait of Malacca, however, the Company must act according to a different principle: "While with one hand we carry to their shores the capital of our merchants, the other should be stretched forth to offer them the means of intellectual improvement." Raffles proceeded to outline a system of conciliation in which educating "the higher orders" – the sons of Malay chiefs – would "attach them more closely to us."[50] The Lieutenant-Governor was not ignorant of the latest education theories: In Bencoolen, he had set up schools on the Lancastrian model. Moreover, like counterparts in India, he proposed to eventually educate a wider range of the populace.[51] Unlike these officials, however, Raffles understood education in fundamentally commercial terms: as a commodity to be bartered for security, goodwill, and other advantages. His views were ambitious, but the ambitions they bespoke dated back to the previous century.[52] It was a question whether these views would take hold in the 1820s.

Events provided an answer in the negative. After various delays, Raffles took steps to establish his college in 1823.[53] Without waiting for approval from London, he endowed lands, collected subscriptions, and commissioned a grand edifice for his "Singapore Institution."[54] But the building was poorly planned and

---

[50] [Sir Thomas Stamford Raffles], *On the Advantage of Affording the Means of Education to the Inhabitants of the Further East* (1819), repr. as Sir Thomas Stamford Raffles, *The First Printing of Sir Stamford Raffles's* Minute on the Establishment of a Malay College at Singapore, ed. John Bastin (Eastbourne, 1999).

[51] Raffles to William Wilberforce, Sept. 1819, in Raffles, *Memoir*, p. 408.

[52] See generally G. G. Hough, "Notes on the Educational Policy of Sir Stamford Raffles," *Journal of the Malaysian Branch of the Royal Asiatic Society* 42 (1969).

[53] For details, see R. L. O'Sullivan, "The Anglo-Chinese College and the Early 'Singapore Institution,'" *Journal of the Malaysian Branch of the Royal Asiatic Society* 61 (1988), pp. 48–52.

[54] Raffles, *Memoir*, Appendix, pp. 74–86; Munshi Abdullah, "The Hikayat Abdullah" (1849), trans. A. H. Hill, *Journal of the Malaysian Branch of the Royal Asiatic Society* 28 (1955), p. 160.

executed.[55] When funding ran out, all that had been built was "a mass of Brick Work," which soon became a "shelter for thieves."[56] By the time of Raffles' death, in 1826, his college too seemed destined for oblivion.[57] According to a report by the Company's resident, John Crawfurd, the institution's problems ran deeper than hasty construction and inadequate funds. The far-flung royalty that Raffles had hoped to attract had not materialized; the need among local inhabitants was for a school or two rather than a college.[58] Crawfurd and other officials saw the institution as ill-situated, befitting perhaps a territorial capital but not an island outpost. In a letter to the directors, the new governor in council declared that its grandiose objects "were not at all adapted to the circumstances of this infant colony."[59] This thinking was reflected in a Malay-language address distributed by the local administration in 1827: From a wish to extend to Singapore "the advantages enjoyed by ... other parts of their Dominions," the Company would allocate funds for elementary instruction.[60] Thus, despite the link between commerce and conciliation, which Raffles had revived, the idea of mass education won out in Singapore. When the Singapore Institution was reestablished in the 1830s, it took the form of a local boys' school.

Just as the Company's authorities in Asia differed and dithered, so too did its authorities in London. In a single dispatch of 1827, they praised the general committee for focusing on the higher classes in Delhi and for instructing all classes in Agra.[61] They at first supported

[55] Philip Jackson to J. A. Maxwell, 14 Jul. [1824], Raffles Archives and Museum, Raffles Institution Records; "Education in Eastern Asia," *Malacca Observer*, repr. in *AJ* 28 (Jul. 1829), p. 106.

[56] Extract General Despatch from Singapore (20 May 1828), BL, IOR F/4/1043/28683, f. 10r; Newspaper, cited in Charles Burton Buckley, *An Anecdotal History of Old Times in Singapore*, 2 vols. (Singapore, 1902), vol. I, p. 127.

[57] For further details, see E. Wijeysingha, *The Eagle Breeds a Gryphon: The Story of the Raffles Institution 1823–1985* (Singapore, 1989), ch. 3.

[58] Crawfurd to Governor-General in Council, 7 Feb. 1826, BL, IOR F/4/1043/28683, ff. 77r–v.

[59] Extract General Despatch from Singapore (20 May 1828), f. 10v.

[60] Address, trans. in Singapore Resident's Diary (25 Jan. 1827), Singapore National Archives, N1, pp. 67–70.

[61] Extract Public Despatch to Bengal (5 Sept. 1827), in PP (1831–2), vol. 735-I, pp. 489–90.

Munro's system and described "the education of the great mass of the population" as "worthy of great encouragement."[62] Yet, on a later occasion, they issued the following admonition to the Madras government:

> The improvements in education ... which most effectually
> contribute to elevate the moral and intellectual condition of
> a people, are those which concern the education of the higher
> classes; of the persons possessing leisure, and natural influence
> over the minds of their countrymen. By raising the standard of
> instruction among these classes, you would eventually produce a
> much greater and more beneficial change in the ideas and feelings
> of the community than you can hope to produce by acting
> directly on the more numerous class.[63]

The chief author of this dispatch was the assistant examiner John Stuart Mill, who, like his father, James, had once approved of mass education.[64] This variance between father and son, and between the son and his former self, illustrated the confused and shifting state of thinking in London. No longer in doubt, at least, was the value of education in attracting support for the Company, including in Britain. By 1826, the directors were boasting of what they had "done for the purpose of extending education generally throughout India." According to the chairman, they were spending in Bengal and its northern dependencies "nearly one lac [lakh] and a half" more than the sum provided for by the Charter Act, not to mention one lakh in Bombay and Madras and a "considerable" amount in Singapore and the other Straits Settlements.[65] On every occasion, the home authorities avowed the ultimate desirability of educating the Indian masses.

---

[62] Extract Public Despatch to Bengal (9 Mar. 1825), in ibid., p. 489.

[63] Public Despatch to Madras (29 Sept. 1830), in *GIED*, p. 126.

[64] Penelope Carson, "Golden Casket or Pebbles and Trash? J.S. Mill and the Anglicist/ Orientalist Controversy," in Martin I. Moir, Douglas M. Peers, and Lynn Zastoupil, eds., *J.S. Mill's Encounter with India* (Toronto, 1999), pp. 157–9.

[65] [Campbell Marjoribanks], Speech in East India House Debate (21 Jun. 1826), *AJ* 22 (1826), p. 117.

They seem to have determined already that any system of conciliation would be temporary.

THE ANGLICIST-ORIENTALIST CONTROVERSY REVISITED

Upon reaching the 1830s, most surveys of Indian education have concerned themselves with the Anglicist-Orientalist controversy. As the previous section has shown, however, the 1820s witnessed a number of other education debates. To the extent that these centered on any one issue, it was the choice between conciliation and mass education. The question then becomes how contention on this issue fed into the later controversy. The answer can be summarized in the name Charles Edward Trevelyan. In Delhi and then in Calcutta, the young official advanced the view that English and mass education went together. He and his "Anglicist" allies were opposed by the "Orientalists," who in truth were wedded less to oriental languages than to the idea of conciliation. What the Charter Act of 1833 accomplished, by ending the Company's trade altogether, was to make its legitimacy rest all the more on its claim to good government. The act, framed largely by Thomas Babington Macaulay, also empowered Governor-General Lord William Bentinck to settle the education question. This Bentinck did in 1835 by endorsing Trevelyan's program, which was now Macaulay's as well. For the moment, English education appeared to be in the ascendant. The more permanent result was the eclipse of the idea of conciliation by that of mass education.

The origins of the Anglicist-Orientalist controversy are properly dated to 1827. In that year, Trevelyan came to Delhi and began "labouring in the cause" that he would carry to victory eight years later.[66] The young Company official was inspired by Evangelical and Utilitarian doctrines – but only in part.[67] As studies of his later

---

[66] Trevelyan to Lord William Bentinck, 30 Apr. 1834, in Bentinck, *The Correspondence of Lord William Cavendish Bentinck*, ed. C. H. Philips, 2 vols. (Oxford, 1977), vol. II, p. 1261.

[67] For these influences, see J. F. Hilliker, "Charles Edward Trevelyan as an Educational Reformer in India 1827–1838," *Canadian Journal of History* 9 (1974), pp. 278–9.

career have discovered, his interests were eclectic, his motivations unusual.[68] "To be widely different from others" was the motto of his fictional double in Anthony Trollope's *The Three Clerks* (1858).[69] It was from his obsession with the "influence of language on national habits of thinking" that the Anglicist position emerged.[70] This position was developed in minutes of the Delhi College Committee of which Trevelyan was the principal author.[71] Its distinctive feature was the twinning of considerations of social reach and of language. The committee held that the masses could be educated only through English and English-inflected vernaculars, and that to preserve Persian, Sanskrit, and Arabic was "to throw the people into the hands of intermediate Agents." These "literary Mohamedans" and presumably pandits, according to the committee, were attached to "the old system" and opposed to any new one. By contrast, "the bulk of the people" were "attached to no previous system" and "ready to adopt our own Literature."[72] Affording them this opportunity, the committee added, would have profound political benefits: It would "tend rapidly ... to amalgamate all classes" and to "form a bond of union between ourselves and them." The combined effect of attaching the people to each other and to their rulers would be to establish "a sort of national character."[73] Trevelyan and his

[68] Jenifer Hart, "Sir Charles Trevelyan at the Treasury," *English Historical Review* 75 (1960); Kevin Theakston, *Leadership in Whitehall* (Basingstoke, 1999), ch. 2; Robin Haines, *Charles Trevelyan and the Great Irish Famine* (Dublin, 2004).

[69] Anthony Trollope, *The Three Clerks: A Novel*, 3 vols. (London, 1858), vol. I, p. 107.

[70] C. E. Trevelyan, *A Treatise on the Means of Communicating the Learning and Civilization of Europe to India* (Calcutta, 1834), p. 14. One source for this idea – and the immediate source for this phrase – was a history of Islam that "enjoyed as extensive a circulation in British India as in the mother country." Charles Mills, *An History of Muhammedanism* (London, 1817), p. 350 n.; [Augustine Skottowe], *A Memoir of the Life and Writings of Charles Mills* (London, 1828), p. 63.

[71] There are at least two reasons to infer that Trevelyan was the principal author: The committee's arguments changed noticeably after he became a member, and many of these arguments appeared again in his later writings. See especially [Charles Edward Trevelyan], Draft Minute [c. 1833–4], Newcastle University Library, CET 102. For the attribution, see J. F. Hilliker, "Trevelyan and the Reform of Indian Education," *Indo-British Review* 6 (1974).

[72] Delhi College Committee to GCPI, 12 Feb. 1829, BL, IOR F/4/1170/30639, pp. 313–39.

[73] Delhi College Committee to GCPI, 14 Apr. 1829, ibid., pp. 372–4.

colleagues thus proposed to make education – for the masses and in English – a vehicle for state-building.

The proposal met with a mixed response. The General Committee of Public Instruction fell back upon the idea of conciliation. It objected, in the first place, to the Delhi officials' plan to create a system of English schools and colleges. To divert funds from the Delhi College for this purpose, the committee alleged, would anger "the most influential Mahomedans, and particularly the men of learning," who "would have the strongest interest in opposing a change that was to deprive them of all credit and subsistence." The committee doubted, moreover, whether qualified teachers and interested students could be found outside of Calcutta. It concluded that it was best to continue introducing English in a piecemeal and peaceable fashion.[74] In this way, the committee sidestepped the arguments of its Delhi subsidiary and upheld its own modest English initiatives. Yet the acknowledgment that English instruction was sought-after, at least in Calcutta, weakened its position. Holt Mackenzie, who had done much to shape the committee's views, now took the unusual step of recording a partial dissent. He held, first, that the demand for English should be investigated, and, second, that English should fully replace Persian as the official language.[75]

Mackenzie's note in support of English and popular education found a receptive audience in Bentinck. Already, by 1829, the new governor-general had expressed a desire to engage with the Indian public. He relaxed controls on the press and invited suggestions from "all Native Gentlemen, Landholders, Merchants and others."[76] Fostering "native agency" was part of a larger project to give the Company's territories what he called "nationality."[77] This project shaped Bentinck's response to the minutes of the general committee

---

[74] GCPI to Governor-General in Council, 2 Jun. 1829, ibid., pp. 341–5.

[75] Mackenzie, Note (3 Jun. 1829), ibid., pp. 350–52.

[76] A. Dobbs, Notice (23 Feb. 1829), *Government Gazette* (2 Mar. 1829), repr. in Ahmed, *Social Ideas*, p. 4 n.

[77] On this project, see John Rosselli, *Lord William Bentinck: The Making of a Liberal Imperialist, 1774–1839* (Berkeley, 1974), pp. 180–89.

and of its Delhi subsidiary. Like Mackenzie, Bentinck endorsed the former for the moment but showed greater enthusiasm for the latter. He wrote of "giving to our Institutions for Native education ... a more popular character."[78] Moreover, he described "encouraging the acquisition of the British language" as "the key to all improvement."[79] If Bentinck had yet to act on the views of the Delhi committee, then he had at least proved sympathetic to them. For Trevelyan, the question was how to secure his commitment.

Prevented from founding his schools, at least temporarily, Trevelyan pressed ahead with other reforms in Delhi. Many of these involved shifting the Company's base of support from nobles and learned elites to a broader public. In 1829, he succeeded in having the resident, Sir Edward Colebrooke, dismissed for corruption. Bound up in the case were larger questions of language and social policy. Whereas Colebrooke had courted the city's Persianate aristocracy, Trevelyan championed its English-leaning middle classes.[80] It was in the context of a turning tide against the old guard – British and Indian – that the English class at Delhi College commenced. "This little class," according to its sponsor, Trevelyan, "was formed amidst the scoffs of the learned natives, and the ... objections of ... European residents."[81] The college maulvis shunned the Muslim students, causing most to unenroll, and the college pandits seem to have pressured the Brahman ones.[82] Hence, from almost the beginning, most of the students came from other social groups:

---

[78] Governor-General in Council to GCPI, 26 Jun. 1829, BL, IOR F/4/1170/30639, pp. 385–92.

[79] Bentinck to Metcalfe, 16 Sept. 1829, in Bentinck, *Correspondence*, vol. I, p. 288.

[80] Prior, Brennan, and Haines, "Bad Language"; Margrit Pernau, *Ashraf into Middle Classes: Muslims in Nineteenth-Century Delhi* (New Delhi, 2013), pp. 91–6.

[81] C. E. Trevelyan, "Memoir," in Mohan Lal, *Journal of a Tour through the Panjab, Afghanistan, Turkistan, Khorasan, and Part of Persia* (Calcutta, 1834), p. ix.

[82] Shahamat Ali, *The Sikhs and Afghans, in Connexion with India and Persia, Immediately before and after the Death of Ranjeet Singh* (London, 1847), pp. viii–ix; Michael H. Fisher, "Mohan Lal Kashmiri (1812–77): An Initial Student of Delhi English College," in Margrit Pernau, ed., *The Delhi College: Traditional Elites, the Colonial State, and Education before 1857* (New Delhi, 2006), p. 241.

> Christian, Mohammedan, and Hindu boys, of every shade of
> colour and variety of descent may be seen standing side by side
> in the same class .... This is a great point gained. The artificial
> institution of taste cannot long survive the period when the
> youth of India ... disregard it.... Habits of friendly communication
> will thus be established between all classes, they will insensibly
> become one people, and the process of enlightening our subjects
> will proceed simultaneously with that of uniting them among
> themselves.[83]

Trevelyan would record this triumphant account in 1838. But as early
as 1830, he observed that "the large and intelligent classes of Kaiths
[Kayasths] and Cashmerians [Kashmiris]" were exchanging Persian
for English.[84] He predicted that, by raising up this middling order,
the English class would serve as "the nucleus of a system which, to
all appearances, is destined to change ... the whole of Upper India."[85]

And yet Trevelyan sought to change the whole of *British* India,
a goal furthered by his transfer to the capital, Calcutta, in 1831.
Before long, he was the chief reformer among the younger officials
and, in particular, "the soul of every scheme for diffusing education
among the natives."[86] Trevelyan's ascent owed to his skill, on the one
hand, in cultivating officials, and, on the other, in cultivating public opinion through the press.[87] These efforts worked in tandem: He
went to great pains to convince Bentinck, especially, that his views
on education were popular.[88] He tried other methods too. When an

---

[83] Charles E. Trevelyan, *On the Education of the People of India* (London, 1838), p. 20.
For evidence on the social makeup of the class, see Margrit Pernau, introduction to
Pernau, ed., *Delhi College*, pp. 27–8.

[84] Trevelyan, *Treatise*, pp. 19–20. He dated this section 21 May 1830.

[85] Trevelyan, "Memoir," p. ix.

[86] Thomas Babington Macaulay to Mrs. Edward Cropper, 7 Dec. 1834, in Thomas
Babington Macaulay, *The Letters of Thomas Babington Macaulay*, ed. Thomas
Pinney, 6 vols. (Cambridge, 1974–81), vol. III, p. 100.

[87] A. D. Webb, "Charles Edward Trevelyan in India: A Study of the Channels of Influence
Employed by a Covenanted Civil Servant in the Translation of Personal Ideas into
Official Policy," *South Asia: Journal of South Asian Studies* new ser. 6 (1983).

[88] Trevelyan to Bentinck, 18 Mar. 183[3], in Bentinck, *Correspondence*, vol. II, p. 777.

Awadhi nobleman came to Calcutta, Trevelyan exhorted him to study English; he also likely assisted him with an ode to Bentinck that celebrated his founding of schools open to "High and Low ... Poor and Rich."[89] Trevelyan may have been the loudest advocate of mass or English education, but increasingly he was joined by other voices. Indian pupils flocked to the English school of the missionary Alexander Duff; pleas for government schools on its model appeared in local newspapers.[90] Such was the state of affairs in March 1833 when Trevelyan wrote the following to Bentinck:

> It is now my intention to apply myself seriously to what I have for a long time past considered the great enterprise of my life. I mean the moral and intellectual renovation of the people of India. I long to see established under your Lordship's auspices a system of education so comprehensive as to embrace every class of public teachers, so elastic as to admit of its being gradually extended to every village in the country and so interwoven with the constitution of the state ... as to furnish the highest motives to intellectual exertion to the whole body of the people ....[91]

If Trevelyan meant to forward his candidacy for the general committee, then he succeeded: An appointment followed in April. And in May, the Anglicist-Orientalist controversy began in earnest. "We have ... arrived at a crisis in the annals of the Education Committee," declared one member, "and the question has become 'whether the natives of India are to remain orientalists or to be made English in their language and literature.'"[92]

---

[89] [Iqbal ud-Daula] Icbal-ood Dowlah, *Icbal-e-Furung or British Prosperity* (Calcutta, 1834), pp. 21, 23, 31, 33.

[90] For examples of such appeals, see *Reformer* (Calcutta; 18 Mar. 1833); "Native Education," *Gyananneshun* (25 Jul. 1833), repr. in Suresh Chandra Moitra, ed., *Selections from Jnanannesan* (Calcutta, 1979), p. 73.

[91] Trevelyan to Bentinck, 18 Mar. 183[3], pp. 776–7.

[92] James Prinsep, Minute (20 May 1833), West Bengal State Archives, GCPI Proceedings, vol. 4, p. 252.

"Orientalists" was a term less often applied to Indians than to Trevelyan's opponents on the general committee. It seems to have been Trevelyan himself who coined this somewhat misleading epithet.[93] Their resistance to mass and English instruction he attributed to their pursuit of a "reputation for oriental learning": They wished to spend the committee's funds on abstruse scholarship instead of on the "education of the people."[94] Trevelyan had a point. With the terminal decline of the College of Fort William, some scholar-officials turned to the committee for patronage.[95] The committee's own secretary, Horace Hayman Wilson, obtained a large grant to prepare and print several works in Sanskrit. But not all so-called Orientalists matched this description. Nor was fame their only motivation. The committee, led by Wilson, still avowed the necessity of "conciliating" the "influential and learned classes." It cited "the limited means at the Committee's disposal, and the inadequacy of any means to the education of a whole people," as well as a political imperative to offset the loss of these scholars' "natural patrons."[96] The Orientalists' preference for India's "learned languages" was thus largely a byproduct of their preference for learned elites. Tellingly, Wilson objected less to the teaching of English at Delhi College than to the supposedly low social class of its superintendent.[97] After the accession of Trevelyan, Wilson did

[93] The term "Anglicists" seems to have originated with B. H. Hodgson, *Preeminence of the Vernaculars; or the Anglicists Answered* (Serampore, 1837).

[94] Trevelyan, Minute (Jan. 1834), pp. 16–26. See also [Trevelyan], Draft Minute [c. 1833–4], ff. 9r–v; Trevelyan to Bentinck [1834] University of Nottingham Libraries, PwJf 2105.

[95] For the decline of the college's literary fund, in particular, see David Kopf, *British Orientalism and the Bengal Renaissance: The Dynamics of Indian Modernization, 1773–1835* (Berkeley, 1969), pp. 220, 234.

[96] *Report on the Colleges and Schools for Native Education, under the Superintendance of the General Committee of Public Instruction in Bengal 1831* (Calcutta, 1832), BL, IOR V/24/946, pp. 44, 47.

[97] For Wilson's disapproval of this "East Indian" (Eurasian) superintendent, John Henry Taylor, see Horace Hayman Wilson, Note [1830], West Bengal State Archives, GCPI Correspondence on Delhi College, vol. 2, part 1, pp. 304–5. Elsewhere, he wrote that he was "as friendly" as Trevelyan to "a wide extension of English." Wilson to Ramkamal Sen, 25 Sept. 1835, cited in Peary Chand Mittra, *Life of Dewan Ramcomul Sen* (Calcutta, 1880), p. 19.

worry that the committee had gone "English-mad" and would alien-
ate "Pundits and Moulvis."[98] Henry Thoby Prinsep, who replaced
him as leader of the Orientalists, began to fervently oppose the promotion of English.[99] In this way, the Orientalist position came to
mirror the Anglicist one. On neither side, however, did issues of
social class simply give way to issues of language.

For all of its rhetorical sprawl, the controversy turned substantially on the same question that had exercised officials for over a
decade. This was clear from the summary arguments of each side
between which Bentinck, in January 1835, was asked to adjudicate.
Whereas the Orientalists declared as their "first great principle ...
that of aiding ... the enlightened and influential Classes," the
Anglicists upheld the government's duty to educate "all classes of its
Indian subjects."[100] Trevelyan persisted in characterizing the divide
as one between a "popular" party and an "anti-popular" party.[101] For
that matter, his adversaries scarcely attempted to shift the terms of
debate. Prinsep and other Orientalists, including his brother James,
could countenance the "peaceful and insensible" spread of English.[102]
Trevelyan, however, would accept nothing less than "radical" social
change. "Our object," he wrote, "is to instruct the people of India by
the united means of English and of the popular languages," not to
"conciliate" the "learned few" by patronizing their studies in Persian,
Sanskrit, and Arabic.[103] This argument prevailed on Bentinck, who
had inclined toward it from the beginning. In February 1835, he broke
the committee's deadlock by endorsing the minute of Trevelyan's
ally Macaulay.

Bentinck was roused to action by events in London as well as
in Calcutta. By ending the Company's trade, the Charter Act of 1833

---

[98] Wilson to Ramkamal Sen, 21 Dec. 1833, in Mittra, *Life*, p. 14.

[99] John Featherston Hilliker, "British Education Policy in Bengal, 1833–1854" (PhD dissertation, University of London, 1968), pp. 93–9.

[100] GCPI to Governor-General in Council, 21 Jan. 1835, in *GIED*, pp. 137, 154.

[101] Trevelyan to Bentinck, 9 Apr. 1834, in Bentinck, *Correspondence*, vol. II, pp. 1238–9.

[102] J. Prinsep, Minute (2 Jan. 1834), in Trevelyan et al., *Application*, p. 35.

[103] Trevelyan, Minute (Jan. 1834), pp. 4, 18, 26.

resolved a longstanding dialectic.[104] As Bentinck put it, "Our character is no longer the inconsistent one of Merchant and Sovereign.... Our future care is that of a vast Territory ...."[105] The Company state endured, in the sense that the corporate structure remained intact and served as an umbrella for private trading interests.[106] Family connections, too, sustained "the nexus between state office and business activity."[107] Yet if the Company was now, to quote one official, "a company of sovereigns," then its legitimacy rested all the more on claims to good government.[108] Its regime in India must appear to be, in Macaulay's words, "an enlightened and paternal despotism."[109] As secretary to the Board of Control, Macaulay played a leading role in drawing up the act and defending it in parliament. Through the recently returned Holt Mackenzie, and through parliamentary reports, he would have become acquainted with the full range of British views on Indian education. Although the act made no explicit provision for education, its entire logic depended upon it. This at least was what Macaulay suggested in the peroration of a climactic speech before the Commons:

> It may be that the public mind of India may expand under our system till it has outgrown that system; that by good government we may educate our subjects into a capacity for better government; that, having become instructed in European knowledge, they may, in some future age, demand European institutions.

[104] On the significance of the act, and for details mentioned below, see Joshua Ehrlich, "The Crisis of Liberal Reform in India: Public Opinion, Pyrotechnics, and the Charter Act of 1833," *MAS* 52 (2018). Since 1813, the Company's monopoly had been limited to the China route. Long before 1833, its share of the India trade had dwindled in consequence.

[105] Lord William Bentinck, Minute (20 Jan. 1834), BL, IOR F/4/1551/62250, p. 83.

[106] Anthony Webster, *The Twilight of the East India Company: The Evolution of Anglo-Asian Commerce and Politics, 1790–1860* (Woodbridge, UK, 2009).

[107] D. A. Washbrook, "India, 1818–1860: The Two Faces of Colonialism," in Andrew Porter, ed., *The Nineteenth Century*, vol. 3 of *The Oxford History of the British Empire* (Oxford, 1999), p. 412.

[108] Charles Metcalfe, Minute (11 Oct. 1829), in Bentinck, *Correspondence*, vol. I, p. 309.

[109] Thomas Babington Macaulay, Speech in HC Deb (10 Jul. 1833), in Macaulay, *The Works of Lord Macaulay*, ed. Lady Trevelyan, 8 vols. (London, 1866), vol. VIII, p. 139.

Macaulay closed by invoking the distant prospect of a self-ruled India that shared "our arts and our morals, our literature and our laws."[110] The speech was a triumph. Macaulay wrote to his sister that it had drawn "such compliments as ... you never heard" from his fellow members of parliament.[111] It not only cemented Macaulay's reputation as an orator but also smoothed the way for his appointment to the Supreme Council. One of his new admirers was Bentinck, who declared himself "delighted with Macaulay's appointment."[112] And no wonder: Among other things, Macaulay had given Bentinck the authority he needed to settle the education question.

The Charter Act, especially as put forward by Macaulay, hardened Bentinck's resolve. He had long favored Trevelyan's views on education but had hesitated to give them his full support. For one thing, he had been ordered to retrench by the home authorities and felt compelled to consult them on important decisions.[113] For another, he feared making enemies of the Orientalists; hence playing "his cards unusually close to his chest."[114] Most importantly, he harbored doubts about the extent of Indian demand for English.[115] The Charter Act altered all of these calculations by authorizing Bentinck to act independently. He was now governor-general of India, not just of Bengal, and could override his council, the other governors, and the Supreme Court if necessary. Along with these powers came expectations, among which the provision of mass education figured prominently. Macaulay would have conveyed this expectation to Bentinck upon his arrival in India in late 1834. Bentinck would have required little convincing: He had declared already that India's "great want" was "knowledge" and "general education ...

---

[110] Ibid., p. 142.

[111] Macaulay to Hannah Macaulay, 11 Jul. 1833, in Macaulay, *Letters*, vol. II, p. 268.

[112] Bentinck to Daniel Wilson, 1 May 1834, in Bentinck, *Correspondence*, vol. II, p. 1264.

[113] Albert H. Imlah, *Lord Ellenborough: A Biography of Edward Law, Earl of Ellenborough, Governor-General of India* (Cambridge, 1939), p. 44 n. 65; C. H. Philips, *The East India Company, 1784–1834*, 2nd edn (Manchester, 1961), p. 262.

[114] Rosselli, *Lord William Bentinck*, p. 220.

[115] See Trevelyan to Bentinck, 9 Apr. 1834, p. 1238.

my panacea."[116] After appointing Macaulay to the general committee, Bentinck endorsed his minute without consulting the home authorities.[117] Nor did he show any compunction about excluding from the council minutes a rebuttal from Prinsep.[118] In a final sign of the impact of the Charter Act, Bentinck signaled that he would no longer wait for "the public mind" to "become better prepared."[119] As the Anglicists put it in their summary argument, the people had no "inherent right ... to demand" an "erroneous education at the expense of the state."[120]

Bentinck's resolution has been remembered as a victory for English, but it was at least as much a victory for mass education. The purpose of Macaulay's minute, for all of its polemical fireworks, was in keeping with the ideas of his now brother-in-law Trevelyan. Macaulay's greatest departure was to focus, like the Orientalists, on teaching a fraction of the people instead of the people at large. Yet what he advocated was not conciliation: He aimed not to patronize old elites but rather to replace them. Like Trevelyan, Macaulay envisioned a system that would bring together students of various social origins and unite them into a new leading class.[121] Like Trevelyan too, and perhaps more sincerely than their opponents, he ultimately hoped to convey "knowledge to the great mass of the population."[122]

[116] Bentinck to G. Norton, 11 Apr. 1834, in James Barber, *A Letter to the Right Hon. Sir John Cam Hobhouse, Bart. M.P. President of the India Board, Etc. Etc. Etc. on Steam-Navigation with India* (London, 1837), pp. 43–4; Bentinck to unknown, 1 Jun. 1834, in Bentinck, *Correspondence*, vol. II, p. 1287. See also Lord William Bentinck, "Lord William Bentinck's Reply to the Society's Address" (8 Apr. 1835), *Transactions of the Agricultural and Horticultural Society of India* 2 (1836), p. 211.

[117] For a severe response, which was never sent, see [John Stuart Mill], Draft Public Despatch (1836), in *GIED*, pp. 225–43.

[118] See Henry Thoby Prinsep, Minute (20 May 1835), in Sharp, ed., *Selections*, pp. 137–9.

[119] Trevelyan to Bentinck, 9 Apr. 1834, p. 1238. See Bentinck, Minute (20 Jan. 1834), pp. 78, 81.

[120] GCPI to Governor-General in Council, 21 Jan. 1835, p. 138 [emphasis removed]. Macaulay made the same claim. Thomas Babington Macaulay, Minute (2 Feb. 1835), in *GIED*, p. 168.

[121] See Trevelyan, *Education*, pp. 135–7, 142.

[122] Macaulay, Minute (2 Feb. 1835), p. 171. Elsewhere, Macaulay described this new class as "conductors of knowledge to the people." Thomas Babington Macaulay, Minute (30 Dec. 1837), in Macaulay, *Macaulay's Minutes on Education in India*, ed. H. Woodrow (Calcutta, 1862), p. 51.

It was this popular program that appealed to Bentinck. Two weeks earlier, he had approved the reformer William Adam's plan to survey schools across the province. He implied that the government's best course of action was to found "a few good institutions" that "natives of all ranks and classes" would attend. He also implied that the "various" other questions under discussion, including the "languages to be cultivated," were of secondary importance. Bentinck's main concern, as ever, was to establish "education upon the largest and most useful basis."[123]

Bentinck's restatement of this concern, as much as his endorsement of English, determined the response by the Orientalists. In his minute, Prinsep subtly but significantly shifted tack: He stressed the good of "the mass of the people" above that of maulvis and pandits. While still finding use for such men as "the teachers of many pupils," he now argued that "we must endeavour to carry the people with us."[124] William Hay Macnaghten too now framed the instruction of learned elites in terms of its benefit to "the great mass of the people." The "grand object," Macnaghten declared, was not that "the few ... should be enlightened but that thro[ugh] their means ... light should be diffused over the whole surface of society."[125] John Tytler, a favorite object of the Committee's patronage, and of Trevelyan's scorn, had expressed this view already.[126] In 1836, it was taken up by Wilson in the pages of the *Asiatic Journal*:

> As long as the learned classes of India are not enlisted in the cause of diffusing sound knowledge, little real progress will be made.... [O]ne able pundit or maulavi, who should ... advocate

---

[123] Bentinck, Minute (20 Jan. 1835), in Bentinck, *Correspondence*, vol. II, pp. 1395–7. Trevelyan and Macaulay also supported Adam's plan. See Trevelyan to Bentinck, 5 Jan. 1835, in ibid., vol. II, p. 1393; Macaulay to Bentinck, undated, University of Nottingham Libraries, PwJf 1327.

[124] Henry Thoby Prinsep, Note (15 Feb. 1835), in *GIED*, pp. 175, 181, 185. His brother James, uniquely among prominent Orientalists, remained opposed to popular education. See James Prinsep, Minute (30 Apr. 1835), BL, IOR F/4/1846/77633, pp. 269–71, 275–6.

[125] NAI, Bengal Public Consultations (22 Apr. 1835), no. 10A.

[126] Tytler to GCPI, 3 Apr. 1834, NAI, Home Miscellaneous, vol. 472, p. 160; Tytler to Wilson, 26 Jan. 1835, BL, Mss Eur E301/2, f. 103v.

the adoption of European knowledge and principles, would work a ... revolution in the minds of his unlettered countrymen ....[127]

Thus, the Orientalists conceded the principle of popular education and sought to salvage merely a supporting role for learned elites.[128] In this, they were helped by a petition against the rumored abolition of the Calcutta Madrasa bearing over eight thousand signatures.[129] By demonstrating popular support for ostensibly elite interests, the petition undercut the Anglicists' premises. No wonder that Macaulay's first response was to accuse Prinsep of engineering the whole affair.[130] The Charter Act authorized Bentinck to override such opposition, but as a practical matter, his plans relied on acquiescence. He ended the controversy with a compromise: The state would not close any school or college so long as the people were "inclined to avail themselves" of it.[131]

CONCLUSION

The end of the Anglicist-Orientalist controversy spelled the end of the idea of conciliation in Company ideology. Mass education, though far from a reality, had become an ideological imperative that precluded scholarly patronage. The General Committee of Public Instruction, with the approval of the governor-general in council, discontinued support for "oriental works."[132] It was clear to Wilson, at least, that the Company now "sought to deter its servants from Oriental studies."[133] It was equally telling that the first Indians

[127] Wilson to ed., 5 Dec. 1835, *AJ*, repr. in *GIED*, p. 216.
[128] William Adam alluded to this change when he wrote that Wilson had not been "always happy or Consistent in applying" the views he expressed in the *Asiatic Journal*. Adam to Wilson, 26 Sept. 1836, BL, Mss Eur E301/2, f. 174v.
[129] Petition (21 Feb. 1835), trans. in *AJ*, repr. in *GIED*, pp. 189–93.
[130] Henry Thoby Prinsep, Autobiography (1865), cited in Sharp, ed., *Selections*, p. 134.
[131] Governor-General in Council, Resolution (7 Mar. 1835), in *GIED*, p. 195.
[132] GCPI to Governor-General in Council, 20 Apr. 1835, in *GIED*, pp. 201–3.
[133] [Horace Hayman Wilson], "The Late John Tytler, Esq., of the Bengal Medical Service," *AJ* new ser. 23 (1837), p. 2. For the attribution, see Gerald Sirkin and Natalie Robinson Sirkin, "The Battle of Indian Education: Macaulay's Opening Salvo Newly Discovered," *Victorian Studies* 14 (1971), p. 413 n. 23.

appointed to the general committee were neither pandits nor maulvis but rather Bhadralok.[134] Scholar-officials and learned elites, once pillars of the Company state, no longer served its purposes.

The idea of conciliation was a relic of the Company's earlier history that proved inconvenient to it in its final incarnation. As Trevelyan put it, "That age with its peculiar exigencies and the policy which they were supposed to require, has long since pas[sed]."[135] By 1853, when parliament examined reputed experts on the education question, Trevelyan's view had long predominated. Wilson was the only witness, among several dozen, who still espoused the idea of conciliation.[136] Alexander Duff spoke for the rest: This idea might have been appropriate to the age of Warren Hastings and Lord Cornwallis, to "so new a conjuncture of affairs," when "we were ... very nearly strangers in the country in our capacity as Governors." Now, however, "that sort of conciliation which was in vogue in those early days" was positively damaging: It served only to align the Company with a "small coterie" of pandits and maulvis "who look down with contempt upon the masses."[137]

Mass education, meanwhile, succeeded more in theory than in practice. Funding remained limited.[138] Lord Auckland's policy represented a step backward.[139] Critics, in the spirit of Edmund Burke, accused the Company of making a mockery of knowledge: now, by framing grand plans for education that embraced but a "small portion of the inhabitants."[140] One described these plans thus:

---

[134] Jana Tschurenev, *Empire, Civil Society, and the Beginnings of Colonial Education in India* (New Delhi, 2019), p. 233.

[135] [Trevelyan], Draft Minute [c. 1833–4], f. 2r.

[136] Horace Hayman Wilson, Testimony (5 Jul. 1853), in PP (1852–3), vol. 627-I, p. 265; Horace Hayman Wilson, Testimony (18 Jul. 1853), in PP (1852–3), vol. 897, p. 6.

[137] Alexander Duff, Testimony (6 Jun. 1853), in PP (1852–3), vol. 627-I, pp. 87–8. See similarly, Thomas Erskine Perry, Testimony (26 May 1853), in ibid., p. 17.

[138] "Sums Spent on Native Education, India, Since 1834," PP (1854), vol. 29, p. 3.

[139] Auckland, Bentinck's permanent successor, nonetheless refused to revive the idea of conciliation. Lord Auckland, Minute (24 Nov. 1839), in *GIED*, pp. 311–15.

[140] "Education," *Meerut Universal Magazine* 1 (1835), pp. 227–8.

> [T]he crude instruction of a few hundred Hindoos and
> Mahomedans, will only teach them to comprehend more clearly
> their depressed and degraded condition—to feel more deeply ...
> the injustice and arrogance of their rulers, and ... to direct the
> physical force of their ... countrymen to the downfal[l] of an
> insatiably rapacious and foreign despotism.[141]

In 1854, upon what would prove to be the final renewal of the Company's charter, a final attempt was made to translate the idea of mass education into reality. The "Intellectual Charter of India," as the plan of that year would come to be known, was inspired by the recent parliamentary testimony, framed by the president of the Board of Control, and endorsed by the governor-general and the directors.[142] Mass education had come to loom large, if not in the Company's budget, then in its ideology. At a time when publics in Britain and India were demanding more from their rulers, this idea provided a basis for claims to good government. The upshot of decades of debate was ably summarized by the directors in their dispatch announcing the new plan: No subject "can have a stronger claim to our attention than ... education" – specifically, "the education of the mass of the people."[143]

---

[141] Robert M[ontgomery] Martin, *Remarks on the East India Company's Administration over One Hundred Millions of British Subjects* (Dublin, 1830), p. 25.

[142] R. J. Moore, "The Composition of 'Wood's Education Despatch,'" *English Historical Review* 80 (1965); R. J. Moore, *Sir Charles Wood's Indian Policy 1853–66* (Manchester, 1966), ch. 6.

[143] Public Despatch to Bengal (19 Jul. 1854), in J. A. Richey, ed., *Selections from Educational Records, Part II: 1840–1859* (Calcutta, 1922), pp. 364, 389.

Epilogue

In 1869, eleven years after the Crown assumed the government of British India, a eulogy of sorts appeared in the pages of the fashionable *Westminster Review*: "The liberality of the Court of Directors of the late East India Company, and their enlightened readiness to promote every kind of scientific and literary exploration in the East, supply one of their highest titles to fame, not to say excite something akin to regret."[1] Just as the *Review* implied, the new regime had backed away from the Company's scientific and humanistic commitments. Education was no longer a priority: The "Intellectual Charter" of 1854 was a dead letter.[2] Nor, for that matter, was the new India Office to revive the old policy of sponsoring scholars. To quote one report, it deemed it generally "inexpedient to expend the revenues of India in literary patronage."[3] If India's British rulers still nurtured ideas about knowledge, then they were ideas of a different kind, which had less to do with cultivating either elites or publics than with asserting a technical mastery over territory.[4] Nostalgia for the Company may have been rare, even in Britain. Among those who expressed it, however, the reasoning of the *Review* remained common.

Modern readers are unlikely to be convinced by claims that the Company was an enlightened promoter of knowledge. Nor has it

---

[1] "Contemporary Literature," *Westminster Review* new ser. 35 (1869), p. 264.

[2] See Tim Allender, *Ruling through Education: The Politics of Schooling in the Colonial Punjab* (Elgin, Ill., 2006).

[3] "Report of the Library Committee" (1877), cited in Sir Malcolm C. C. Seton, *The India Office* (London, 1926), p. 252.

[4] See C. A. Bayly, *Empire and Information: Intelligence Gathering and Social Communication in India, 1780–1870* (Cambridge, 1996), ch. 10; Jon Wilson, *India Conquered: Britain's Raj and the Chaos of Empire* (London, 2016), ch. 9.

been the contention of this book that they ought to be. These claims are still worth revisiting, however, in part because they so closely resemble ones made by business corporations today. The history of the Company in general commands attention because, now too, relations between states and companies are in flux. Company states may be unlikely to return anytime soon.[5] To fixate on this narrow point, however, is to miss the broader one. In many spheres, ranging from the military to infrastructure, the roles of states and companies have increasingly overlapped.[6] "Corporate responsibility," "corporate governance," even "corporate sovereignty" have become common expressions. In this "knowledge age," the "knowledge sector" – including science, publishing, and education – has emerged as perhaps the key site of corporate encroachment. What lessons might participants in debates on this growing phenomenon glean from earlier debates involving the Company?

At one level, the record of these debates reinforces the reigning skepticism about corporate knowledge. Critics, from the time of Warren Hastings onwards, made a number of now-familiar allegations. Some charged the Company with seeking to monopolize intellectual goods, much as it did material ones. Others accused it of corrupting or destroying once-proud scholarly institutions. Many claimed that its commercial character prevented it from being a good steward or patron of knowledge. Yet these critics also tended to appreciate something that their modern counterparts have ignored: in a word, ideology. Running through the knowledge debates of the Company was a general understanding that it was not its business, in a narrow sense, but rather its legitimacy that was primarily at stake. Attending not only to the practical or instrumental but also to the

---

[5] Andrew Phillips and J. C. Sharman, *Outsourcing Empire: How Company-States Made the Modern World* (Princeton, 2020), pp. 215–22.

[6] Alfred D. Chandler and Bruce Mazlish, eds., *Leviathans: Multinational Corporations and the New Global History* (Cambridge, 2005); Joshua Barkan, *Corporate Sovereignty: Law and Government Under Capitalism* (Minneapolis, 2013); John Mikler, *The Political Power of Global Corporations* (Cambridge, 2018); Swati Srivastava, *Hybrid Sovereignty in World Politics* (Cambridge, 2022).

ideological aspects of corporate involvement with knowledge may open up more thoroughgoing and effective lines of critique.

At the same time, to recognize that companies are not "merely profit-maximizing machines" is to refute a basic assumption of their modern critics. To understand them as partly political bodies with a need for legitimacy is to allow that they might be made accountable to outside constituencies.[7] The Company's enlightened promises were enforceable, at least to some extent, when political classes in Britain and India took them seriously. Scholars and friends of knowledge accomplished more when they held the Company to these promises than when they dismissed the possibility of its meeting them. To conceptualize companies as purely economic in nature is thus to foreclose a powerful means of reforming their behavior. A well-earned distrust of companies is compatible with a sense that it may be in the best interests of knowledge to expect more rather than less from them.

One overarching conclusion to be drawn from this book is that the relations among states, companies, and knowledge are malleable. The state-led knowledge order now threatened by business corporations dates back no further than the nineteenth century. To create this order, states had to contend with preexisting notions of what would now be called corporate social responsibility.[8] Company-states benefited in the interim because they could play to knowledge's affinities to trade as well as sovereignty. Indeed, it was in its dual character that the Company patronized scholars and, later, sponsored mass education. From a future vantage point, the state's leading role in such activities – if not the state itself – may look merely "intermezzate."[9] Along with the "historicity, flexibility, and

[7] Timothy Alborn, *Conceiving Companies: Joint-Stock Politics in Victorian England* (London, 1998), pp. 1–2.

[8] For this concept's antecedents, see William A. Pettigrew and David Chan Smith, eds., *A History of Socially Responsible Business, c. 1600–1950* (Basingstoke, 2017).

[9] For this suggestion about the state, see Sophus A. Reinert, "Rivalry: Greatness in Early Modern Political Economy," in Philip J. Stern and Carl Wennerlind, eds., *Mercantilism Reimagined: Political Economy in Early Modern Britain and Its Empire* (Oxford, 2014), p. 362.

contingency of any assumed distinctions between public and private," the Company's debates attest to the long presence of ideas about knowledge in corporate ideology.[10] Such ideas may not inspire; nevertheless, they instruct. Corporate involvement with knowledge can be made to look very different than it does today.

---

[10] Philip J. Stern, "English East India Company-State and The Modern Corporation: The Google of Its Time?," in Thomas Clarke, Justin O'Brien, and Charles R. T. O'Kelley, eds., *The Oxford Handbook of the Corporation* (Oxford, 2019), p. 85.

Bibliography

MANUSCRIPTS

Canada

Dalhousie University Archives, Halifax, Nova Scotia
James Dinwiddie Fonds

India

Maharashtra State Archives, Mumbai, Maharashtra
Bombay General Volumes

National Archives of India, New Delhi, Delhi
Bengal Public Consultations
Bengal Public Proceedings
Home Miscellaneous
  Proceedings of the College of Fort William
  Report of the General Committee of Public Instruction: Bengal
    Enclosures

National Library of India, Kolkata, West Bengal
Vincent-Francklin Correspondence

Tamil Nadu Archives, Chennai, Tamil Nadu
Madras Public Consultations

Victoria Memorial Hall, Kolkata, West Bengal
Hyde Notebooks

West Bengal State Archives, Kolkata, West Bengal
Bengal Revenue Proceedings

General Committee of Public Instruction
> Correspondence on Delhi College
> Proceedings

Singapore

National Archives of Singapore
Straits Settlements Records
> Singapore Resident's Diary

Raffles Archives and Museum
Raffles Institution Records

United Kingdom

British Library, London, England
Asia, Pacific, and Africa Collections
> European Manuscripts
>> Barlow Papers
>> Charles Francis Greville Papers
>> Elphinstone Papers
>> Henry Wellesley Papers
>> Letters to H. H. Wilson
>> Macpherson Collection
>> Records of the East India Company Library
>> Tipu Sultan Papers
> India Office Records
>> E/4: Correspondence with India
>> F/3: Draft Despatches Submitted to the Board
>> F/4: Board's Collections
>> H: Home Miscellaneous
>> J: Records of the East India College, Haileybury
> Islamic Manuscripts
>> Letters from Anand Rao Gaekwad and Fateh Singh Rao Gaekwad
> Oriental Manuscripts
>> Ali Ibrahim Khan, *Tarikh-i Chait Singh*
Western Manuscripts
> Anderson Papers
> Blechynden Papers

Erskine Diary
Gibbon Papers
Hardwicke Papers
Hastings Papers
Holland House Papers
Leyden and Erskine Papers
Liverpool Papers
Mackintosh Papers
Vansittart Papers
Wellesley Papers

Cambridge South Asian Archive, Cambridge University, Cambridge, England
Macpherson Family Papers (microfilm)

Cambridge University Library, Cambridge, England
Additional Manuscripts
    Edmonstone Papers
Islamic Manuscripts
    Letter to the Marqu[es]s Wellesley

Centre for Buckinghamshire Studies, Aylesbury, England
Grenville Papers

Edinburgh University Library, Edinburgh, Scotland
Carlyle Papers
Ferguson Papers

Glasgow City Archives, Mitchell Library, Glasgow, Scotland
Bogle Papers

John Rylands Library, University of Manchester, Manchester, England
Philipps Collection

Linnean Society of London, London, England
Smith Correspondence

Mount Stuart, Bute, Scotland
Marquess of Hastings Papers

National Library of Scotland, Edinburgh, Scotland
Irvine Papers
Letters of Baptist Missionaries
Leyden Papers
Melville Papers
Minto Papers
Walker of Bowland Papers

National Records of Scotland, Edinburgh, Scotland
Buchanan Family Papers

Natural History Museum, London, England
Buchanan Manuscripts

Newcastle University Library, Newcastle, England
Trevelyan Papers

Public Record Office of Northern Ireland, Belfast,
Northern Ireland
Castlereagh Papers

Reelig House, Inverness-shire, Scotland
Fraser Papers

Staffordshire County Record Office, Stafford, England
Dartmouth Papers

The National Archives, Kew, England
Chatham Papers
Cornwallis Papers

University of Nottingham Libraries, Nottingham, England
Bentinck Papers

United States

Beinecke Library, Yale University, New Haven, Connecticut
Osborn Collection

Cleveland Public Library, Cleveland, Ohio
East India Company Manuscript Collection

Huntington Library, San Marino, California
Hastings Manuscripts

Ames Library of South Asia, University of Minnesota, Minneapolis, Minnesota
Ames Rare Collection

PRINTED PRIMARY SOURCES

A Preliminary View of the Establishment of the Honourable East-India Company in Hertfordshire for the Education of Young Persons Appointed to the Civil Service in India. [Hertfordshire,] 1806.

[Abu al-Fazl.] Ayeen Akbery: Or, The Institutes of the Emperor Akber, trans. Francis Gladwin. 3 vols. Calcutta, 1783–6.

Adam, William. *Adam's* Reports on Vernacular Education in Bengal and Behar, *Submitted to Government in 1835, 1836 and 1838,* ed. J. Long. Calcutta, 1868.

"An Account of the Life and Character of Tofuzzel Hussein Khan." *Asiatic Annual Register* [5] (1804), "Characters": 1–8.

An Authentic Copy of the Correspondence in India between the Country Powers and the Honourable the East India Company's Servants. 6 vols. London, 1787.

Annual Register, or a View of the History, Politics, and Literature for the Year 1797 (1800).

Arbuthnot, Alexander J., ed. *Papers Relating to Public Instruction.* Madras, 1855.

Asiatic Annual Register.

Asiatic Journal.

Bacon, Francis. *The Advancement of Learning (1605),* ed. Michael Kiernan. Oxford: Oxford University Press, 2000.

Barber, James. *A Letter to the Right Hon. Sir John Cam Hobhouse, Bart. M.P. President of the India Board, Etc. Etc. Etc. on Steam-Navigation with India.* London, 1837.

Beatson, Alexander. *A View of the Origin and Conduct of the War with Tippoo Sultaun*. London, 1800.

Bentham, Jeremy. *Plan of Parliamentary Reform*. London, 1817.

Bentinck, William. "Lord William Bentinck's Reply to the Society's Address" (8 Apr. 1835), *Transactions of the Agricultural and Horticultural Society of India* 2 (1836): 210–11.

Bentinck, William. *The Correspondence of Lord William Cavendish Bentinck*, ed. C. H. Philips. 2 vols. Oxford: Oxford University Press, 1977.

Bharatchandra Ray. *In Praise of Annada* (1752), trans. France Bhattacharya. 2 vols. Cambridge, MA: Harvard University Press, 2017–20.

Bolts, William. *Considerations on India Affairs*. 2 vols. London, 1772–5.

Bond, E. A., ed. *Speeches of the Managers and Counsel in the Trial of Warren Hastings*. 4 vols. London, 1859–61.

Brissot, Jacques-Pierre. *London Literary Lyceum; or, an Assembly and Correspondence Established at London*. London, 1783.

Bruce, John. *Annals of the Honorable East-India Company, from Their Establishment by the Charter of Queen Elizabeth, 1600, to the Union of the London and English East-India Companies, 1707-8*. 3 vols. London, 1810.

Bruce, John. *Report on the Negociation, Between the Honorable East-India Company and the Public, Respecting the Renewal of the Company's Exclusive Privileges of Trade, for Twenty Years from March, 1794*. London, 1811.

[Bruce, John.] *Historical View of Plans, for the Government of British India, and Regulation of Trade to the East Indies*. London, 1793.

Buchanan, Claudius. *Memoir of the Expediency of an Ecclesiastical Establishment for British India*. London, 1805.

Buchanan, Claudius. *Christian Researches in Asia: With Notices of the Translation of the Scriptures into the Oriental Languages*. Cambridge, 1811.

[Buchanan, Claudius, ed.] *The College of Fort William in Bengal*. London, 1805.

Buchanan, Francis. *A Journey from Madras through the Countries of Mysore, Canara, and Malabar*. 3 vols. London, 1807.

[Buchanan, Francis] Francis Hamilton. *Genealogies of the Hindus, Extracted from Their Sacred Writings*. Edinburgh, 1819.

[Buchanan, Francis.] *The History, Antiquities, Topography, and Statistics of Eastern India*, ed. [Robert] Montgomery Martin. 3 vols. London, 1838.

Burke, Edmund. *The Correspondence of Edmund Burke*, ed. Thomas Copeland. 10 vols. Chicago: University of Chicago Press, 1958–78.

Burke, Edmund. *The Writings and Speeches of Edmund Burke*, gen. ed. Paul Langford. 9 vols. Oxford: Oxford University Press, 1981–2015.

Calendar of Persian Correspondence. 11 vols. Calcutta and Delhi, 1911–69.

Carey, W. et al. *Proposals for a Subscription for Translating the Holy Scriptures.* Serampore, 1806.

Copy of a Proposed Dispatch to the Bengal Government, Approved by Twenty-Three of the Twenty-Four Directors of the Hon. East-India Company, Dated April 3, 1805. London, 1806.

Cornwallis, Marquis. *Correspondence of Charles, First Marquis of Cornwallis,* ed. Charles Ross. 2nd edn. 3 vols. London, 1859.

Crabb, George. *English Synonymes Explained, in Alphabetical Order; with Copious Illustrations and Examples Drawn from the Best Writers.* London, 1816.

Creon [pseud.]. "The State of Asiatic Affairs, as Represented by a Writer Well Acquainted with the Concerns of Government." *Gentleman's Magazine* 39 (Aug. 1769): 374–5.

"Curious Oriental Literature." *Literary Gazette; and Journal of Belles Lettres, Arts, and Sciences, etc.* (18 Nov. 1837): 737–9.

de Quincey, Thomas. *The Works of Thomas De Quincey,* ed. Frederick Burnwick. 21 vols. London: Pickering and Chatto, 2000.

de Staël, Germaine. *Correspondance Générale.* 9 vols. Paris and Geneva, 1960–2017.

Dow, Alexander. *The History of Hindostan.* 2 vols. London, 1768–72.

[Duff, Alexander.] "The Early or Exclusively Oriental Period of Government Education in Bengal." *Calcutta Review* 3 (1845): 211–63.

Duncan, Jonathan. "Historical Remarks on the Coast of Malabar, with some Description of the Manners of Its Inhabitants." *Asiatick Researches* 5 (Calcutta, 1798): 1–36.

Dundas, Henry, and Lord Wellesley. *Two Views of British India: The Private Correspondence of Mr. Dundas and Lord Wellesley, 1798–1801,* ed. Edward Ingram. Bath: Adams and Dart, 1970.

"Education." *Meerut Universal Magazine* 1 (1835): 227–35.

"Education in Eastern Asia." *Malacca Observer.* Repr. in *Asiatic Journal* 28 (Jul. 1829): 105–6.

Elphinstone, Mountstuart. *Selections from the Minutes and Other Official Writings of the Honourable Mountstuart Elphinstone, Governor of Bombay,* ed. George W. Forrest. London, 1884.

[Emerson, John Swift.] *One Year of the Administration of His Excellency the Marquess of Wellesley in Ireland.* London, 1823.

English Review.

Farrington, Anthony, ed. *The Records of the East India College Haileybury & Other Institutions.* London: H.M.S.O., 1976.

Ferguson, Adam. *The Correspondence of Adam Ferguson,* ed. Vincenzo Merolle. 2 vols. London: Routledge, 1995.

First, Second, and Third Reports of the Select Committee, Appointed by the Court of Directors of the East India Company, to Take into Consideration the Export Trade from Great Britain to the East Indies. London, 1793.

Firishta. *Tarikh-i Firishta*, trans. John Briggs, as *History of the Rise of the Mahomedan Power in India, till the Year A.D. 1612.* 4 vols. London, 1829.

Fontana, Nicolas. "On the Nicobar Isles and the Fruit of the Mellori." *Asiatick Researches* 3 (Calcutta, 1792): 149–63.

Forrest, George W., ed. *Selections from the Letters, Despatches, and Other State Papers Preserved in the Foreign Department of the Government of India, 1772–1785.* 3 vols. Calcutta, 1899.

Fort William – India House Correspondence. 21 vols. Delhi: National Archives of India, 1949–85.

Francis, Philip. *Letter from Mr. Francis to Lord North, Late Earl of Guildford* [17 Sept. 1777]. London, 1793.

[Francis, Philip]. *A Letter from Warren Hastings, Esq., Dated 21st of February, 1784, with Remarks and Authentic Documents.* London, 1786.

Fraser-Mackintosh, Charles, ed. *Letters of Two Centuries, Chiefly Connected with Inverness and the Highlands, from 1616 to 1815.* Inverness, 1890.

Ghulam Husain Khan Tabataba'i. *Siyar al-Muta'akhkhirin.* 2 vols. Calcutta, 1833.

[Ghulam Husain Khan Tabataba'i] Seid-Gholam-Hossein-Khan. *A Translation of the Seir Mutaqharin; or, View of Modern Times*, trans. Nota Manus [Haji Mustapha]. 4 vols. Calcutta, 1789–90.

Gilchrist, John. *Dictionary, English and Hindoostanee.* 2 vols. Calcutta, 1787–98.

G[ilchrist], J[ohn] B[orthwick]. Dr. Gilchrist's Statement of His Case and Conduct, bound with Jonathan Scott and John Borthwick Gilchrist, *Introductory Address to the Honorable Court of Proprietors of the East India Company* [Hertford, 1806], UCL Library Special Collections, Hume Tracts, vol. 119.

Gleig, G. R. *Memoirs of the Life of the Right Hon.* Warren Hastings. 3 vols. London, 1841.

Gordon, Peter. *The Oriental Repository at the India House.* London, 1835.

[Gordon, Peter.] "The Oriental Repository at the India House." Alexander's East India and Colonial Magazine 10–11 (1835-6), X, 61–6, 130–42, 415–27, 542–53, XI, 124–32, 217–27, 318–21, 399–403, 410–14.

Graham, Maria. *Journal of a Residence in India.* Edinburgh, 1812.

Grand, G. F. *The Narrative of the Life of a Gentleman Long Resident in India* (1814), ed. Walter K. Firminger. Calcutta, 1910.

Grant, Charles. *Observations on the State of Society among the Asiatic Subjects of Great-Britain.* London, 1797.

Hager, Joseph. *A Dissertation on the Newly Discovered Babylonian Inscriptions.* London, 1801.

Halhed, Nathaniel Brassey. *A Grammar of the Bengal Language.* Hoog[h]ly, 1778.

Halhed, Nathaniel Brassey, trans. *A Code of Gentoo Laws, or, Ordinations of the Pundits.* London, 1776.

Hamilton, Charles, trans. *The Hedaya, or Guide; A Commentary on the Mussulman Laws.* 4 vols. London, 1791.

Hamilton, Eliza. *Translation of the Letters of a Hindoo Rajah.* 2 vols. London, 1796.

Hastings, Marquess of. *Summary of the Administration of the Indian Government, from October 1813, to January 1823.* London, 1824.

Hastings, Marquess of. *The Private Journal of the Marquess of Hastings,* ed. Marchioness of Hastings. 2 vols. London, 1858.

Hastings, Warren. *A Narrative of the Insurrection Which Happened in the Zemeedary of Banaris.* Calcutta, 1782.

Hastings, Warren. *The Letters of Warren Hastings to His Wife,* ed. Sydney C. Grier. London, 1905.

Hastings, Warren. *Selections from the State Papers of the Governors-General of India: Warren Hastings,* ed. G. W. Forrest. 2 vols. Oxford, 1910.

Hastings, Warren. *Warren Hastings' Letters to Sir John Macpherson,* ed. Henry Dodwell. London: Faber and Gwyer, 1927.

Hastings, Warren. "A Letter of Warren Hastings on the Civil Service of the East India Company" (19 Jul. 1801), ed. W. H. Hutton, *English Historical Review* 44 (1929): 633–41.

[Hastings, Warren.] *A Proposal for Establishing a Professorship of the Persian Language in the University of Oxford.* [c. 1766.]

[Hastings, Warren, ed.] *Debates of the House of Lords, on the Evidence Delivered in the Trial of Warren Hastings in Consequence of His Acquittal.* London, 1797.

[Hawkesworth, John.] *Asiaticus: In Two Parts.* Calcutta, 1803.

"Her Majesty's East India House." *East India Magazine* (Mar. 1841): 219–21.

Heyne, Benjamin. *Tracts, Historical and Statistical, on India.* London, 1814.

Hickey, William. *Memoirs of William Hickey,* ed. Alfred Spencer. 5th edn. 4 vols. London: Hurst and Blackett, 1950.

Hodgson, B. H. *Preeminence of the Vernaculars; or the Anglicists Answered.* Serampore, 1837.

Hughes, William Essington, ed. *Monumental Inscriptions and Extracts from Registers of Births, Marriages, and Deaths, at St. Anne's Church, Soho.* London, 1905.

[Inayat-Allah Kamboh] Einaiut Oolah. *Bahar-Danush; or, Garden of Knowledge. An Oriental Romance*, trans. Jonathan Scott. 3 vols. Shrewsbury, 1799.

[Iqbal ud-Daula] Icbal-ood Dowlah. *Icbal-e-Furung or British Prosperity*. Calcutta, 1834.

Johnson, J. *The Oriental Voyager; or, Descriptive Sketches and Cursory Remarks, on a Voyage to India and China*. London, 1807.

Johnson, Samuel. *A Dictionary of the English Language*. 2 vols. London, 1755.

Johnson, Samuel. *The Letters of Samuel Johnson*, ed. Bruce Redford. 5 vols. Princeton: Princeton University Press, 1992–4.

Johnston, Alexander. "Biographical Sketch of the Literary Career of the Late Colonel Colin Mackenzie." *Journal of the Royal Asiatic Society of Great Britain and Ireland* 1 (1834): 333–64.

Jones, William. *A Grammar of the Persian Language*. London, 1771.

Jones, William. *The Letters of Sir William Jones*, ed. Garland Cannon. 2 vols. Oxford: Oxford University Press, 1970.

[Jones, William.] "The Introduction." *Asiatick Researches* 1 (Calcutta, 1788): iii–viii.

Karam Ali. *Muzaffarnama* [c. 1772–3]. Patna: Khuda Baksh Oriental Public Library, 1992.

Keir, Archibald. *Thoughts on the Affairs of Bengal*. London, 1772.

Kerr, J. *A Review of Public Instruction in the Bengal Presidency, from 1835 to 1851*. 2 vols. Calcutta, 1853.

Lamb, Alistair, ed. *Bhutan and Tibet: The Travels of George Bogle and Alexander Hamilton, 1774–1777*. Vol. 1. Hertingfordbury, UK: Roxford Books, 2002.

Leyden, John. *The Poetical Works of Dr. John Leyden*. London, 1875.

Macaulay, Thomas Babington. *Macaulay's Minutes on Education in India*, ed. H. Woodrow. Calcutta, 1862.

Macaulay, Thomas Babington. *The Works of Lord Macaulay*, ed. Lady Trevelyan. 8 vols. London, 1866.

Macaulay, Thomas Babington. *The Letters of Thomas Babington Macaulay*, ed. Thomas Pinney. 6 vols. Cambridge: Cambridge University Press, 1974–81.

Mackintosh, Sir James. *Memoirs of the Life of the Right Honourable Sir James Mackintosh*, ed. Robert James Mackintosh. 2nd edn. 2 vols. London, 1836.

Macpherson, David. *Annals of Commerce, Manufactures, Fisheries, and Navigation*. 4 vols. London, 1805.

[Macpherson, John.] *Documents Explanatory of the Case of Sir John Macpherson, Baronet, as Governor General of Bengal*. [London, 1800.]

Malthus, T. R. *Statements Respecting the East-India College*. London, 1817.

[Marsh, Charles.] "Society in India." *New Monthly Magazine* 22-3 (1828): XXII, 224-36, 327-40, 464-72, XXIII, 67-74, 336-41.

Martin, Robert M[ontgomery]. *Remarks on the East India Company's Administration over One Hundred Millions of British Subjects.* Dublin, 1830.

Maulavi Ikram 'Ali. *Ikhwanu-S-Safa; or, Brothers of Purity* [1810], trans. John Platts. London, 1869.

Maurice, Thomas. *Indian Antiquities.* 7 vols. London, [1793]-1800.

Mill, James. *The History of British India.* 3 vols. London, 181[8].

Mills, Charles. *An History of Muhammedanism.* London, 1817.

Minto, Earl of. *Lord Minto in India: Life and Letters of Gilbert Elliot, First Earl of Minto, from 1807 to 1814,* ed. Countess of Minto. London, 1880.

Minutes of Evidence Taken at the Trial of Warren Hastings. 11 vols. London, 1788-95.

Mir Amman. *Bāgh o Bahār; or Tales of the Four Darweshes* [1804], trans. Duncan Forbes. London, 1857.

[Mir Sher Ali Afsus]. *The Araish-i-Mahfil; or, Ornament of the Assembly,* trans. Henry Court. Allahabad, 1871.

[Mir Sher Ali Afsus] Meer Sher Ulee Ufsos, trans. *The Rose Garden of Hindoostan.* Calcutta, 1802.

Mirza Abu Taleb Khan. *The Travels of Mirza Abu Taleb Khan,* trans. Charles Stewart. 2 vols. London, 1810.

"Mirza Abu Taleb Khan." *Asiatic Annual Register* [3] (1802), "Miscellaneous Tracts": 100-101.

Mirza Abul Hassan Khan. *A Persian at the Court of King George 1809-10: The Journal of Mirza Abul Hassan Khan,* ed. and trans. Margaret Morris Cloake. London: Barrie and Jenkins, 1988.

Moitra, Suresh Chandra, ed. *Selections from Jnanannesan.* Calcutta: Prajna, 1979.

Montesquieu. *The Spirit of the Laws* (1748), ed. and trans. Anne M. Cohler, Basia C. Miller, and Harold S. Stone. Cambridge: Cambridge University Press, 1989.

Monthly Magazine.

Moolla Rustom Bin Kaikobad, *Contents of the George Nameh, Composed in Verses in the Persian Language.* [Bombay,] 1836.

Morning Chronicle.

Morning Post.

Morrison, John. *The Advantages of an Alliance with the Great Mogul.* London, 1774.

Mulla' Feruz Bin Ka'wus. *The George-Námah,* ed. Mulla' Rustam Bin Kaikoba'd. 3 vols. Bombay, 1837.

Munshi Abdullah. "The Hikayat Abdullah" (1849), trans. A. H. Hill. *Journal of the Malaysian Branch of the Royal Asiatic Society* 28 (1955): 5-345.

Original Papers Relative to the Disturbances in Bengal: Containing Every Material Transaction from 1759 to 1764. 2 vols. London, 1765.

Orme, Robert. *Historical Fragments of the Mogul Empire*. London, 1805.

Parliamentary Papers. London.

Parliamentary Debates from the Year 1803. London, 1803–.

"Particular Account of the Nuddeah University." *Calcutta Monthly Register and India Repository* (Jan. 1791): 136–9.

Parulekar, R. V., ed. *Selections from the Records of the Government of Bombay: Education*. 3 vols. Bombay: Asia Publishing House, 1953–7.

Pearce, Robert Rouiere. *Memoirs and Correspondence of the Most Noble Richard Marquess Wellesley*. 3 vols. London, 1846–7.

Pearson, Hugh. *Memoirs of the Life and Writings of the Rev. Claudius Buchanan*. 2 vols. Oxford, 1817.

Perera, S. G., ed. *The Douglas Papers*. Colombo: Ceylon Observer Press, 1933.

Pickett, Catherine. *Bibliography of the East India Company*. 2 vols. London: British Libary, 2011–15.

Pownall, Thomas. *The Right, Interest, and Duty, of the State, as Concerned in the Affairs of the East Indies*. London, 1773.

Price, Joseph. *A Short Commercial and Political Letter from Mr. Joseph Price to the Right Honourable Charles James Fox*. London, 1783.

Primitiae Orientalis [vol. 1 titled *Essays by the Students of the College of Fort William*]. 3 vols. Calcutta, 1802–4.

Proceedings of the Asiatic Society. 4 vols. Calcutta: Asiatic Society, 1980–2000.

Puddester, Robert P. *Medals of British India with Rarity and Valuations: Volume One: Commemorative and Historical Medals from 1750 to 1947*. London: Spink, 2002.

Raffles, Sophia. *Memoir of the Life and Public Services of Sir Thomas Stamford Raffles*. London, 1830.

[Raffles, Sir Thomas Stamford.] *On the Advantage of Affording the Means of Education to the Inhabitants of the Further East* (Serampore, 1819). Repr. as *The First Printing of Sir Stamford Raffles's Minute on the Establishment of a Malay College at Singapore*, ed. John Bastin. Eastbourne: [John Bastin], 1999.

Rám Ráz, *Essay on the Architecture of the Hindús*. London, 1834.

[Ramkamal Sen] Ram Comul Sen. *A Dictionary in English and Bengalee*. 2 vols. Serampore, 1834.

Rammohun Roy. *The Correspondence of Raja Rammohun Roy*, ed. Dilip Kumar Biswas. 2 vols. Calcutta: Saraswat Library, 1992–4.

Ramsbotham, R. B., ed. "Pages from the Past: Extracts from the Records of the Government of India." *Bengal Past and Present* 29 (1925): 207–16.

Reformer (Calcutta).

Rehatsek, Edward. *Catalogue Raisonné of the Arabic, Hindostani, Persian, and Turkish MSS. in the Mulla Firuz Library*. Bombay, 1873.

Rennell, James. *Memoir of a Map of Hindoostan*. London, 1783.

Rennell, James. *Memoir of a Map of Hindoostan*. 2nd edn. London, 1785.

Report on the Colleges and Schools for Native Education, under the Superintendance of the General Committee of Public Instruction in Bengal. 1831. Calcutta, 1832. British Library, IOR V/24/946.

Report on the Manuscripts of J. B. Fortescue, Esq., Preserved at Dropmore. 9 vols. London, 1892–1915.

Richey, J. A., ed. *Selections from Educational Records, Part II: 1840–1859*. Calcutta: Superintendent Government Printing, 1922.

Rickards, R. *India; or Facts Submitted to Illustrate the Character and Condition of the Native Inhabitants*. 2 vols. London, 1829–32.

Rieu, Charles. *Catalogue of the Persian Manuscripts in the British Museum*. 3 vols. London, 1879.

Robertson, William. *An Historical Disquisition Concerning the Knowledge which the Ancients Had of India*. London, 1791.

Roebuck, Thomas. *Annals of the College of Fort William*. Calcutta, 1819.

Roebuck, Thomas. *A Collection of Proverbs and Proverbial Phrases, in the Persian and Hindoostanee Languages*, ed. H. H. Wilson. Calcutta, 1824.

Russell, Patrick. *An Account of Indian Serpents, Collected on the Coast of Coromandel*. London, 1796.

Salim Allah. *Tarikh-i Bangala* (c. 1760–4), trans. Francis Gladwin, as *A Narrative of the Transactions in Bengal*. Calcutta, 1788.

Sargent, J. *The Life of the Rev. T. T. Thomason*. London, 1833.

Scott, David. *The Correspondence of David Scott*, ed. C. H. Philips. 2 vols. London: Royal Historical Society, 1951.

Scott, John, ed. *Copies of the Several Testimonials Transmitted from Bengal by the Governor and Council, Relating to Warren Hastings, Esq. Late Governor General of Bengal*. London, 1789.

Scott, Jonathan. *Observations on the Oriental Department of the Hon. Company's East India College, at Hertford*. Hertford, [1806]. British Library, IOR H/488, pp. 671–724.

Selections from the Calcutta Gazettes. 5 vols. Calcutta, 1864–8.

Sen, Surendranath and Umesha Mishra, eds. *Sanskrit Documents: Being Sanskrit Letters and Other Documents Preserved in the Oriental Collection at the National Archives of India*. Allahabad: Ganganatha Jha Research Institute, 1951.

Shahamat Ali. *The Sikhs and Afghans, in Connexion with India and Persia, Immediately Before and After the Death of Ranjeet Singh*. London, 1847.

Sharp, H., ed. *Selections from Educational Records, Part I: 1781–1839*. Calcutta, 1920.

Shaw, Thomas. "On the Inhabitants of the Hills Near Rájamahall." *Asiatick Researches* 4 (Calcutta, 1795): 45–107.

[Sherer, Moyle.] *Sketches of India: Written by an Officer for Fire-Side Travellers at-Home*. London, 1821.

Shore, John. *The Literary History of the Late Sir William Jones, in a Discourse*. London, 1795.

Shore, John (as Lord Teignmouth). *Memoirs of the Life, Writings, and Correspondence, of Sir William Jones*. London, 1804.

Sinclair, John. *Memoirs of the Life and Works of Sir John Sinclair, Bart*. 2 vols. Edinburgh, 1837.

[Skottowe, Augustine.] *A Memoir of the Life and Writings of Charles Mills*. London, 1828.

Smith, Adam. *An Inquiry into the Nature and Causes of the Wealth of Nations*. 2 vols. London, 1776.

Smith, Adam. *The Correspondence of Adam Smith*, ed. Ernest Campbell Mossner and Ian Simpson Ross. 2nd edn. Oxford: Oxford University Press, 1987.

Smith, Robert Percy. *Early Writings of Robert Percy Smith*, ed. R. V. S. Chiswick, 1850.

"Some Account of a Hindu Temple, and a Bust, of which Elegant Engravings are Placed in the Oriental Library of the Hon. East India Company, Leadenhall Street." *European Magazine* 42 (Dec. 1802): 448–9.

Stewart, Charles. *A Descriptive Catalogue of the Oriental Library of the Late Tippoo Sultan of Mysore*. Cambridge, 1809.

Stewart, John. "An Account of the Kingdom of Thibet. In a Letter from John Stewart, Esquire, F. R. S. to Sir John Pringle, Bart. P. R. S." *Philosophical Transactions of the Royal Society of London* 47 (1777): 465–92.

Stewart, John. "A Letter from John Stewart, Secretary and Judge Advocate of Bengal, 1773," ed. L. S. Sutherland. *Indian Archives* 10 (1956): 1–12.

Teignmouth, Lord. *Memoir of the Life and Correspondence of John Lord Teignmouth*. 2 vols. London, 1843.

[Thiruverkadu Muttiah] Teroovercadoo Mootiah. "An Historical and Chronological Journal, of the Life of Teroovercadoo Mootiah." *Oriental Repository* 2 (1797): 559–70.

The Case of Sir John Macpherson, Baronet, Late Governor-General of India, Containing a Summary Review of his Administration and Services Prepared by Friends from Authentic Documents. London, 1808.

The First Report of the Calcutta School Book Society. Calcutta, 1818.

The Merits of Mr. Pitt and Mr. Hastings, as Ministers in War and in Peace, Impartially Stated. London, 1794.

The Parliamentary History of England, from the Earliest Period to the Year 1803. 36 vols. London, 1806–20.

The Second Report of the Calcutta School Book Society's Proceedings. Calcutta, 1819.

The Second Report of the Madras School-Book Society. Madras, 1827.

Thompson, George Nesbitt. "The Nesbitt-Thompson Papers." Bengal Past and Present 8-23 (1914–21): VIII, 145-55, XVI, 1–19, 208–25, XVII, 79–120, XVIII, 178–200, XIX, 1–30, XX, 1–51, XXI, 19–76, XXIII, 38–83.

Thoughts on Improving the Government of the British Territorial Possessions in the East Indies. London, 1780.

Times (London).

Trevelyan, Charles E. *A Treatise on the Means of Communicating the Learning and Civilization of Europe to India.* Calcutta, 1834.

Trevelyan, Charles E. "Memoir." In Mohan Lal, Journal of a Tour through the Panjab, *Afghanistan, Turkistan, Khorasan, and Part of Persia,* ix–xviii. Calcutta, 1834.

Trevelyan, Charles E. *On the Education of the People of India.* London, 1838.

Trevelyan, C[harles] E. et al. *The Application of the Roman Alphabet to All the Oriental Languages.* Serampore, 1834.

Trollope, Anthony. *The Three Clerks: A Novel.* 3 vols. London, 1858.

Tucker, Henry St. George. "The Education of the Civil Service" (1843). In Tucker, *Memorials of Indian Government,* ed. John William Kaye, 430–34. London, 1853.

"Twelfth Annual Report of the Council." *Journal of the Royal Asiatic Society of Great Britain and Ireland* 2 (1835): xxiii–xxvi.

Valentia, Viscount. *Voyages and Travels to India, Ceylon, the Red Sea, Abyssinia, and Egypt.* 3 vols. London, 1809.

[Vennelakanti Subbarao] Vennelacunty Soob Row. *The Life of Vennelacunty Soob Row,* ed. Vennelacunty Venkata Gopal Row. Madras, 1873.

Virgil. *The Georgics of Virgil: A Translation,* trans. David Ferry. New York: Farrar, Straus and Giroux, 2005.

Watson, Richard. *Anecdotes of the Life of Richard Watson.* London, 1817.

Wellesley, Marquess. *Letters of the Marquis Wellesley Respecting the College of Fort William.* London, 1812.

Wellesley, Marquess. *The Despatches, Minutes, and Correspondence, of the Marquess Wellesley, K. G., During His Administration in India,* ed. Robert Montgomery Martin. 5 vols. London, 1836–7.

Wellesley, Marquess. *The Wellesley Papers,* ed. L. S. Benjamin. 2 vols. London, 1914.

Westminster Review.

Whishaw, John. *The "Pope" of Holland House: Selections from the Correspondence of John Whishaw and His Friends, 1813–1840*, ed. Lady Seymour. London, 1906.

Wilberforce, Robert Isaac and Samuel Wilberforce. *The Life of William Wilberforce.* 5 vols. London, 1838.

Wilkins, Charles, trans. *The Bhāgvǎt Gēētā.* London, 1785.

Wilks, Mark. *Historical Sketches of the South of India, in an Attempt to Trace the History of Mysoor.* 3 vols. London, 1817.

Wilson, Horace Hayman. *A Dictionary, Sanscrit and English: Translated, Amended and Enlarged, from an Original Compilation Prepared by Learned Natives for the College of Fort William.* Calcutta, 1819.

[Wilson, Horace Hayman.] "The Late John Tytler, Esq., of the Bengal Medical Service." *Asiatic Journal* new ser. 23 (1837): 1–16.

Zastoupil, Lynn and Martin Moir, eds. *The Great Indian Education Debate: Documents Relating to the Orientalist-Anglicist Controversy, 1781–1843.* Richmond, UK: Curzon, 1999.

SECONDARY SOURCES

Abid, Arif. "A Poisoned Chalice." *3 Quarks Daily* (2006). https://3quarksdaily .com/3quarksdaily/2006/03/nawab_tafazzul_.html.

Ahmad, Naheed F. "The Elphinstone College, Bombay, 1827–1890: A Case Study in 19th Century English Education." In Mushirul Hasan, ed., *Knowledge, Power and Politics: Educational Institutions in India*, 389–425. New Delhi: Roli, 1998.

Ahmed, A. F. Salahuddin. *Social Ideas and Social Change in Bengal, 1818–35.* 2nd edn. Calcutta: Ṛddhi, 1976.

Alam, Muzaffar. *The Crisis of Empire in Mughal North India: Awadh and the Punjab, 1707–48.* 2nd edn. New Delhi: Oxford University Press, 2013.

Alam, Muzaffar and Sanjay Subrahmanyam. Introduction to Alam and Subrahmanyam eds., *The Mughal State, 1526–1750*, 1–71. Delhi: Oxford University Press, 1998.

Alam, Muzaffar and Seema Alavi. Introduction to Alam and Alavi, trans., *A European Experience of the Mughal Orient: The I'jāz-i Arsalānī (Persian Letters, 1773–1779) of Antoine-Louis Henri Polier*, 1–91. New Delhi: Oxford University Press, 2001.

Alborn, Timothy. *Conceiving Companies: Joint-Stock Politics in Victorian England.* London: Routledge, 1998.

Alborn, Timothy. "Boys to Men: Moral Restraint at Haileybury College." In Brian Dolan, ed., *Malthus, Medicine, and Morality: "Malthusianism" after 1798*, 33–55. Amsterdam: Rodopi, 2000.

Allender, Tim. *Ruling through Education: The Politics of Schooling in the Colonial Punjab*. Elgin, IL: New Dawn Press, 2006.

Arberry, A. J. *The Library of the India Office: A Historical Sketch*. London: India Office, 1938.

Archer, Mildred. "India and Natural History: The Role of the East India Company, 1785–1858." *History Today* 9 (1959): 736–43.

Armitage, David. *The Ideological Origins of the British Empire*. Cambridge: Cambridge University Press, 2000.

Arnold, David. "Plant Capitalism and Company Science: The Indian Career of Nathaniel Wallich." *Modern Asian Studies* 42 (2008): 899–928.

Ballantyne, Tony. "Colonial Knowledge." In Sarah Stockwell, ed., *The British Empire: Themes and Perspectives*, 177–97. Malden, MA: Blackwell, 2008.

Ballhatchet, Kenneth. *Social Policy and Social Change in Western India 1817–1830*. Oxford: Oxford University Press, 1957.

Ballhatchet, Kenneth. "The Elphinstone Professors and Elphinstone College, 1827–1840." In C. H. Philips and Mary Doreen Wainwright, eds., *Indian Society and the Beginnings of Modernisation, c. 1830–1850*, 159–63. London: School of Oriental and African Studies, 1976.

Barkan, Joshua. *Corporate Sovereignty: Law and Government under Capitalism*. Minneapolis: University of Minnesota Press, 2013.

Bastin, John. *Sir Stamford Raffles and Some of His Friends and Contemporaries: A Memoir of the Founder of Singapore*. Singapore: World Scientific, 2019.

Bayly, C. A. *Indian Society and the Making of the British Empire*. Cambridge: Cambridge University Press, 1988.

Bayly, C. A. *Imperial Meridian: The British Empire and the World, 1780–1830*. London: Longman, 1989.

Bayly, C. A. *Empire and Information: Intelligence Gathering and Social Communication in India, 1780–1870*. Cambridge: Cambridge University Press, 1996.

Bayly, C. A. "Orientalists, Informants and Critics in Benares, 1790–1860." In Jamal Malik, ed., *Perspectives of Mutual Encounters in South Asian History, 1760–1860*, 97–127. Leiden: Brill, 2000.

Bayly, C. A. *Recovering Liberties: Indian Thought in the Age of Liberalism and Empire*. Cambridge: Cambridge University Press, 2012.

Bayly, Susan. *Caste, Society and Politics in India from the Eighteenth Century to the Modern Age*. Cambridge: Cambridge University Press, 1999.

Bearce, George D. *British Attitudes towards India, 1784–1858*. Oxford: Oxford University Press, 1961.

Beckingham, C. F. "A History of the Royal Asiatic Society, 1823–1973." In Stuart Simmonds and Simon Digby, eds., *The Royal Asiatic Society: Its History and Treasures*, 1–77. Leiden: Brill, 1979.

Bednarski, Andrew. *Holding Egypt: Tracing the Reception of the Description de l'Égypte in Nineteenth-Century Britain*. London: Golden House, 2005.

Bell, Evans. *Memoir of General John Briggs*. London, 1885.

Benite, Zvi Ben-Dor, Stefanos Geroulanos, and Nicole Jerr. Introduction to Benite, Geroulanos, and Jerr, eds., *The Scaffolding of Sovereignty: Global and Aesthetic Perspectives on the History of a Concept*, 1–49. New York: Columbia University Press, 2017.

Benton, Lauren. *A Search for Sovereignty: Law and Geography in European Empires, 1400–1900*. Cambridge: Cambridge University Press, 2010.

Biel, Justin. "Edge of Enlightenment: The Akbar Tradition and 'Universal Toleration' in British Bengal." *Modern Asian Studies* 53 (2019): 1956–2006.

Bingle, Richard John. "The Decline of the Marquess of Hastings." In Donovan Williams and E. Daniel Potts, eds., *Essays in Indian History in Honour of Cuthbert Collin Davies*, 172–92. New York: Asia Publishing House, 1973.

Binnema, Ted. *"Enlightened Zeal": The Hudson's Bay Company and Scientific Networks, 1670–1870*. Toronto: University of Toronto Press, 2014.

Blake, David M. "Colin Mackenzie: Collector Extraordinary." *British Library Journal* 17 (1991): 128–50.

Bok, Derek. *Universities in the Marketplace: The Commercialization of Higher Education*. Princeton: Princeton University Press, 2003.

Bose, Sugata. *A Hundred Horizons: The Indian Ocean in the Age of Global Empire*. Cambridge, MA: Harvard University Press, 2006.

Bourke, Richard. *Empire and Revolution: The Political Life of Edmund Burke*. Princeton: Princeton University Press, 2015.

Bowen, H. V. *The Business of Empire: The East India Company and Imperial Britain, 1756–1833*. Cambridge: Cambridge University Press, 2006.

Bowen, John. "The East India Company's Education of Its Own Servants." *Journal of the Royal Asiatic Society of Great Britain and Ireland* 87 (1955): 105–23.

Bowyer, T. H. "Anderson, David (1751–1825)." Oxford Dictionary of National Biography (2004). https://doi.org/10.1093/ref:odnb/63498.

Braddick, Michael J. *State Formation in Early Modern England, c. 1550–1700*. Cambridge: Cambridge University Press, 2000.

Brockington, J. L. "Warren Hastings and Orientalism." In Geoffrey Carnall and Colin Nicholson, eds., *The Impeachment of Warren Hastings: Papers from a Bicentenary Commemoration*, 91–108. Edinburgh: Edinburgh University Press, 1989.

Brown, I. M. "John Leyden (1775–1811): His Life and Works." PhD dissertation, University of Edinburgh, 1955.

Brown, Rebecca M. "Inscribing Colonial Monumentality: A Case Study of the 1763 Patna Massacre Memorial." *Journal of Asian Studies* 65 (2006): 91–113.

Brown, Stewart J. "William Robertson, Early Orientalism and the *Historical Disquisition* on India of 1791." *Scottish Historical Review* 88 (2009): 289–312.

Buckley, Charles Burton. *An Anecdotal History of Old Times in Singapore*. 2 vols. Singapore, 1902.

Burke, Peter. *A Social History of Knowledge*. 2 vols. Cambridge: Polity, 2000–2012.

Butler, Iris. *The Eldest Brother: The Marquess Wellesley, the Duke of Wellington's Eldest Brother*. London: Hodder and Stoughton, 1973.

Calkins, Philip B. "The Formation of a Regionally Oriented Ruling Group in Bengal, 1700–1740." *Journal of Asian Studies* 29 (1970): 799–806.

Cannon, Garland. *The Life and Mind of Oriental Jones: Sir William Jones, the Father of Modern Linguistics*. Cambridge: Cambridge University Press, 1990.

Carnall, Geoffrey. "Robertson and Contemporary Images of India." In Stewart J. Brown, ed., *William Robertson and the Expansion of Empire*, 210–30. Cambridge: Cambridge University Press, 1997.

Carson, Penelope. "Golden Casket or Pebbles and Trash? J.S. Mill and the Anglicist/Orientalist Controversy." In Martin I. Moir, Douglas M. Peers, and Lynn Zastoupil, eds., *J.S. Mill's Encounter with India*, 149–72. Toronto: University of Toronto Press, 1999.

Carson, Penelope. *The East India Company and Religion, 1698–1858*. Woodbridge, UK: Boydell, 2012.

Cassels, Nancy Gardner. *Social Legislation of the East India Company: Public Justice versus Public Instruction*. New Delhi: Sage, 2010.

Chancey, Marla Karen. "In the Company's Secret Service: Neil Benjamin Edmonstone and the First Indian Imperialists, 1780–1820." PhD dissertation, Florida State University, 2003.

Chandler, Alfred D. and Bruce Mazlish, eds. *Leviathans: Multinational Corporations and the New Global History*. Cambridge: Cambridge University Press, 2005.

Chandra, Prakash. "The Establishment of the Fort William College." *Calcutta Review* 51 (1934): 160–71.

Chassé, Daniel Speich. "The History of Knowledge: Limits and Potentials of a New Approach." History of Knowledge (3 Apr. 2017). https://historyofknowledge .net/2017/04/03/the-history-of-knowledge-limits-and-potentials-of-a-new-approach/.

Chatterjee, Kumkum. *Merchants, Politics and Society in Early Modern India: Bihar, 1733–1820.* Leiden: Brill, 1996.

Chatterjee, Kumkum. *The Cultures of History in Early Modern India: Persianization and Mughal Culture in Bengal.* New Delhi: Oxford University Press, 2009.

Chatterjee, Nandini. "Hindu City and Just Empire: Banaras and India in Ali Ibrahim Khan's Legal Imagination." *Journal of Colonialism and Colonial History* 15 (2014).

Chatterjee, Nandini. "*Mahzar-nama*s in the Mughal and British Empires: The Uses of an Indo-Islamic Legal Form." *Comparative Studies in Society and History* 58 (2016): 379–406.

Chatterjee, Partha. *The Black Hole of Empire: History of a Global Practice of Power.* Princeton: Princeton University Press, 2012.

Chaudhury, Sushil. "Merchants, Companies and Rulers: Bengal in the Eighteenth Century." *Journal of the Economic and Social History of the Orient* 31 (1988): 74–109.

Clark, Anna and Aaron Windel. "The Early Roots of Liberal Imperialism: 'The Science of a Legislator' in Eighteenth-Century India." *Journal of Colonialism and Colonial History* 14 (2013).

Cohn, Bernard S. "Recruitment and Training of British Civil Servants in India, 1600–1800." In Cohn, ed., *An Anthropologist among the Historians and Other Essays*, 500–53. Delhi: Oxford University Press, 1987.

Cohn, Bernard S. "Law and the Colonial State." In *Cohn, Colonialism and Its Forms of Knowledge: The British in India*, 57–75. Princeton: Princeton University Press, 1996.

Colebrooke, Sir T. E. *The Life of H. T. Colebrooke.* London, 1873.

Collins, Gregory M. "The Limits of Mercantile Administration: Adam Smith and Edmund Burke on Britain's East India Company." *Journal of the History of Economic Thought* 41 (2019): 369–92.

Cook, Harold J. *Matters of Exchange: Commerce, Medicine, and Science in the Dutch Golden Age.* New Haven: Yale University Press, 2007.

Cottom, Tressie McMillan. *Lower Ed: The Troubling Rise of For-Profit Colleges in the New Economy.* New York: The New Press, 2018.

Covernton, A. L. "The Educational Policy of Mountstuart Elphinstone." *Journal of the Bombay Branch of the Royal Asiatic Society* new ser. 1 (1925): 53–73.

Curley, David L. "Maharaja Krisnacandra, Hinduism, and Kingship in the Contact Zone of Bengal." In Richard B. Barnett, ed., *Rethinking Early Modern India*, 85–117. New Delhi: Manohar, 2002.

Curley, Thomas M. *Sir Robert Chambers: Law, Literature, and Empire in the Age of Johnson*. Madison: University of Wisconsin Press, 1998.

Curzon, George Nathaniel. *British Government in India: The Story of the Viceroys and Government Houses*. 2 vols. London: Cassell, 1925.

Cutts, Elmer H. "Early Nineteenth Century Chinese Studies in Bengal." *Indian Historical Quarterly* 20 (1944): 114–31.

Dalrymple, William. *The Anarchy: The East India Company, Corporate Violence, and the Pillage of an Empire*. London: Bloomsbury, 2019.

Darnton, Robert. "The Grub Street Style of Revolution: J.-P. Brissot, Police Spy." *Journal of Modern History* 40 (1968): 301–27.

Das, Sisir Kumar. *Sahibs and Munshis: An Account of the College of Fort William*. Repr. edn. Calcutta: Papyrus, 2001.

Dasgupta, Ratan. "Maharaja Krishnachandra: Religion, Caste and Polity in Eighteenth Century Bengal." *Indian Historical Review* 38 (2011): 225–42.

Datta, Rajat. *Society, Economy, and the Market: Commercialization in Rural Bengal, c. 1760–1800*. Delhi: Manohar, 2000.

Datta, Rajat. "The Commercial Economy of Eastern India under Early British Rule." In H. V. Bowen, Elizabeth Mancke, and John G. Reid, eds., *Britain's Oceanic Empire: Atlantic and Indian Ocean Worlds, c. 1550–1850*, 340–69. Oxford: Oxford University Press, 2012.

Davies, C. C. "Warren Hastings and the Younger Pitt." *English Historical Review* 70 (1955): 609–22.

De, Rohit and Robert Travers, eds. Petitioning and Political Cultures in South Asia. Special Issue of *Modern Asian Studies* 53 (2019).

Desmond, Ray. *The India Museum, 1801–1879*. London: H.M.S.O., 1982.

Desmond, Ray. *The European Discovery of the Indian Flora*. Oxford: Oxford University Press, 1992.

Dirks, Nicholas B. Foreword to Bernard S. Cohn, *Colonialism and Its Forms of Knowledge: The British in India*, ix–xvii. Princeton: Princeton University Press, 1996.

Dirks, Nicholas B. *The Scandal of Empire: India and the Creation of Imperial Britain*. Cambridge, MA: Harvard University Press, 2006.

Dodson, Michael S. *Orientalism, Empire, and National Culture: India, 1770–1870*. Basingstoke: Palgrave Macmillan, 2007.

Drayton, Richard. *Nature's Government: Science, Imperial Britain, and the 'Improvement' of the World*. New Haven: Yale University Press, 2000.

Drucker, Peter F. *The Age of Discontinuity: Guidelines to Our Changing Society*. New York: Harper and Row, 1969.

Edney, Matthew H. *Mapping an Empire: The Geographical Construction of British India, 1765–1843*. Chicago: University of Chicago Press, 1997.

Ehrlich, Joshua. "The Crisis of Liberal Reform in India: Public Opinion, Pyrotechnics, and the Charter Act of 1833." *Modern Asian Studies* 52 (2018): 2013–55.

Ehrlich, Joshua. "Empire and Enlightenment in Three Letters from Sir William Jones to Governor-General John Macpherson." *Historical Journal* 62 (2019): 541–51.

Ehrlich, Joshua. "Plunder and Prestige: Tipu Sultan's Library and the Making of British India." *South Asia: Journal of South Asian Studies* 43 (2020): 478–92.

Ehrlich, Joshua. "New Lights on Raja Krishnachandra and Early Hindu-European Intellectual Exchange." *Journal of the Royal Asiatic Society* 3rd ser. 31 (2021): 159–71.

Elliott, J. H. "A Europe of Composite Monarchies." *Past and Present* 137 (1992): 48–71.

Ellis, Catriona. "History of Colonial Education: Key Reflections." In Padma M. Sarangapani and Rekha Pappu, eds., *Handbook of Education Systems in South Asia*, 363–89. Singapore: Springer, 2021.

Embree, Ainslie Thomas. *Charles Grant and British Rule in India*. London: George Allen and Unwin, 1962.

Erikson, Emily. *Between Monopoly and Free Trade: The English East India Company, 1600–1757*. Princeton: Princeton University Press, 2014.

Feiling, Keith. *Warren Hastings*. London: Macmillan, 1954.

Fisher, Michael H. *A Clash of Cultures: Awadh, the British, and the Mughals*. New Delhi: Manohar, 1987.

Fisher, Michael H. "The Office of Akhbār Nawīs: The Transition from Mughal to British Forms." *Modern Asian Studies* 27 (1993): 45–82.

Fisher, Michael H. "Mohan Lal Kashmiri (1812–77): An Initial Student of Delhi English College." In Margrit Pernau, ed., *The Delhi College: Traditional Elites, the Colonial State, and Education before 1857*, 231–66. New Delhi: Oxford University Press, 2006.

Foster, William. *The East India House: Its History and Associations*. London: John Lane, 1924.

Foster, William. *John Company*. London: John Lane, 1926.

Foucault, Michel. *Discipline and Punish: The Birth of the Prison*, trans. Alan Sheridan. 2nd edn. New York: Vintage Books, 1995.

Franklin, Michael J. "'The Hastings Circle': Writers and Writing in Calcutta in the Last Quarter of the Eighteenth Century." In Emma J. Clery, Caroline Franklin, and Peter D. Garside, eds., *Authorship, Commerce and the Public: Scenes of Writing, 1750–1850*, 186–202. Basingstoke: Palgrave Macmillan, 2002.

Franklin, Michael J. *Orientalist Jones: Sir William Jones, Poet, Lawyer, and Linguist, 1746–1794.* Oxford: Oxford University Press, 2011.

Franklin, Michael J., ed. *Romantic Representations of British India.* Abingdon, UK: Routledge, 2005.

Freitag, Jason. *Serving Empire, Serving Nation: James Tod and the Rajputs of Rajasthan.* Leiden: Brill, 2009.

Fry, Michael. *The Dundas Despotism.* Edinburgh: John Donald, 1992.

Frykenberg, Robert Eric. *Guntur District 1788–1848: A History of Local Influence and Central Authority in South India.* Oxford: Oxford University Press, 1965.

Frykenberg, Robert Eric "Modern Education in South India, 1784–1854: Its Roots and Its Role as a Vehicle of Integration under Company Raj." *American Historical Review* 91 (1986): 37–65.

Furber, Holden. *Henry Dundas, First Viscount Melville, 1742–1811: Political Manager of Scotland, Statesman, Administrator of British India.* Oxford: Oxford University Press, 1931.

Furber, Holden. *John Company at Work: A Study of European Expansion in India in the Late Eighteenth Century.* Cambridge, MA: Harvard University Press, 1948.

Gabriel, Ruth. "Learned Communities and British Educational Experiments in North India: 1780–1830." PhD dissertation, University of Virginia, 1979.

Gambles, Anna. *Protection and Politics: Conservative Economic Discourse, 1815–1852.* Woodbridge, UK: Boydell Press, 1999.

Gilding, Ben Joseph. "British Politics, Imperial Ideology, and East India Company Reform, 1773–1784." PhD dissertation, University of Cambridge, 2019.

Gillespie, Stuart. "Warren Hastings as a Translator of Latin Poetry." *Translation and Literature* 26 (2017): 199–213.

Gillispie, Charles Coulston. *Science and Polity in France: The Revolutionary and Napoleonic Years.* Princeton: Princeton University Press, 2004.

Green, William A. and John P. Deasy, Jr. "Unifying Themes in the History of British India, 1757–1857: An Historiographical Analysis." *Albion* 17 (1985): 15–45.

Grove, Richard H. *Green Imperialism: Colonial Expansion, Tropical Island Edens and the Origins of Environmentalism, 1600–1860.* Cambridge: Cambridge University Press, 1995.

Guha, Ranajit. *A Rule of Property for Bengal: An Essay on the Idea of Permanent Settlement.* 2nd edn. New Delhi: Orient Longman, 1982.

Haines, Robin. *Charles Trevelyan and the Great Irish Famine.* Dublin: Four Courts Press, 2004.

Hancher, Michael. "Reading and Writing the Law: Macaulay in India." In Michael Freeman and Fiona Smith, eds., *Law and Language: Current Legal Issues*, 187–200. Oxford: Oxford University Press, 2013.

Hanifi, Shah Mahmoud, ed., *Mountstuart Elphinstone in South Asia: Pioneer of British Colonial Rule*. London: Hurst and Company, 2019.

Haque, Ishrat. *Glimpses of Mughal Society and Culture: A Study Based on Urdu Literature, in the 2nd Half of the 18th Century*. New Delhi: Concept, 1992.

Hardy, P. *Introduction to William Erskine, A History of India under the Two First Sovereigns of the House of Taimur, Baber and Humayun*, vol. I, vii–xvii. Repr. 2 vols. Karachi: Oxford University Press, 1974.

Harrington, Jack. *Sir John Malcolm and the Creation of British India*. Basingstoke: Palgrave Macmillan, 2010.

Harris, Steven J. "Long-Distance Corporations, Big Sciences, and the Geography of Knowledge." *Configurations* 6 (1998): 269–304.

Harrison, Mark. "The Calcutta Botanic Garden and the Wider World, 1817–46." In Uma Das Gupta, ed., *Science and Modern India: An Institutional History, c.1784–1947*, 235–53. Delhi: Pearson Education, 2011.

Hart, Jenifer. "Sir Charles Trevelyan at the Treasury." *English Historical Review* 75 (1960): 92–110.

Hasan, Farhat. *State and Locality in Mughal India: Power Relations in Western India, c. 1572–1730*. Cambridge: Cambridge University Press, 2004.

Herbert, Eugenia W. *Flora's Empire: British Gardens in India*. Philadelphia: University of Pennsylvania Press, 2011.

Hilliker, John Featherston. "British Education Policy in Bengal, 1833–1854." PhD dissertation, School of Oriental and African Studies, University of London, 1968.

Hilliker, John Featherston. "Charles Edward Trevelyan as an Educational Reformer in India 1827–1838." *Canadian Journal of History* 9 (1974): 275–91.

Hilliker, John Featherston. "Trevelyan and the Reform of Indian Education." *Indo-British Review* 6 (1974): 68–74.

Hoock, Holger. *Empires of the Imagination: Politics, War and the Arts in the British World, 1750–1850*. London: Profile, 2010.

Hough, G. G. "Notes on the Educational Policy of Sir Stamford Raffles." *Journal of the Malaysian Branch of the Royal Asiatic Society* 42 (1969): 155–60.

Hutchins, Francis G. *The Illusion of Permanence: British Imperialism in India*. Princeton: Princeton University Press, 1967.

Imlah, Albert H. *Lord Ellenborough: A Biography of Edward Law, Earl of Ellenborough, Governor-General of India*. Cambridge: Cambridge University Press, 1939.

Ingram, Edward. "The Geopolitics of the First British Expedition to Egypt – III: The Red Sea Campaign, 1800–1801." *Middle Eastern Studies* 31 (1994–5): 146–69.

Irschick, Eugene F. *Dialogue and History: Constructing South India, 1795–1895*. Berkeley: University of California Press, 1994.

Jasanoff, Maya. *Edge of Empire: Lives, Culture, and Conquest in the East, 1750–1850*. New York: Vintage, 2005.

Jeanneney, Jean-Noël. *Google and the Myth of Universal Knowledge*, trans. Teresa Lavender Fagan. Chicago: University of Chicago Press, 2007.

Jokic, Olivera. "Commanding Correspondence: Letters and the 'Evidence of Experience' in the Letterbook of John Bruce, the East India Company Historiographer." *The Eighteenth Century* 52 (2011): 109–36.

Kapila, Shruti. Preface to Kapila, ed., An Intellectual History for India. Special Issue of *Modern Intellectual History* 4 (2007): 3–6.

Kaye, John William. *Lives of Indian Officers*. 2 vols. London, 1867.

Keen, Paul. *The Crisis of Literature in the 1790s: Print Culture and the Public Sphere*. Cambridge: Cambridge University Press, 2004.

Kejariwal, Om Prakash. *The Asiatic Society of Bengal and the Discovery of India's Past*. Delhi: Oxford University Press, 1988.

Khan, Abdul Majed. *The Transition in Bengal, 1756–1775: A Study of Saiyid Muhammad Reza Khan*. Cambridge: Cambridge University Press, 1969.

Khan, Gulfishan. *Indian Muslim Perceptions of the West During the Eighteenth Century*. Karachi: Oxford University Press, 1998.

Khan, M. Siddiq. "William Carey and the Serampore Books (1800–1834)." *Libri* 11 (1961): 197–280.

Khan, Shayesta. *A Biography of Ali Ibrahim Khan (circa 1740–1793): A Mughal Noble in the Administrative Service of the British East India Company*. Patna: Khuda Baksh Oriental Public Library, 1992.

Kinra, Rajeev. "Handling Diversity with Absolute Civility: The Global Historical Legacy of Mughal Ṣulḥ-i Kull." *Medieval History Journal* 16 (2013): 251–95.

Kinra, Rajeev. *Writing Self, Writing Empire: Chandar Bhan Brahman and the Cultural World of the Indo-Persian State Secretary*. Berkeley: University of California Press, 2015.

Kinra, Rajeev. "The Learned Ideal of the Mughal *Wazīr*: The Life and Intellectual World of Prime Minister Afzal Khan Shirazi (d. 1639)." In Paul M. Dover, ed., *Secretaries and Statecraft in the Early Modern World*, 177–205. Edinburgh: Edinburgh University Press, 2016.

Kinra, Rajeev. "Revisiting the History and Historiography of Mughal Pluralism." *ReOrient* 5 (2020): 137–82.

Knights, Mark. *Trust and Distrust: Corruption in Office in Britain and its Empire, 1600–1850.* Oxford: Oxford University Press, 2021.

Kopf, David. *British Orientalism and the Bengal Renaissance: The Dynamics of Indian Modernization 1773–1835.* Berkeley: University of California Press, 1969.

Krimsky, Sheldon. *Science in the Private Interest: Has the Lure of Profits Corrupted Biomedical Research?.* Oxford: Oxford University Press, 2003.

LaCroix, Alison L. *The Ideological Origins of American Federalism.* Cambridge, MA: Harvard University Press, 2010.

Laird, M. A. *Missionaries and Education in Bengal 1793–1837.* Oxford: Oxford University Press, 1972.

Lawson, Philip and Jim Phillips. "'Our Execrable Banditti': Perceptions of Nabobs in Mid-Eighteenth Century Britain." *Albion* 16 (1984): 225–41.

Leask, Nigel. "Francis Wilford and the Colonial Construction of Hindu Geography, 1799–1822." In Amanda Gilroy, ed., *Romantic Geographies: Discourses of Travel 1775–1844,* 204–22. Manchester: Manchester University Press, 2000.

Llewellyn-Jones, Rosie. *A Very Ingenious Man, Claude Martin in Early Colonial India.* Delhi: Oxford University Press, 1992.

Macdonald, Paul K. *Networks of Domination: The Social Foundations of Peripheral Conquest in International Politics.* Oxford: Oxford University Press, 2014.

MacGregor, Arthur. *Company Curiosities: Nature, Culture and the East India Company, 1600–1874.* London: Reaktion Books, 2018.

Maclean, James Noel Mackenzie. "The Early Political Careers of James 'Fingal' Macpherson (1736–1796) and Sir John Macpherson, Bart. (1744–1821)." PhD dissertation, University of Edinburgh, 1967.

Macpherson, W. C., ed. *Soldiering in India, 1764–1787.* Edinburgh: Blackwood, 1928.

Majeed, Javed. *Ungoverned Imaginings: James Mill's The History of British India and Orientalism.* Oxford: Oxford University Press, 1992.

Mantena, Rama Sundari. *The Origins of Modern Historiography in India: Antiquarianism and Philology, 1780–1880.* Basingstoke: Palgrave Macmillan, 2012.

Marchand, Suzanne. "How Much Knowledge Is Worth Knowing? An American Intellectual Historian's Thoughts on the Geschichte des Wissens." *Berichte zur Wissenschafts-Geschichte* 42 (2019): 126–49.

Markham, Clements R. *Major James Rennell and the Rise of Modern English Geography.* London, 1895.

Marshall, P. J. *The Impeachment of Warren Hastings*. Oxford: Oxford University Press, 1965.

Marshall, P. J. *Problems of Empire: Britain and India 1757–1813*. London: Allen and Unwin, 1968.

Marshall, P. J. "Warren Hastings as Scholar and Patron." In Anne Whiteman, J. S. Bromley, and P. G. M. Dickson, eds., *Statesmen, Scholars and Merchants: Essays in Eighteenth-Century History Presented to Dame Lucy Sutherland*, 242–62. Oxford: Oxford University Press, 1973.

Marshall, P. J. *East Indian Fortunes: The British in Bengal in the Eighteenth Century*. Oxford: Oxford University Press, 1976.

Marshall, P. J. *Bengal: The British Bridgehead: Eastern India 1740–1828*. Cambridge: Cambridge University Press, 1987.

Marshall, P. J. *Trade and Conquest: Studies on the Rise of British Dominance in India*. Aldershot: Variorum, 1993.

Marshall, P. J. *"A Free Though Conquering People": Eighteenth-Century Britain and Its Empire*. Aldershot: Variorum, 2003.

Marshall, P. J. Introduction to Marshall, ed., *The Eighteenth Century in Indian History: Revolution or Evolution?*, 2–49. Delhi: Oxford University Press, 2003.

Marshall, P. J. "Johnson, Richard, (1753–1807)." Oxford Dictionary of National Biography (2004). https://doi.org/10.1093/ref:odnb/63514.

Marshall, P. J. *The Making and Unmaking of Empires: Britain, India, and America c. 1750–1783*. Oxford: Oxford University Press, 2005.

Marshall, P. J. "The Shaping of the New Colonial Regime in Bengal." In Mahmudul Huque, ed. *Bangladesh: History, Politics, Economy, Society and Culture*, 15–40. Dhaka: University Press Limited, 2016.

McAleer, John. "Exhibiting the 'Strangest of All Empires': The East India Company, East India House, and Britain's Asian Empire." In Stephanie Barczewski and Martin Farr, eds., *The Mackenzie Moment and Imperial History: Essays in Honour of John M. Mackenzie*, 25–45. Basingstoke: Palgrave Macmillan, 2019.

McDaniel, Iain. *Adam Ferguson in the Scottish Enlightenment: The Roman Past and Europe's Future*. Cambridge, MA: Harvard University Press, 2013.

McElroy, George. "Ossianic Imagination and the History of India: James and John Macpherson as Propagandists and Intriguers." In Jennifer J. Carter and Joan H. Pittock, eds., *Aberdeen and the Enlightenment: Proceedings of a Conference Held at the University of Aberdeen*, 363–74. Aberdeen: Aberdeen University Press, 1987.

McLane, John R. *Land and Local Kingship in Eighteenth-Century Bengal*. Cambridge: Cambridge University Press, 1993.

McLaren, Martha. *British India and British Scotland, 1780–1830: Career Building, Empire Building, and a Scottish School of Thought on Indian Governance.* Akron: University of Akron Press, 2001.

McNeely, Ian F. with Lisa Wolverton. *Reinventing Knowledge: From Alexandria to the Internet.* New York: W. W. Norton, 2008.

Metcalf, Thomas R. *Ideologies of the Raj.* Cambridge: Cambridge University Press, 1995.

Mikler, John. *The Political Power of Global Corporations.* Cambridge: Polity, 2018.

Mirowski, Philip. *Science-Mart: Privatizing American Science.* Cambridge, MA: Harvard University Press, 2011.

Mishra, Rupali. *A Business of State: Commerce, Politics, and the Birth of the East India Company.* Cambridge, MA: Harvard University Press, 2018.

Misra, G. S. "Napoleon's Egyptian Expedition and Its Repercussions on Wellesley's Policy." *Journal of the Uttar Pradesh Historical Society* new ser. 3 (1955): 62–80.

Mittra, Peary Chand. *Life of Dewan Ramcomul Sen.* Calcutta, 1880.

Moin, A. Azfar, ed. Sulh-i Kull as an Oath of Peace: Mughal Political Theology in History, Theory, and Comparison. Special Issue of *Modern Asian Studies* 56 (2022).

Moir, Martin. "The Examiner's Office: The Emergence of an Administrative Elite in East India House (1804–1858)." *India Office Library and Records Report for 1977* (1979): 25–42.

Moir, Martin "The Examiner's Office and the Drafting of East India Company Despatches." In Kenneth Ballhatchet and John Harrison, eds., *East India Company Studies: Papers Presented to Professor Sir Cyril Philips*, 123–52. Hong Kong: Asian Research Service, 1986.

Monckton Jones, Mary E. *Warren Hastings in Bengal, 1772–4.* Oxford, 1918.

Moore, Robin J. "The Composition of 'Wood's Education Despatch.'" *English Historical Review* 80 (1965): 70–85.

Moore, Robin J. *Sir Charles Wood's Indian Policy 1853–66.* Manchester: Manchester University Press, 1966.

Morris, Henry. *The Life of Charles Grant: Sometime Member of Parliament for Inverness-Shire and Director of the East India Company.* London, 1904.

Mosca, Mathew. *From Frontier Policy to Foreign Policy: The Question of India and the Transformation of Geopolitics in Qing China.* Stanford: Stanford University Press, 2013.

Mukherjee, S. N. *Sir William Jones: A Study in Eighteenth-Century British Attitudes to India.* Cambridge: Cambridge University Press, 1968.

Mukherjee, Tilottama. *Political Culture and Economy in Eighteenth-Century Bengal*. New Delhi: Orient Blackswan, 2013.

Mulsow, Martin and Lorraine Daston. "History of Knowledge." In Marek Tamm and Peter Burke, eds., *Debating New Approaches to History*, 159–87. London: Bloomsbury, 2019.

Nair, Savithri Preetha. *Raja Serfoji II: Science, Medicine and Enlightenment in Tanjore*. New Delhi: Routledge, 2012.

Narain, V. A. *Jonathan Duncan and Varanasi*. Calcutta: Firma K. L. Mukhopadhyay, 1959.

Nechtman, Tillman W. *Nabobs: Empire and Identity in Eighteenth-Century Britain*. Cambridge: Cambridge University Press, 2010.

Nicholls, George. *Sketch of the Rise and Progress of the Benares Patshalla or Sanskrit College*. Allahabad, 1907.

Ng, Su Fang. "Indian Interpreters in the Making of Colonial Historiography: New Light on Mark Wilks's Historical Sketches of the South of India (1810–1817)." *English Historical Review* 84 (2019): 821–54.

Norval, Aletta J. "The Things We Do with Words – Contemporary Approaches to the Analysis of Ideology." *British Journal of Political Science* 30 (2000): 314–36.

O'Sullivan, Ronnie L. "The Anglo-Chinese College and the Early 'Singapore Institution.'" *Journal of the Malaysian Branch of the Royal Asiatic Society* 61 (1988): 45–62.

Ogborn, Miles. *Indian Ink: Script and Print in the Making of the English East India Company*. Chicago: University of Chicago Press, 2007.

Östling, Johan et al. Introduction to Östling et al., eds., *Circulation of Knowledge: Explorations in the History of Knowledge*, 9–33. Lund: Nordic Academic Press, 2018.

Oz-Salzberger, Fania. "Civil Society in the Scottish Enlightenment." In Sudipta Kaviraj and Sunil Khilnani, eds., *Civil Society: History and Possibilities*, 58–83. Cambridge: Cambridge University Press, 2001.

Patterson, Jessica. *Religion, Enlightenment and Empire: British Interpretations of Hinduism in the Eighteenth Century*. Cambridge: Cambridge University Press, 2021.

Peers, Douglas M. *Between Mars and Mammon: Colonial Armies and the Garrison State in 19th-Century India*. London: Tauris, 1995.

Peers, Douglas M. "Colonial Knowledge and the Military in India, 1780–1860." *Journal of Imperial and Commonwealth History* 33 (2005): 157–80.

Penson, Lilian M. "The Bengal Administrative System, 1786–1818." In *The Cambridge History of India*, vol. V, 433–61. 6 vols. Cambridge: Cambridge University Press, 1922–37.

Pernau, Margrit. Introduction to Pernau, ed., *The Delhi College: Traditional Elites, the Colonial State, and Education before 1857*, 1–32. New Delhi: Oxford University Press, 2006.

Pernau, Margrit. *Ashraf into Middle Classes: Muslims in Nineteenth-Century Delhi*. New Delhi: Oxford University Press, 2013.

Pettigrew, William A. "Corporate Constitutionalism and the Dialogue between the Global and Local in Seventeenth-Century English History." *Itinerario* 39 (2015): 487–501.

Pettigrew, William A. and David Chan Smith, eds. *A History of Socially Responsible Business, c. 1600–1950*. Basingstoke: Palgrave Macmillan, 2017.

Philips, C. H. *The East India Company, 1784–1834*. 2nd edn. Manchester: Manchester University Press, 1961.

Phillimore, R. H. *Historical Records of the Survey of India*. 5 vols. Dehra Dun: Survey of India, 1945–68.

Phillips, Andrew and J. C. Sharman. *Outsourcing Empire: How Company-States Made the Modern World*. Princeton: Princeton University Press, 2020.

Pinch, William R. *Peasants and Monks in British India*. Berkeley: University of California Press, 1996.

Pinch, William R. "Same Difference in India and Europe." *History and Theory* 38 (1999): 389–407.

Pocock, J. G. A. "Empire, State and Confederation: The War of American Independence as a Crisis in Multiple Monarchy." In John Robertson, ed., *A Union for Empire: Political Thought and the British Union of 1707*, 318–48. Cambridge: Cambridge University Press, 1995.

Pocock, J. G. A. "The Politics of Historiography." *Historical Research* 78 (2005): 1–14.

Port, M. H. and R. G. Thorne. "Smith, Robert Percy (1770–1845)." In Thorne, ed., *The House of Commons 1790–1820*, vol. V, 201–3. 5 vols. London: History of Parliament Trust, 1986.

Prakash, Om. "The English East India Company and India." In H. V. Bowen, Margarette Lincoln, and Nigel Rigby, eds., *The Worlds of the East India Company*, 1–18. Woodbridge, UK: The Boydell Press, 2002.

Prior, Katherine, Lance Brennan, and Robin Haines. "Bad Language: The Role of English, Persian and other Esoteric Tongues in the Dismissal of Sir Edward Colebrooke as Resident of Delhi in 1829." *Modern Asian Studies* 35 (2001): 75–112.

Proudfoot, William Jardine. *Biographical Memoir of James Dinwiddie*. Liverpool, 1868.

Rabitoy, Neil. "System v. Expediency: The Reality of Land Revenue Administration in the Bombay Presidency, 1812–1820." *Modern Asian Studies* 9 (1975): 529–46.

Raj, Kapil. *Relocating Modern Science: Circulation and the Construction of Knowledge in South Asia and Europe, 1650–1900.* Basingstoke: Palgrave Macmillan, 2007.

Raj, Kapil. "Mapping Knowledge Go-Betweens in Calcutta, 1770–1820." In Simon Schaffer et al., eds., *The Brokered World: Go-Betweens and Global Intelligence, 1770–1820,* 105–50. Sagamore Beach, MA: Science History Publications, 2009.

Raman, Bhavani. *Document Raj: Writing and Scribes in Early Colonial South India.* Chicago: University of Chicago Press, 2012.

Ranking, G. S. A. "History of the College of Fort William from Its First Foundation." Bengal Past and Present 7–24 (1911–22): VII, 1–29, XXI, 160–200, XXII, 120–58, XXIII, 1–37, 84–153, XIV, 112–38.

Rao, Parimala V. *Beyond Macaulay: Education in India, 1780–1860.* New Delhi: Routledge, 2019.

Rao, Velcheru Narayana. "Print and Prose: Pundits, *Karanams,* and the East India Company in the Making of Modern Telugu." In Stuart Blackburn and Vasudha Dalmia, eds., *India's Literary History: Essays on the Nineteenth Century,* 146–66. New Delhi: Permanent Black, 2004.

Ratcliff, Jessica. "Hand-in-Hand with the Survey: Surveying and the Accumulation of Knowledge Capital at India House during the Napoleonic Wars." *Notes and Records: The Royal Society Journal of the History of Science* 73 (2019): 149–66.

Raven, James. *Judging New Wealth: Popular Publishing and Responses to Commerce in England, 1750–1800.* Oxford: Oxford University Press, 1992.

Ray, Pradyot Kumar. *Dewan Ramcomul Sen and His Times.* Calcutta: Modern Book Agency, 1990.

Ray, Rajat Kanta. "Colonial Penetration and the Initial Resistance: The Mughal Ruling Class, the English East India Company and the Struggle for Bengal 1756–1800." *Indian Historical Review* 12 (1988): 1–105.

Reinert, Sophus A. "Rivalry: Greatness in Early Modern Political Economy." In Philip J. Stern and Carl Wennerlind, eds. *Mercantilism Reimagined: Political Economy in Early Modern Britain and Its Empire,* 348–70. Oxford: Oxford University Press, 2014.

Rendall, Jane. "The Political Ideas and Activities of Sir James Mackintosh (1765–1832): A Study in Whiggism between 1789 and 1832." PhD dissertation, University of London, 1972.

Rendall, Jane. "Scottish Orientalism: From Robertson to James Mill." *Historical Journal* 25 (1982): 43–69.

Robb, Peter. "Completing 'Our Stock of Geography', or an Object 'Still More Sublime': Colin Mackenzie's Survey of Mysore, 1799–1810." *Journal of the Royal Asiatic Society* 3rd ser. 8 (1998): 181–206.

Roberts, P. E. *India Under Wellesley*. London: G. Bell, 1929.

Robins, Nick. *The Corporation That Changed the World: How the East India Company Shaped the Modern Multinational*. 2nd edn. London: Pluto Press, 2012.

Robinson, Tim. *William Roxburgh: The Founding Father of Indian Botany*. Chichester: Phillimore, 2008.

Rocher, Rosane. *Alexander Hamilton, 1762–1824: A Chapter in the Early History of Sanskrit Philology*. New Haven: American Oriental Society, 1968.

Rocher, Rosane. *Orientalism, Poetry, and the Millennium: The Checkered Life of Nathaniel Brassey Halhed, 1751–1830*. Delhi: Motilal Banarsidass, 1983.

Rocher, Rosane. "The Career of Rādhākānta Tarkavāgīśa, an Eighteenth-Century Pandit in British Employ." *Journal of the American Oriental Society* 109 (1989): 627–33.

Rocher, Rosane. "British Orientalism in the Eighteenth Century: The Dialectics of Knowledge and Government." In Carol A. Breckenridge and Peter van der Veer, eds., *Orientalism and the Postcolonial Predicament: Perspectives on South Asia*, 215–49. Philadelphia: University of Pennsylvania Press, 1993.

Rocher, Rosane and Ludo Rocher. *The Making of Western Indology: Henry Thomas Colebrooke and the East India Company*. Abingdon, UK: Routledge, 2012.

Rosselli, John. *Lord William Bentinck: The Making of a Liberal Imperialist, 1774–1839*. Berkeley: University of California Press, 1974.

Rothschild, Emma. *Economic Sentiments: Adam Smith, Condorcet, and the Enlightenment*. Cambridge, MA: Harvard University Press, 2001.

Rothschild, Emma. "Language and Empire, c.1800." *Historical Research* 78 (2005): 208–29.

Roy, Tirthankar. *The East India Company: The World's Most Powerful Corporation*. New Delhi: Portfolio, 2012.

Ruch, Richard S. *Higher Ed, Inc.: The Rise of the For-Profit University*. Baltimore: Johns Hopkins University Press, 2001.

Said, Edward. *Orientalism*. New York: Pantheon, 1978.

Sanial, S. C. "History of the Calcutta Madrassa." *Bengal Past and Present* 8 (1914): 83–111, 225–50.

Schaffer, Simon. "The Asiatic Enlightenments of British Astronomy." In Schaffer et al., eds., *The Brokered World: Go-Betweens and Global Intelligence, 1770–1820*, 49–104. Sagamore Beach, MA: Science History Publications, 2009.

Schaffer, Simon. "The Bombay Case: Astronomers, Instrument Makers and the East India Company." *Journal for the History of Astronomy* 43 (2012): 151–80.

Schmitthenner, Peter L. *Telugu Resurgence: C. P. Brown and Cultural Consolidation in Nineteenth-Century South India*. New Delhi: Manohar, 2001.

Schwab, Raymond. *La Renaissance Orientale*. Paris: Payot, 1950.

Sen, Joydeep. *Astronomy in India, 1784–1876*. London: Pickering and Chatto, 2014.

Sen, Neil. "Warren Hastings and British Sovereign Authority in Bengal, 1774–80." *Journal of Imperial and Commonwealth History* 25 (1997): 59–81.

Sen, Sudipta. *Distant Sovereignty: National Imperialism and the Origins of British India*. New York: Routledge, 2002.

Seton, Sir Malcolm C. C. *The India Office*. London: G. P. Putnam's Sons, 1926.

Shovlin, John. *Trading with the Enemy: Britain, France, and the 18th-Century Quest for a Peaceful World Order*. New Haven: Yale University Press, 2021.

Sinha, Devi P. *Educational Policy of the East India Company in Bengal to 1854*. Calcutta: Punthi Pustak, 1964.

Sirkin, Gerald and Natalie Robinson Sirkin. "The Battle of Indian Education: Macaulay's Opening Salvo Newly Discovered." *Victorian Studies* 14 (1971): 407–28.

Sivasundaram, Sujit. *Islanded: Britain, Sri Lanka, and the Bounds of an Indian Ocean Colony*. Chicago: University of Chicago Press, 2013.

Skinner, Quentin. "Meaning and Understanding in the History of Ideas." *History and Theory* 8 (1969): 3–53.

Skinner, Quentin. "A Genealogy of the Modern State." *Proceedings of the British Academy* 162 (2009): 325–70.

Smith, George. *The Life of William Carey, D.D.* 2nd edn. London, 1887.

Sonenscher, Michael. *Capitalism: The Story Behind the Word*. Princeton: Princeton University Press, 2022.

Srivastava, Sushil. "Constructing the Hindu Identity: European Moral and Intellectual Adventurism in 18th Century India." *Economic and Political Weekly* 33 (1998): 1181–9.

Srivastava, Swati. *Hybrid Sovereignty in World Politics*. Cambridge: Cambridge University Press, 2022.

Stein, Burton. *Thomas Munro: The Origins of the Colonial State and His Vision of Empire*. Delhi: Oxford University Press, 1989.

Stern, Philip J. "'A Politie of Civill and Military Power': Political Thought and the Late Seventeenth-Century Foundations of the East India Company-State." *Journal of British Studies* 47 (2008): 253–83.

Stern, Philip J. *The Company-State: Corporate Sovereignty and the Early Modern Foundations of the British Empire in India*. Oxford: Oxford University Press, 2011.

Stern, Philip J. "English East India Company-State and The Modern Corporation: The Google of Its Time?," in Thomas Clarke, Justin O'Brien, and Charles

R. T. O'Kelley, eds., *The Oxford Handbook of the Corporation*, 75–92. Oxford: Oxford University Press, 2019.

Sterndale, Reginald Craufuird. *An Historical Account of "The Calcutta Collectorate."* 2nd edn. Alipore: West Bengal Govt. Press, 1958.

Stokes, Eric. *The English Utilitarians and India.* Oxford: Oxford University Press, 1959.

Subrahmanyam, Sanjay. "Of Imârat and Tijârat: Asian Merchants and State Power in the Western Indian Ocean, 1400 to 1750." *Comparative Studies in Society and History* 37 (1995): 750–80.

Subrahmanyam, Sanjay. *Europe's India: Words, People, Empires, 1500–1800.* Cambridge, MA: Harvard University Press, 2017.

Sutherland, Gillian. "Education." In F. M. L. Thompson, ed., *Social Agencies and Institutions*, vol. 3 of *The Cambridge Social History of Britain, 1750–1950*, 119–69. Cambridge: Cambridge University Press, 1990.

Sutherland, Lucy S. *The East India Company in Eighteenth-Century Politics.* Corr. edn. Oxford: Clarendon Press, 1962.

Teltscher, Kate. *The High Road to China: George Bogle, the Panchen Lama and the First British Expedition to Tibet.* London: Bloomsbury, 2006.

Theakston, Kevin. *Leadership in Whitehall.* Basingstoke: Palgrave Macmillan, 1999.

Thomas, Adrian P. "The Establishment of the Calcutta Botanic Garden: Plant Transfer, Science and the East India Company, 1786–1806." *Journal of the Royal Asiatic Society of Great Britain and Ireland* 3rd ser. 16 (2006): 165–77.

Tilly, Charles. *Coercion, Capital, and European States, AD 990–1990.* Malden, MA: Blackwell, 1992.

Trautmann, Thomas R. *Aryans and British India.* Berkeley: University of California Press, 1997.

Trautmann, Thomas R. *Languages and Nations: The Dravidian Proof in Colonial Madras.* Berkeley: University of California Press, 2006.

Trautmann, Thomas R. Introduction to Trautmann, ed., *The Madras School of Orientalism: Producing Knowledge in Colonial South India*, 1–25. New Delhi: Oxford University Press, 2009.

Travers, Robert. "Death and the Nabob: Imperialism and Commemoration in Eighteenth-Century India." *Past and Present* 196 (2007): 83–124.

Travers, Robert. *Ideology and Empire in Eighteenth-Century India: The British in Bengal.* Cambridge: Cambridge University Press, 2007.

Travers, Robert. "The Connected Worlds of Haji Mustapha (c. 1730–91): A Eurasian Cosmopolitan in Eighteenth-Century Bengal." *Indian Economic and Social History Review* 52 (2015): 297–333.

Travers, Robert. *Empires of Complaints: Mughal Law and the Making of British India, 1765–1793*. Cambridge: Cambridge University Press, 2022.

Tribe, Keith. *The Economy of the Word: Language, History, and Economics*. Oxford: Oxford University Press, 2015.

Tschurenev, Jana. *Empire, Civil Society, and the Beginnings of Colonial Education in India*. New Delhi: Cambridge University Press, 2019.

Turner, Henry S. *The Corporate Commonwealth: Pluralism and Political Fictions in England, 1516–1651*. Chicago: University of Chicago Press, 2016.

Vaughn, James M. *The Politics of Empire at the Accession of George III: The East India Company and the Crisis and Transformation of Britain's Imperial State*. New Haven: Yale University Press, 2019.

Veevers, David. *The Origins of the British Empire in Asia, 1600–1750*. Cambridge: Cambridge University Press, 2020.

Veluthat, Kesavan. "The Kēraḷōlpatti as History." In Veluthat, *The Early Medieval in South India*, 129–46. New Delhi: Oxford University Press, 2009.

Venkatachalapathy, A. R. "'Grammar, the Frame of Language': Tamil Pandits at the College of Fort St. George." In Thomas R. Trautmann, ed., *The Madras School of Orientalism: Producing Knowledge in Colonial South India*, 113–25. New Delhi: Oxford University Press, 2009.

Vicziany, Marika. "Imperialism, Botany and Statistics in Early Nineteenth-Century India: The Surveys of Francis Buchanan (1762–1829)." *Modern Asian Studies* 20 (1986): 625–660.

Viswanathan, Gauri. *Masks of Conquest: Literary Study and British Rule in India*. New York: Columbia University Press, 1989.

Wagoner, Phillip B. "Precolonial Intellectuals and the Production of Colonial Knowledge." *Comparative Studies in Society and History* 45 (2003): 783–814.

Washbrook, David. "India, 1818–1860: The Two Faces of Colonialism." In Andrew Porter, ed., *The Nineteenth Century*, vol. 3 of *The Oxford History of the British Empire*, 395–421. Oxford: Oxford University Press, 1999.

Washburn, Jennifer. *University Inc.: The Corporate Corruption of Higher Education*. New York: Basic Books, 2006.

Watson, Mark F. and Henry J. Noltie. "Career, Collections, Reports and Publications of Dr Francis Buchanan (Later Hamilton), 1762–1829: Natural History Studies in Nepal, Burma (Myanmar), Bangladesh and India (Part 2)." *Annals of Science* (in press).

Watt, James. *British Orientalisms, 1759–1835*. Cambridge: Cambridge University Press, 2019.

Webb, A. D. "Charles Edward Trevelyan in India: A Study of the Channels of Influence Employed by a Covenanted Civil Servant in the Translation of Personal Ideas into Official Policy." *South Asia: Journal of South Asian Studies* new ser. 6 (1983): 15–33.

Webster, Anthony. *The Twilight of the East India Company: The Evolution of Anglo-Asian Commerce and Politics, 1790–1860*. Woodbridge, UK: The Boydell Press, 2009.

White, James. "On the Road: The Life and Verse of Mir Zeyn al-Din 'Eshq, a Forgotten Eighteenth-Century Poet." *Iranian Studies* 53 (2020): 789–820.

Wickwire, Franklin and Mary Wickwire. *Cornwallis: The Imperial Years*. Chapel Hill: University of North Carolina Press, 1980.

Wijeysinha, Eugene. *The Eagle Breeds a Gryphon: The Story of the Raffles Institution 1823–1985*. Singapore: Pioneer Book Centre, 1989.

Wilkinson, Callie. "The East India College Debate and the Fashioning of Imperial Officials, 1806–1858." *Historical Journal* 60 (2017): 943–69.

Wilson, C. R. "Introductory Account of the Early History of the English in Bengal." In Wilson, ed., *The Early Annals of the English in Bengal*, vol. I, 1–216. 3 vols. Calcutta, 1895–1917.

Wilson, Jon E. "Early Colonial India Beyond Empire." *Historical Journal* 50 (2007): 951–70.

Wilson, Jon E. *The Domination of Strangers: Modern Governance in Eastern India, 1780–1835*. Basingstoke: Palgrave Macmillan, 2008.

Wilson, Jon E. *India Conquered: Britain's Raj and the Chaos of Empire*. London: Simon and Schuster, 2016.

Winterbottom, Anna. *Hybrid Knowledge in the Early East India Company World*. Basingstoke: Palgrave Macmillan, 2016.

Withington, Phil. *The Politics of Commonwealth: Citizens and Freemen in Early Modern England*. Cambridge: Cambridge University Press, 2005.

Withington, Phil. *Society in Early Modern England: The Vernacular Origins of Some Powerful Ideas*. London: Polity, 2010.

Wolffhardt, Tobias. *Unearthing the Past to Forge the Future: Colin Mackenzie, the Early Colonial State and the Comprehensive Survey of India*, trans. Jane Rafferty. New York: Berghahn, 2018.

Wright, Dennis. "Descendants of Capt Francis Irvine, 1786–1855." Self-published booklet, 2014.

Index